Praise for the Gookins and this book

"As I was reading, I could hear Sandy's voice — light-hearted and full of humor. The lessons about looking your children in the eye and paying attention to them talk really hit home!"
— Denise Delozier, dental hygienist and mother of four

"I thoroughly enjoyed it and know it has great potential."
— Jodi Wilson, teacher and mother of four

"*Parenting for Dummies* skips the long-winded theories and explanations and cuts to the chase, giving practical, wise parenting advice you can use right now."

— Deborah A. Wilburn, Senior Editor, *Working Mother Magazine*

The tone of the overall book is wonderful. It's personal, a handholding charmer, and never condescending.
— Diana Korte, contributing writer to *Mothering Magazine;* mother of four and grandmother of two

Good emphasis on humor and consistency. Nice, easy reading. I like the concepts of unity, discipline, and punishment. Good emphasis on safety issues. This is a book all parents need to read.
— Dr. Mary Jo Shaw, pediatrician, mother of three

"Gookin writes in a humorous, informal style that entertains as it teaches."
— Craig Crossman, nationally syndicated computer columnist

Praise for . . . For Dummies Books

"Easy to read and understand. It's not necessary to read cover to cover to have comprehension."
— Lesley McCrom, Edmonton, Alta.

"Puts terms in language I can understand."
— H. Hopkinson, Orleans, Ont.

"It's simplicity married to detail with humor and personalized style — FAB."
— Peter Czajkowski, London, England

"Clear, concise, informative, and humorous. I read it cover to cover."
— M. Byrne, Etobicoke, Ont.

"Appreciated answers to all 'dumb' questions. . . "
— Lorraine Gosselin, Montreal, Que.

"Light approach to important information."
— David Bartle, Salt Spring Island, B.C.

"Simplicity of explanations, yet extent of information."
— Zelig Spillman, Thornhill, Ont.

"Easy to read and understandable. Everyone above the age of 14 should read and own this book!!!"
— John Cakars, Berkely, CA

"Plain language for average people."
— Jeff Holt, Montreal, Que.

"I recommend the *Dummies* series of books to my customers — they enjoy them, too!"
— Loies Shanahan, Rocky Mtn. House, Alta.

"It explained everything that I needed to know in words I understood."
— Erin Grundy, Pickering, Ont.

"Easy to locate information, comprehensive, easy to read and understand. Up-to-date!!"
— Tom Johnson, Niagara Falls, Ont.

"Down to earth and enjoyable to read."
— Ray Gorzynski, Sudbury, Ont.

TM

References for the Rest of Us

PARENTING
FOR
DUMMIES™

PARENTING
FOR
DUMMIES™

by **Sandra Hardin Gookin**
edited by **Dan Gookin**

IDG Books Worldwide, Inc.
An International Data Group Company

Foster City, CA ♦ Chicago, IL ♦ Indianapolis, IN ♦ Braintree, MA ♦ Dallas, TX

Parenting For Dummies™

Published by
IDG Books Worldwide, Inc.
An International Data Group Company
919 E. Hillsdale Blvd.
Suite 400
Foster City, CA 94404

Library of Congress Catalog Card No.: 95-78775

ISBN: 1-56884-383-6

Printed in the United States of America

10 9 8 7 6 5 4 3 2 1

1B/RW/QY/ZV

Distributed in the United States by IDG Books Worldwide, Inc.

Distributed by Macmillan Canada for Canada; by Computer and Technical Books for the Caribbean Basin; by Contemporanea de Ediciones for Venezuela; by Distribuidora Cuspide for Argentina; by CITEC for Brazil; by Ediciones ZETA S.C.R. Ltda. for Peru; by Editorial Limusa SA for Mexico; by Transworld Publishers Limited in the United Kingdom and Europe; by Al-Maiman Publishers & Distributors for Saudi Arabia; by Simron Pty. Ltd. for South Africa; by IDG Communications (HK) Ltd. for Hong Kong; by Toppan Company Ltd. for Japan; by Addison Wesley Publishing Company for Korea; by Longman Singapore Publishers Ltd. for Singapore, Malaysia, Thailand, and Indonesia; by Unalis Corporation for Taiwan; by WS Computer Publishing Company, Inc. for the Philippines; by WoodsLane Pty. Ltd. for Australia; by WoodsLane Enterprises Ltd. for New Zealand.

For general information on IDG Books Worldwide's books in the U.S., please call our Consumer Customer Service department at 800-762-2974. For reseller information, including discounts and premium sales, please call our Reseller Customer Service department at 800-434-3422.

For information on where to purchase IDG Books Worldwide's books outside the U.S., contact IDG Books Worldwide at 415-655-3021 or fax 415-655-3295.

For information on translations, contact Marc Jeffrey Mikulich, Director, Foreign & Subsidiary Rights, at IDG Books Worldwide, 415-655-3018 or fax 415-655-3295.

For sales inquiries and special prices for bulk quantities, write to the address above or call IDG Books Worldwide at 415-655-3200.

For information on using IDG Books Worldwide's books in the classroom, or ordering examination copies, contact Jim Kelly at 800-434-2086.

For authorization to photocopy items for corporate, personal, or educational use, please contact Copyright Clearance Center, 222 Rosewood Drive, Danvers, MA 01923, or fax 508-750-4470.

About the Gookins

Sandra Hardin Gookin is the mother of four boys. She holds a degree in Speech Communications from Oklahoma State University. It's this background in communications that has been the basis for her theories on parenting. That . . . and lots of experience resulting in parenting methods that not only work, but are painless.

Dan Gookin has written more than 30 books on computers, translated into over 25 languages. His often-imitated style is light, humorous, and yet very informative. His most recent titles include *Real World Windows 95,* the best-selling *DOS For Dummies*, 2nd Edition, and *Word For Windows 6 For Dummies.* Dan holds a degree in communications from UCSD.

Dan and Sandy currently live with their several boys in the as-yet-untamed state of Idaho.

ABOUT
IDG
BOOKS
WORLDWIDE

Welcome to the world of IDG Books Worldwide.

IDG Books Worldwide, Inc., is a subsidiary of International Data Group, the world's largest publisher of computer-related information and the leading global provider of information services on information technology. IDG was founded more than 25 years ago and now employs more than 7,500 people worldwide. IDG publishes more than 235 computer publications in 67 countries (see listing below). More than 60 million people read one or more IDG publications each month.

Launched in 1990, IDG Books Worldwide is today the #1 publisher of best-selling computer books in the United States. We are proud to have received 8 awards from the Computer Press Association in recognition of editorial excellence, and our best-selling ...For Dummies™ series has more than 17 million copies in print with translations in 25 languages. IDG Books Worldwide, through a recent joint venture with IDG's Hi-Tech Beijing, became the first U.S. publisher to publish a computer book in the People's Republic of China. In record time, IDG Books Worldwide has become the first choice for millions of readers around the world who want to learn how to better manage their businesses.

Our mission is simple: Every one of our books is designed to bring extra value and skill-building instructions to the reader. Our books are written by experts who understand and care about our readers. The knowledge base of our editorial staff comes from years of experience in publishing, education, and journalism — experience which we use to produce books for the '90s. In short, we care about books, so we attract the best people. We devote special attention to details such as audience, interior design, use of icons, and illustrations. And because we use an efficient process of authoring, editing, and desktop publishing our books electronically, we can spend more time ensuring superior content and spend less time on the technicalities of making books.

You can count on our commitment to deliver high-quality books at competitive prices on topics consumers want to read about. At IDG Books Worldwide, we value quality, and we have been delivering quality for more than 25 years. You'll find no better book on a subject than an IDG book.

John J. Kilcullen

John Kilcullen
President and CEO
IDG Books Worldwide, Inc.

WINNER
*Eighth Annual
Computer Press
Awards ➢ 1992*

WINNER
*Ninth Annual
Computer Press
Awards ➢ 1993*

**IDG
BOOKS**
WORLDWIDE

IDG Books Worldwide, Inc., is a subsidiary of International Data Group, the world's largest publisher of computer-related information and the leading global provider of information services on information technology. International Data Group publishes over 235 computer publications in 67 countries. More than sixty million people read one or more International Data Group publications each month. The officers are Patrick J. McGovern, Founder and Board Chairman; Kelly Conlin, President; Jim Casella, Chief Operating Officer. International Data Group's publications include: **ARGENTINA'S** Computerworld Argentina, Infoworld Argentina; **AUSTRALIA'S** Computerworld Australia, Computer Living, Australian PC World, Australian Macworld, Network World, Mobile Business Australia, Publish!, Reseller, IDG Sources; **AUSTRIA'S** Computerwelt Oesterreich, PC Test; **BELGIUM'S** Data News (CW); **BOLIVIA'S** Computerworld; **BRAZIL'S** Computerworld, Connections, Game Power, Mundo Unix, PC World, Publish, Super Game; **BULGARIA'S** Computerworld Bulgaria, PC & Mac World Bulgaria, Network World Bulgaria; **CANADA'S** CIO Canada, Computerworld Canada, InfoCanada, Network World Canada, Reseller; **CHILE'S** Computerworld Chile, Informatica; **COLOMBIA'S** Computerworld Colombia, PC World; **COSTA RICA'S** PC World; **CZECH REPUBLIC'S** Computerworld, Elektronika, PC World; **DENMARK'S** Communications World, Computerworld Danmark, Computerworld Focus, Macintosh Produktkatalog, Macworld Danmark, PC World Danmark, PC Produktguide, Tech World, Windows World; **ECUADOR'S** PC World Ecuador; **EGYPT'S** Computerworld (CW) Middle East, PC World Middle East; **FINLAND'S** MikroPC, Tietoviikko, Tietoverkko; **FRANCE'S** Distributique, GOLDEN MAC, Le Guide du Monde Informatique, Le Monde Informatique, Telecoms & Reseaux; **GERMANY'S** Computerwoche, Computerwoche Focus, Computerwoche Extra, Electronic Entertainment, Gamepro, Information Management, Macwelt, Netzwelt, PC Welt, Publish, Publish; **GREECE'S** Publish & Macworld; **HONG KONG'S** Computerworld Hong Kong, PC World Hong Kong; **HUNGARY'S** Computerworld SZT, PC World; **INDIA'S** Computers & Communications; **INDONESIA'S** Info Komputer; **IRELAND'S** ComputerScope; **ISRAEL'S** Beyond Windows, Computerworld Israel, Multimedia, PC World Israel; **ITALY'S** Computerworld Italia, Lotus Magazine, Macworld Italia, Networking Italia, PC World Italia; **JAPAN'S** Computerworld Today, Information Systems World, Macworld Japan, Nikkei Personal Computing, SunWorld Japan, Windows World; **KENYA'S** East African Computer News; **KOREA'S** Computerworld Korea, Macworld Korea, PC World Korea; **LATIN AMERICA'S** GamePro; **MALAYSIA'S** Computerworld Malaysia, PC World Malaysia; **MEXICO'S** Compu Edicion, Compu Manufactura, Computacion/Punto de Venta, Computerworld Mexico, MacWorld, Mundo Unix, PC World, Windows; **THE NETHERLANDS'** Computer! Totaal, Computable (CW), LAN Magazine, Lotus Magazine, MacWorld; **NEW ZEALAND'S** Computer Buyer, Computerworld New Zealand, Network World, New Zealand PC World; **NIGERIA'S** PC World Africa; **NORWAY'S** Computerworld Norge, Lotusworld Norge, Macworld Norge, Maxi Data, Networld, PC World Ekspress, PC World Nettverk, PC World Norge, PC World's Produktguide, Publish& Multimedia World, Student Data, Unix World, Windowsworld; **PAKISTAN'S** PC World Pakistan; **PANAMA'S** PC World Panama; **PERU'S** Computerworld Peru, PC World; **PEOPLE'S REPUBLIC OF CHINA'S** China Computerworld, China Infoworld, China PC Info Magazine, Computer Fan, PC World China, Electronics International, Electronics Today/Multimedia World, Electronic Product World, China Network World, Software World Magazine, Telecom Product World; **PHILIPPINES'** Computerworld Philippines, PC Digest (PCW); **POLAND'S** Computerworld Poland, Computerworld Special Report, Networld, PC World/Komputer, Sunworld; **PORTUGAL'S** Cerebro/PC World, Correio Informatico/Computerworld, MacIn; **ROMANIA'S** Computerworld, PC World, Telecom Romania; **RUSSIA'S** Computerworld-Moscow, Mir - PK (PCW), Sety (Networks); **SINGAPORE'S** Computerworld Southeast Asia, PC World Singapore; **SLOVENIA'S** Monitor Magazine; **SOUTH AFRICA'S** Computer Mail (CIO),Computing S.A.,Network World S.A., Software World; **SPAIN'S** Advanced Systems, Amiga World, Computerworld Espana, Communicaciones World, Macworld Espana, NeXTWORLD, Super Juegos Magazine (GamePro), PC World Espana, Publish; **SWEDEN'S** Attack, ComputerSweden, Corporate Computing, Macworld, Mikrodatorn, Natverk & Kommunikation, PC World, CAP & Design, Datalngenjoren, Maxi Data,Windows World; **SWITZERLAND'S** Computerworld Schweiz, Macworld Schweiz, PC Tip; **TAIWAN'S** Computerworld Taiwan, PC World Taiwan; **THAILAND'S** Thai Computerworld; **TURKEY'S** Computerworld Monitor, Macworld Turkiye, PC World Turkiye; **UKRAINE'S** Computerworld, Computers+Software Magazine; **UNITED KINGDOM'S** Computing /Computerworld, Connexion/Network World, Lotus Magazine, Macworld, Open Computing/Sunworld; **UNITED STATES'** Advanced Systems, AmigaWorld, Cable in the Classroom, CD Review, CIO, Computerworld, Computerworld Client/Server Journal, Digital Video, DOS World, Electronic Entertainment Magazine (E2), Federal Computer Week, Game Hits, GamePro, IDG Books Worldwide, Infoworld, Laser Event, Macworld, Maximize, Multimedia World, Network World, PC Letter, PC World, Publish, SWATPro, Video Event; **URUGUAY'S** PC World Uruguay; **VENEZUELA'S** Computerworld Venezuela, PC World; **VIETNAM'S** PC World Vietnam.
05/17/95

Dedication

This book is dedicated to you, our reader. We thank you for taking enough interest in your children to want to be the best parent possible. There is nothing in this world more important than your job as parent, and we applaud you for your efforts.

Credits

Vice President & Publisher
Kathleen A. Welton

Executive Editor
Sarah Kennedy

Managing Editor
Stephanie Britt

Brand Manager
Stacy Collins

Executive Assistant
Jamie Klobuchar

Editorial Assistants
Stacey Holden Prince
Kevin Spencer

Production Director
Beth Jenkins

**Supervisor of
Project Coordination**
Cindy L. Phipps

Supervisor of Page Layout
Kathie S. Schnorr

Pre-Press Coordinator
Steve Peake

Associate Pre-Press Coordinator
Tony Augsburger

Media/Archive Coordinator
Paul Belcastro

Project Editor
Bill Helling

Editor
Tamara S. Castleman

Technical Reviewers
Chris J. Boyatzis, Ph.D.
Debra Englander
Diana Korte
Robin Coons
Denise Delozier
Dr. Mary Jo Shaw
Jody Wilson
Jeanne Wolverton

Project Coordinator
Valery Bourke

Production Staff
Gina Scott
Carla C. Radzikinas
Patricia R. Reynolds
Melissa D. Buddendeck
Dwight Ramsey
Robert Springer
Theresa Sánchez-Baker
Elizabeth Cárdenas-Nelson
Jae J. Cho
Dominique DeFelice
Maridee Ennis
Angela F. Hunckler
Laura Puranen
Michael Sullivan

Proofreader
Jennifer Kaufeld

Indexer
Sherry Massey

Cover Design
Kavish + Kavish

Acknowledgments

This book came together with a sincere desire to help parents with topics that have very few right and wrong answers. But it takes a lot of really great people to put this kind of effort together, and those are the people we'd like to thank.

Thank you Matt Wagner of Waterside Productions for schmoozing this book into the hands of John Kilcullen and Kathy Welton of IDG books. Thanks to John and Kathy for accepting this idea and publishing it. Thank you Bill Helling for doing such a great job of editing this book and making us look like we really do know what a hanging participle is and how to correctly use punctuation,.!?

We want to thank our parents for teaching us all something very special: Shirley for the firm belief that family is the most important thing you can have (and that you *always* stand up for your kids), Virgil for not yelling even though he had plenty of reasons to, Jonnie for the love and respect of reading, and Bob for how to pull an engine out of a Volkswagen.

We have to mention our boys Jordan, Simon, Jonah, and Jeremiah. You've all been great test rats for us to practice on. We hope you don't grow up to be resentful of the fact we put your lives in a book.

And to all the *many* people who reviewed this book, thank you for your comments. We read them all, even though we may not have agreed with you:

Chris J. Boyatzis, Ph.D.	father of Jeniss (soon-to-be) and stepfather of Janine (9)
Michelle Brock	former day care operator and still concerned about tomorrow's adults
Melissa Buddendeck	mother of Andy (2) and Sarah (4)
Tamara S. Castleman	poet
Robin Coons	licensed practical nurse; mother of Justin (16) and Jessica (8)
Denise Delozier	certified dental assistant; mother of Megan (13), Malary (10), Madalyn (8), and Bryar (3)
Terri Edelman	new godmother to Ryan Parker Lefebvre (7 mos.)
Debra Englander	mother of Elise (6)
Richard Graves	new father of Ericka (7 mos.)
Paula Hershman	possible future parent
Diana Korte	mother of Aren (29), Drew (31), Juliana (27), and Neil (33); grandmother of Akio (3) and Hope (2)
Beth Lefebvre	new mother of Ryan (7 mos.)

Stacey Holden Prince	big sister to Gerry, Trista, and Greg
Anna Rohrer	mother of three teenagers and a United States Marine: Brian (20), Amie (18), Reilly (15), and Mark (14)
Helen Saraceni	mother of two adult children who survived Mom's trials and errors
Dr. Mary Jo Shaw	pediatrician, mother of Kellen (9), Christopher (6), and Mason (3)
Jennifer Wallis	aunt extraordinaire
Jody Wilson	teacher; mother of Jeff (14), Molly (13), and Tim (9)
Bronwyn Wolf	day care curriculum specialist, parent-to-be
Jeanne Wolverton	professional volunteer, mother of Bill (33), Kay (30), Andy (29); grandmother of Christopher (4) and Drew (1)

(The Publisher would like to give special thanks to Patrick J. McGovern and Bill Murphy, without whom this book would not have been possible.)

Contents at a Glance

Cartoons at a Glance

By Rich Tennant

page 44

page 301

page 162

page 203

page 135

page 7

page 325

page 61

page 112

Table of Contents

Foreword

. . . .

*W*hile the tone of this book would suggest that it's targeted for one subset of the population — the dummies — the fact is that when it comes to parenting, we're all, at one time or another, *clueless*.

For me, that moment of reckoning came early on. So early, in fact, that I hadn't even left the hospital yet. I was so naive when my son, now 15, was born, that I panicked when I first noticed what looked like two pinpricks on his chest. You can imagine my chagrin when the hospital nurse told me those were his nipples.

Okay, so I got off to a slow start. If you're about to become a parent or already have young children, you're apt to feel perplexed and a little overwhelmed at times, too. Don't worry: It's normal. The mere fact that you've picked up this book indicates that help is on the way.

Written by a mother of four who has navigated her way through her share of the perils of parenting — such as those interminable moments when your child whines, for what seems like five minutes (or maybe it's more like five hours) — *Parenting For Dummies* skips the long-winded theories and explanations and cuts to the chase, giving practical, wise parenting advice you can use right now.

In fact, sitting down with this book is a lot like having lunch with a really cool best friend who is there to offer you calm, reassuring, confident guidance. Without pulling any punches, or scaring you needlessly about what will happen if you don't successfully manage every last one of your toddler's hissy fits, this book explains just what you need to know to raise well-behaved, well-adjusted, happy kids. I encourage you to read it and apply its very sound advice. You'll benefit from it — and so will your children!

Deborah A. Wilburn
Senior Editor, *Working Mother* magazine

Introduction

$\bullet$

*W*elcome to *Parenting For Dummies*, a book that takes away all the psychological bull and all the historical blah-blah — and gets down to what it takes to be a good parent.

The idea here is simple: You're a smart person who loves your children and wants to raise them in the best way possible. But there's too much bunk and bullhockey out there that makes you feel like you must be doing something wrong. All you want is to find out how to work with your children during all the stages and phases they'll go through. And you want to do this without turning gray prematurely or sending your children off to military school.

This book covers the basics of raising your child (what you need to start with and what you need to keep going with your kids — until one day they're off on their own, asking *you* questions about raising their own kids) without the psychological hype, growth charts, and other goop that only gets in the way of being a good parent.

About This Book

This book isn't meant to be read from front to back. It's a reference for people who have children aged newborn to around ten years old, although the first six chapters pertain to kids of all ages. Each chapter has self-contained information about parenting. You don't have to read the whole thing to understand what's going on; just go to the chapter and section that interests you. Typical sections include:

- Talking and being heard (It's not always the same)
- The art of keeping your cool
- The perils and joys of bed time
- The Crying Baby flowchart
- Guidelines for co-parenting (the two-party system)
- Dining out with children (other than McDonald's)
- Finding good child care
- Discipline techniques

You won't learn the history of potty training here, or the pyschological effects of bottlefeeding vs. breastfeeding. But you will learn some excellent guidelines and helpful hints on getting your kids to bed, finding a good doctor, and making your home as safe as it can be. You know — practical stuff. The examples you read in the book have really happened to our family. The names have been changed to protect the not-so-innocent.

Foolish Assumptions

The only assumption made in this book is that you have kids, are going to have kids, would like to have kids, know somebody who has kids, live next to somebody who has kids, or were yourself once a kid. Whatever the subject is when dealing with kids, this is your reference.

For ourselves, you may notice that there are two people listed on the cover. That's right, we're married. We don't claim to be *parenting experts*. Our belief is that there is no such person. But we have four children and tons of parenting experience. So a lot of this book's information has been practiced in real-world situations. It really works.

How This Book Is Organized

This book has five major parts. Each part has at least six chapters. Inside each chapter are sub-sections that (hopefully) apply to the topic at hand. Even though this book is arranged so that you can pick it up and start reading from any point, the book is outlined here for you:

Part I: The Basic, Important Stuff

This first section is the backbone of the whole parenting topic. It contains information on how to speak, listen, and interact with your children — the basic, important stuff.

Part II: Getting to the Nitty Gritty

This part of the book starts getting into parenting topics like food, bedtime, bathtime, and your new job of teacher. It's about the day-to-day interraction experiences you'll share with your children.

Part III: Dealing with Babies

Babies are in a class of their own so they deserve their own special section (which we would have written in gender-neutral yellow, had we thought of it sooner). There's a great chapter on *cranky babies,* which every parent really needs — and wants — to read.

Part IV: Help for Desperate Parents

Topics covered in this section cover specific subjects such as finding good child care, arranging health care, and dealing with those fights and squabbles. It's crime and punishment all over again! Every parent will face these topics at some time or another. It's inevitable.

Part V: The Part of Tens

This part of the book contains several chapters containing lists of ten somethings-or-another. For example, ten choking hazards, ten don'ts, ten things to do everyday, ten reasons for bragging about your kids, and so on.

Part VI: The Appendixes

Checklists and questionnares galore. Appendixes A through E have complete lists of helpful checklists and questionnares to get you through the tedious tasks of shopping, packing, and interviewing.

Icons Used in This Book

Helpful Hints — These are hints, guides, and suggestions that you won't find in other books. They come from ourselves and other parents like us who *know* they work because we use or do them. These are things your grandmother would normally pass down to you.

Remember — A reminder so you don't forget.

Warning — A reminder of what to look out for.

FYI — Tidbits of information that will help you while you learn how to work with your children.

Parents Approved — Names of books, phone numbers, or products that are currently used by these parents — who think that they're great.

Words of Wisdom — Quotes by people, some who are famous, most who are not.

Contacting the Author

Finally, if you'd like to write me, I love to hear from you. Feel free to tell about your personal parenting adventures, how you've overcome some situations, or just to ask for more detailed information that may not be covered in this book.

The best way to contact me is through an online account. You can expect the fastest feedback this way. Obviously, this works best if you have a computer and modem.

On Prodigy, contact:

```
pkhg47b
```

Or on CompuServe, you can write to me at:

```
76201,3211
```

Via the Internet, write to either:

```
pkgh47b@prodigy.com
```

OR

`76201.3211@compuserve.com`

Via the US Mail service (which was devised in the 18th century, by the way), contact us care of the publisher:

Sandy & Dan Gookin
c/o IDG Books
919 E. Hillsdale Blvd., Ste 400
Foster City, CA 94404

Where to Go from Here

This book is designed to work as a reference where you can look up the topic that concerns you, read about it, then go on with your life. I strongly suggest that you — whatever you do — read Chapters 1 through 6 first (maybe not in order, but read them). The information they contain is extremely important. It deals with your general approach to your children and the basic guidelines on how you handle them, no matter what situation you're in. Please, read these chapters. Then read whatever tickles your fancy. But don't try to change a diaper and read the book at the same time. This isn't a truly hands-on book — if you catch our meaning.

Being a parent is the most important thing you will do in your life. Nothing else will be as important or have as much effect on the world. Don't take this job or responsibility lightly.

Part I
The Basic, Important Stuff

The 5th Wave — By Rich Tennant

"Six of Jennifer's goldfish died today, and, well, I just don't think it's worth the three of us keeping our reservations at Takara's Sushi Restaurant tonight."

In this part...

Sometimes the answer to a puzzle is amazingly easy.
Take Alexander the Great, for example. He was faced
with the fabled Gordian Knot. (It was like one of those knots
your kids get in their shoelaces.) Whoever could untie the
knot would rule Asia. Many had tried, but none had suc-
ceeded. So finally along came Alexander, and he cut the knot
in half with his sword. Cheating? Maybe. But it worked.
Sometimes the best solutions are the simplest, which is the
thrust of this part of the book: The most basic, important
part of being a parent is communication — though having a
sword handy helps.

Chapter 1
Winning *The Parenting Game*

· ·

· ·

Admit it, you're not in charge. Your children are. And both of you know it. Children draw you in and then pounce for the attack. They know when to cry. They know how to get you to say "Yes." They know when you're not looking. It's like playing a game of chess with someone with an IQ of 300. But you don't want to destroy your opponents. You want to love them and hopefully raise them properly.

Welcome to *The Parenting Game.* The object here is not total victory, but a mutual solution that keeps everyone happy. You want to raise a child who turns into a well-adjusted adult, and you want to do it without being escorted away by men in white coats while wearing a jacket that has way-too-long sleeves. But you can't play without the proper parenting skills. That's precisely what this chapter shows you.

Welcome to The Parenting Game

In *The Parenting Game,* you're *not* going to do everything right. Keep this in mind because it's very important that you realize you won't be perfect. You'll lose your temper, you may yell, you may give in to whining every now and then (although you lose points for that), and you'll feed your kids cake for dinner at *least* once. That's all OK. There is no perfect parent, and all you can do is try your best. The game ain't over until your children become adults (or until the fat lady sings). If they're happy, wholesome people — or at least pretend to be or can fool a psychologist — you've won.

So the object is to learn how to perfect your parenting skills. To do that you'll have to understand two basic things:

✔ Parenting is a job that you can never quit.

✔ Parenting means playing some new and exciting roles.

There are some who say that the game never ends. It would be nice to have an answer to the question, "At what age are your children completely independent?" Alas, the answer is, "Never."

The American Dream is not owning your own house. The American Dream is getting your children out of your house. — Congressman Dick Armey.

Welcome to a job you can never quit

Your parenting job doesn't start at 8 a.m. and end at 5 p.m. It's a 24-hour job. If you have an outside job, that doesn't mean that when you get home your job is over. Instead, you come home and instantly change into your parenting "uniform" and go back to work. There is no time off!

✔ Don't use silk as a part of your parenting uniform; puke stains.

Your job consists of the following duties and responsibilities to your kids: love them, feed them, take care of them when they're sick, play with them, educate them, discipline them, be a good friend to them, and occasionally do something really goofy to embarrass them in front of their friends. You can't slack off, you can't quit, and there aren't too many tax breaks. Your parenting job is your responsibility, regardless if you have an outside job.

Of course, there is a bonus plan. In return, your kids will love you back, frustrate you, make you laugh, maybe make you cry, anger you, and make you really proud of them.

If you're a parent who is fortunate enough to be able to stay home with the kids, you may need to give your partner (who isn't at home all day) some *gentle guidance* as to what needs to be done. Like walking into an ongoing project, it's hard to know where to start. Don't be afraid to say, "Jessica just woke up from her nap; would you mind changing her diaper?"

Necessary vocabulary

Puke is one of many words that you'll find yourself using to describe your child's projectiles. Here are some more, just so that you get comfortable with these graphic descriptions: throw-up, barf, upchuck, regurgitate, heave, spit up, toss your cookies, blow lunch. Do you get the idea?

Both parents must be involved in raising children. If your partner has the attitude that it's not his or her job, feel free to hit this person upside the head. (OK. Hitting is bad, so at least have a heart to heart talk with your partner.) Refer to Chapter 19, "Guidelines for Co-Parenting (The Two-Party System)."

The three duties of a parent

The next thing you need to understand about the parenting game is that you'll be taking on some new and important duties. You just can't "be yourself" any more, not if you expect to raise those well-adjusted kids everyone yearns for.

To win the game, and to become the highly touted, relaxed type of parent, you need to be three things:

1. a positive role model

2. a teacher

3. a friend

The positive role model

A *role model* is someone you look up to and try to be like. Maybe it's that woman down the street who raised five kids all to become doctors. Maybe it's a fictional character. Batman was a great role model. Even when Batgirl was about to be dipped in bubbling hot oil, he still drove the speed limit. Or maybe your role model is your own mother or father. Whoever it is, it's someone you want to be like, someone who is liked.

The reason for being a positive role model is obvious: Your children look to you as an example of how to behave. Whatever your habits and actions are, you can be sure that your li'l thumb-sucker is looking at you and gathering that this is the behavior to imitate. What you do has a direct impact — positive or negative.

Bad habits are inherited. Do you curse, or have a bad habit that you wouldn't be proud to see your kids sharing with their friends? Then change that habit. Do you think kids know better than to use foul language? No. Some parents say: "Do as I say and not as I do." This attitude is bogus and doesn't work in real life. Don't do or say anything you wouldn't want your child doing or saying in school.

A *good role model* doesn't have to be someone who is perfect in every way. If you can walk on water, great. Otherwise, you should try to do things you know are right. You'll get upset. That happens. The important part is to apologize later, or explain to your kids why you got upset. It's healthy for kids to know that their parents get upset or mad. Everyone does. *How* you handle being upset is what's important.

A *bad role model* doesn't necessarily mean being a bad person. Bad role models are typically workaholics, alcoholics, drug users, or any person who puts material things ahead of their families — the oblivious parent type.

Being a good role model means no smoking, cursing, getting drunk, lying, cheating, crossing the street on a red light, stealing, yelling, (*think of your own nasty habit here*), and so on.

The ever-present teacher

Everything you do and say is soaked up by your child's brain. This happens whether you want it to or not, so welcome to your second role as parent, that of *teacher*. (And if you think school teachers are under paid, guess what! In your new role of teacher, you'll work harder than any teacher without the benefit of a meager paycheck.)

From the day your children are born, they are watching and learning from your actions and behavior. It's sort of a scary thought, isn't it? Your wee ones learn when you talk to them, do things with them, and are with them. You'll teach them how to respond to spilled milk, how to react to a joke, what to do when they fall down — and all the other things in life we deal with.

If you're calm, relaxed, and don't over react to things like a broken dish, your children will most likely be calm and relaxed. If you're nervous and tense, your children will most likely be nervous and tense.

Chapter 8, "Your New Job — Teacher," delves into the subject of teaching your children.

A scholar is of all persons the most unfit to teach young children. A mother is the infant's true guide to knowledge. — Edward Bulwer-Lytton

The good friend

How can parents be *friends* and still be parents? Children and their parents may go together like oil and water, but it can be done. It means spending time together doing things. Playing, laughing, and crying together. Good parents make things fun, just as a good friend does.

Being a good friend to your children also means accepting them for who they are. It's not harping on or pointing out their weaknesses, but helping them to build up the things they're good at. By encouraging them, you not only prove that you're a good friend, but you also help them develop their self confidence.

Always praise your kids; and praise everyone else's kids while you're at it. Of course, this means realistic praise. A kind word or a pat on a back can be considered praise. A snide comment to a kid — even if you're doing it for joke value among your own friends — has two negative results: It belittles the kid, and it teaches other kids that it's okay to do what you're doing.

A good friend remembers what we were and sees what we can be. — Janette Oke

Let your kids "help" you. Even if that means letting them stir flour all over your counter when you cook. Going to the store and cleaning house together can also be fun. This strategy not only teaches them work can be fun, but they're also learning skills — and you're spending time developing your relationship.

Think about your best friend. How did this person become your best friend? You probably just spent a lot of time together, had fun, and the next thing you knew, you were friends. The same thing can happen with your children. Raising kids is not the time to be selfish with your time or energy. It's the time when you *make time* for your kids.

If your children are your friends, they're more likely to open up to you with their problems and concerns about school, peer pressure, or the other things that bother kids. You will be more approachable if your kids look to you not only as a parent, but also a friend.

Introducing the Five Basic Parenting Skills

To play *The Parenting Game* properly, you need to know five basic skills. Rolling dice here is optional. If you get these five basic skills down, you should be able to handle most situations that arise. They are:

- ✔ Speak and listen with care.
- ✔ Be consistent.
- ✔ Follow through.
- ✔ Remain patient.
- ✔ Learn to manage behavior.

Like the simplicity of cutting the Gordian Knot, these rules are really all you need to become an effective, happy parent and raise those *perfect* kids you see in the catalogs.

Your responsibility as a parent is not as great as you might imagine. You need not supply the world with the next conqueror of disease or major motion picture star. If your child simply grows up to be someone who does not use the word "collectible" as a noun, you can consider yourself an unqualified success. — Fran Leibowitz

Speak and Listen with Care

You need an effective way to express your ideas, wants, and desires to your kids. That's communication. Speak clearly, precisely, and without a lot of babbling. Take the time to listen. In any relationship — even with your hair stylist — if you don't, won't, or can't communicate effectively, you're doomed. Doomed! Doomed! Doomed!

Being specific is the opposite of being vague, and most people are vague. Don't you hate talking to people who seem neither here nor there about what they want? Vagueness may be a blessing when you're a politician or some big corporate executive about to be skewered on *60 Minutes*, but it can be hazardous in *The Parenting Game.*

You have to be specific about your wants and desires when you talk to your children. They don't always have the same frame of reference that you do. So when you say, "Go clean your room," you have to be specific about what "clean" means. You may mean surgical clean, and they may think they only need to make the path to their bed and closet wider.

Babble. *Abba blabba abba dabba blah* is the disease of the 90s, where we have talk radio, talk shows, and talk-talk-talk without getting anything done. People like to hear themselves talk. Kids don't like to hear you talk. They would rather you just get to the point. If you're too long-winded, their minds wander off to battle against *The Forces of Evil,* and they won't hear half of what you're saying. But communication also means listening. It's a two-way street: You talk. You listen. Without listening, talking isn't communication. It's filling the room with noise while you recycle air through your lungs. Kids pick up on this real quick.

The basic rules of communications are that you be specific about what you want and that you don't babble when you say it.

> ✔ Be specific!
>
> ✔ Get to the point!

Yes, sometimes it helps to phrase things in cryptic lawyer-speak. But when you say, "We're going to the grocery store, so I want you to behave," do you mean, "We are going to the store. Do not touch anything, do not ask for anything, do not yell or scream, do not poke the hamburger meat, and please sit quietly in the cart"? Be specific about what you want. "Behave" may have different meanings to you and your kids.

Speaking to a young child is easy. He reaches for an apple, you say, "No." He starts to touch the apple again, and you say, "No." This activity may go on until you figure out that you should move him away from the apples. Don't babble: "Sweetheart, please don't touch the apple. If you touch the pretty red apple, they may all fall on the ground causing your dear, sweet mother an enormous amount of embarrassment." What he hears is, "Sweetheart, blah apple blah blah. . . ."

Communication is the key to your relationship with your children. Refer to Chapter 2, "Communicating with Your Child."

For a fun book to read to your kids that shows how words can mean different things, try *The King Who Rained* by Fred Gwynne (The Trumpet Club).

Waver not, lest ye topple (being consistent)

Think of a top. It spins until it wobbles, and then it falls down. While it spins, it's being consistent. When it slows down, it stops being consistent. It wobbles and falls. Being consistent is setting rules and not going back or changing those rules. It's not being wishy-washy with your kids. Even when the whining gets to you (and it *will*), you need to be firm. This is so important that I'm going to bullet it:

▮ ✔ Be consistent — don't get tired and start to wobble.

This is perhaps the toughest part of being a parent. When your child crawls on the dinning room table, you take him down *every time* he crawls back up. Don't pretend you don't see him after a while. You may be tired of this game, but he has the energy of the Energizer Bunny and just keeps on going. Every time you take him off the table you're being consistent.

Being consistent sounds easy, like one of the easiest rules of *The Parenting Game.* But your kids have one up on you. They're cute; they cry; they beg; tiny arms reach up; tear-filled eyes beg for mercy; boo-boo lips protrude. Don't give in. Be strong. Be consistent. Your kids really want that from you. They need it.

There are a thousand examples of being consistent. Bed times need to be consistent. You have to be firm on the denial of candy if you've already told them they can't have any more. God made little kids cute so we wouldn't kill them when they cry. But this plays in their favor when tear-filled eyes beg for more candy. Just say no! (Consistently.)

Being consistent and following through are sort of like cousins marrying; the two concepts are related in a weird kind of way. If you are not consistent, and you don't practice follow-through, you'll have problems with your kids. Guaranteed! Read Chapter 3, "Being a Consistent Parent."

Do what you say, and think before you say it (the art of follow-through)

Follow-through means doing what you said. It means sticking to your original word, an important offshoot of being consistent. The key here is to think before you say something. Do you really mean *sit down or no dinner?* You had better mean it if you expect to live up to your follow-through.

Don't say, "Do that one more time and you'll regret it." It sounds nice because it gives you an out; you're not bound to do anything linked to that threat. But it's better if you say instead, "Do that one more time, and Vicky can't spend the night tonight." Then punish children properly when they disobey.

> ✔ *Think* before you say something.
>
> ✔ Consistently follow through or your children will never believe you again.

It also helps to make your punishment realistic. For example, instead of saying "Do that one more time and I'll ground you for a *millennium*," say "Do that one more time and you'll be grounded for a *week*." Then ground them for a week. If you tell your six-year-old that you'll take his ball away if he throws it again in the house, take his ball away the next time he throws it in the house.

For more information on following through with what you say, please read Chapter 4, "Follow Through."

Learn the virtue of patience

Who couldn't use more patience? You must maintain patience and control with your kids. Don't let things upset you; crying babies, poopy diapers that have overflowed onto your nice white Battenburg bedspread (and yes, thank you Dan for laying Jonah there to begin with), being late, a toddler who seems to be dragging his feet — these things happen. You must have patience with your kids. You'll go crazy if you don't.

> ✔ Patience means taking more time than is necessary to do something.
>
> ✔ Patience means letting your daughter take two hours to pick out the most perfect Barbie doll so she can go home and cut off Barbie's hair.
>
> ✔ Patience is something that you develop. It takes time and practice.

To learn more about making patience a part of your character, read Chapter 5, "The Art of Keeping Your Cool."

Behavior-management skills

Idle hands get into trouble. If your children are bored with nothing to do, they'll find their own entertainment: sorting all your CDs; crawling into the fireplace, getting sooty, then crawling on the carpet; painting the cabinets with peanut butter. These activities aren't the kid's fault: They're due to improper behavior management on the parent's behalf.

Behavior management is keeping your children busy and occupied *most* of the time. It's good to give them their own free time so they can use their imagination and create their own fun, but if you burden them with activities when they start acting bored, they won't have the time to get into things they shouldn't. And, while you're at it, praise them when they do something great like help you pick up toys or do something kind for their sibling. Praise will reinforce in your kids that what they just did made you very happy. Since kids like to please their parents, they'll do it again to get more praise from you.

You may look at this as manipulation, which wouldn't be far from the truth. Remember that children are the masters of manipulation. Therefore it's your job to outmanipulate them from the start. Manipulating your children's behavior, or behavior management, is keeping your children happy, safe, and out of *trouble* by being a part of their daily activities, attitudes, and environment.

So behavior management involves some simple concepts:

- ✔ keeping idle hands busy
- ✔ giving lots of attention
- ✔ offering praise

Chapter 6, "Behavior Management," discusses what rewarding good behavior, constant praise, lots of hugs and kisses, and organized play can do to keep your child out of mischief.

Find Your Sense of Humor in the Lost and Found

Children are funny. They're goofy. If they weren't, Erma Bombeck would be known only in her own neighborhood and maybe just for her bowling average. There is humor in everything, though it may not be obvious to you when it happens.

WARNING: The perils of negative attention

Your kids will do anything they can to get your attention. Even if that means *negative attention.* If you don't work to keep them busy, give them lots of positive attention, and praise them often for their good deeds, they'll start doing anything just to get that attention. If they find that pouring water on the floor will get your attention (even if it's negative attention), they'll do it.

Without being evil, children have an uncanny ability to push all your buttons. You really need to be able to laugh at the things that ordinarily would drive you up the wall. Relax. Don't concern yourself with the fact that your two-year-old has poured baby powder all over the place. Instead, grab the camera. It's going to be a funny story in a few hours so you might as well "Kodak-moment" it before you clean the little one up.

Anger is our first reaction because what kids do is unexpected and we usually have to clean it up. So what? Stop, take several deep breaths, look at that sweet face, and smile. Anger is wasted energy and that energy should be spent somewhere else.

Let your kids be kids. They goof up. They make messes. Accept that fact and never assume they're doing something "to get you." Part of the joy of being a parent is sitting back and watching your kids do all the goofy things your parents accused you of doing when you were a kid. (Besides, you can't tell the funny story when it has the sad ending of "and then I beat the *crap* out of him.")

Stop before you react to anything and take a deep breath. Deep breathing (or maybe it's just stopping and letting your brain work for a minute) helps you to realize that whatever you are looking at is really not that awful. You may even get so mad that you have to excuse yourself and tell your children that you're upset and you'll have to discuss the situation later when you've had time to cool down. Make sure you resolve the situation that day. If you let too much time go by, your kids will have forgotten the whole thing.

Concern for your children is good. But don't be so protective of your children that you forget how fun kids can really be. Laughing is great. It makes you feel good, it relieves stress, and it makes life a lot more fun.

Is There an End to This Game?

The Parenting Game is never really over. Soon your kids will be older and have kids of their own. Then you'll start all over with the I-told-you-so's, which are a grandparent's right (and which you're probably getting enough of right now).

Being a parent can be hard. It takes effort. Trying to be consistent, always thinking about the proper ways to communicate with your child, cleaning up messes, and working to keep your little ones busy isn't always easy. Take heart. You can get through all this with your smile.

All the parents of the world are going through the same things you're going through, so you're not alone. Everyone will have the same problems you have and get to a point when they just want to throw their hands up and give up. Just keep your sense of humor, whatever you do.

The day you bring your little bundle of joy home from the hospital is the happiest day of your life. However, the new Mommy is exhausted, sore, and probably feeling a little emotionally unstable thanks to her hormones. Daddy is also tired. You both will sit and look at your new baby and wonder, "Now what?" Then that little, beautiful baby opens its little cherub mouth and begins to wail. So what do you do? Smile. Continue smiling through all the years that you are lucky enough to be a parent.

Three parental types

There are three different types of parents: the Worry Warts, the Oblivious, and the Relaxed. You don't really choose one of these as much as you become one. For example, everyone really wants to be a "relaxed" parent. However, if you don't understand your children or play *The Parenting Game* by the proper rules, you'll lapse into one of the other two nasty types. This is bad since the type of parent you are (or become) directly reflects what type of child you raise.

Parentius worry-wartius: This worry-wart parent is a nervous wreck. And in return, they typically raise nervous kids. You know the type: They cry more often, tend to whine a lot, and no one wants to play with them. And then there are their kids.

Worry-warts are fussers. They stew and pitch fits about things. They dwell on every little thing, from feeding a baby right (and the food only goes in one end), to trying to buy the affection of their child.

Warning signs for worry-wart parents include being over-protective of your children; not letting your children take chances or risks; not allowing them to be independent; stifling their creativity by wanting to help them do everything; and making clucking sounds in the presence of their friends.

Parentius oblivious. Oblivious parents are the opposite of the worry-warts, they're just a wee bit too nonchalant about their children. The main reason for this is most likely that these parents don't take the parenting job seriously. They think it's too much trouble. They figure kids can take care of themselves. Most important, they give higher priority to other things in their life (like work). They've never learned that nothing should be more important than their children.

Warning signs for oblivious parents include not knowing where your kids are, who they're with, or what they're doing; feeling your kids are responsible at any age; feeling your kids are a burden; not being involved in their activities (or not even being able to recite what their activities are); and not reading this book.

Parentius relaxus. This is the type of parent you want to be. A relaxed parent is a happy parent, and these parents raise (or at least attempt to raise) well-adjusted kids.

Don't go overboard on the happy concept. It's tough. For example, don't picture Carol Brady as your ideal happy parent. (That's sick.) Instead, all you need to do is follow a few simple rules, take on a few new roles, and understand that your kids are out to foil any attempt you make at becoming the perfect parent.

Delightful warning signs you're becoming a relaxed, happy parent include keeping track of your kid's eating habits without buying a hospital-grade food sterilizer; paying attention to the number of bowel movements li'l diaper-bottom has per day, his fluid intake, his attitude and behavior; watching that your house is safe and secure without installing a time clock; not panicking; caring; allowing your kids to take risks and chances as long as they're not in danger; working to help build their self confidence and self esteem.

TV parental types

Worry-wart TV parents:

Dr. Crusher in *Star Trek: The Next Generation*

Daren Stevens in *Bewitched* (Samantha was cool. She didn't worry.)

Rob and Laura Petrie in *The Dick Van Dyke Show*

Captain Stubbing in *The Love Boat*

Oblivious TV parents:

Alice and George Mitchell in *Dennis The Menace*

Homer and Marge Simpson in *The Simpsons*

Roseanne in *Roseanne*

All the parents in *Rugrats*

The parents of *Beavis and Butthead* (They'd have to be.)

Al and Peg Bundy in *Married With Children*

Relaxed TV parents:

Mike and Carol Brady in *The Brady Bunch*

Ward and June Cleaver in *Leave It to Beaver*

Donna Reed in *The Donna Reed Show*

Brian Keith in *Family Affair*

Robert Young in *Father Knows Best*

Cliff and Clair Huxtable in *The Cosby Show*

Bill Bixby in *The Courtship of Eddy's Father*

Your lesson for the day

Communication is more than just talking to your kids. It's being a great listener, too.

Chapter 2

Communicating with Your Child

● ●

In This Chapter

▶ Talking effectively

▶ Explaining to your children what is to be expected

▶ Teaching communication skills

▶ Answering questions

▶ Using alternate forms of communication to get your point across

● ●

*I*t's always been easier to ignore someone than to pay attention. Children have this ignoring thing down pretty well, so you really have to work at getting them to listen. Part of the problem is that children have the attention span of a hummingbird (or at least it *seems* that way).

This chapter covers things that you can do to make your kids listen to you. It doesn't necessarily mean they'll mind you (that's something completely different, covered in Chapter 3, "Being a Consistent Parent"), but they'll hear what you're saying. This chapter also lets you know how to avoid problems because of lack of communication — in addition to providing some ideas on how to teach your kids to be good communicators.

Talking and Being Heard (It's Not Always the Same)

— "I've informed you a googolplex to abstain from vexing your sibling."

— "Huh, Mom?"

When you talk to your kids, you have to keep a few things in mind.

If you have something to say and you want to be heard, do the following:

- ✔ Get down on your children's level.
- ✔ Use simple words.
- ✔ Get to the point.
- ✔ Don't yell.

Get down on your children's level

If you really want your kids to hear you when you talk, physically get down on their level. If you can't squat, pick them up and put them on your lap. Look them right in the eyes. It's hard to avoid someone who's in your face — and that's exactly what you want to do. Get in someone's face.

Look your children in the eye, speak calmly and slowly, and say what you have to say.

Don't be vague, babble, and try to impress your children with your fabulous expanded vocabulary.

Encourage your children to look *you* in the eye. Kids can be standing right in front of you and have a bobbly head like those dogs that sit in the rear window of old-lady cars. *Bobble, bobble, bobble.* They're not paying attention.

You certainly don't need to get on your children's level to say "Good morning," or "Are you hungry?" Save this kind of action for *serious* conversations such as, "Now, Simon, what did you do with Mommy's keys?" or, "Do you understand why you got into trouble for hitting your brother over the head with the bat?" But don't forget that the most important part of communicating is being a good listener. Communication can't go both ways if you're doing *all* the talking and *none* of the listening.

MEGO: My Eyes Glaze Over

You stand there and talk to your kids, and they're all MEGO when communication falls apart. MEGO also occurs when you break the communication rules — you don't keep things brief and to the point. If you talk and MEGO hits, you've lost 'em.

Have you ever been talking to someone and you know she isn't listening because she's staring at you a little too intensely? She hears you but isn't listening. Kids do this all the time. (They're masters of this behavior.) You know — the lights are on, but no one's home.

God gave us two ears and one mouth so that we can listen twice as much as we talk. — old proverb by someone important

Use simple words

As adults, we're sometimes brave enough to say, "What *exactly* does that mean?" We do this hoping we don't sound too much like a dork. Kids, on the other hand, will smile at you and nod — or better yet — stare at you with a blank look on their faces.

Talk to your kids using words they understand. It's easier to get your point across when your kids know what you're talking about. If you don't think that they understand, ask them to explain back what you said. This is a great test to see how well you are getting your message across.

If you don't talk to your kids using words they understand, you may as well be speaking Swahili. That's why you hear a lot of successful parents talking in short, blunt sentences using simple commands. (Although they sometimes sound like they're talking to a pet: "Sit. Stay. No, no, no! Stop, stop, stop! Good boy.")

At some point you'll have to expand your vocabulary; you shouldn't always talk on a pre-school level. When you start to introduce new words to your children, take the time to ask if they understand what you just said. A lot of times they'll smile meekly and say "Yes" insincerely.

Real-life examples you need not read

What you say: "Jordan, you need to be *responsible* and put your dirty clothes in the clothes hamper every night."

What he hears: "Jordan, you need to be *rah-pitty-blah* and put your dirty clothes in the clothes hamper every night."

What you say: "Don't *piddle*. You're supposed to clean your room."

What he hears: "Don't *pid hole*. You're supposed to clean your room."

What you say: "Don't be *sarcastic* to your sister."

What he hears: "Don't be *sark a stick* to your sister."

Always ask children if they understand. If they seem unsure or hesitate, ask them to explain it back to you. That's really the only way you'll ever discover if you're getting your point across. Of course, you may have a child who doesn't hesitate to ask you what certain words mean. Then there's no question as to what is understood.

Get to the point

Pretend that you're on a conversation egg timer. If you don't say what you need to say within a short period of time, you've lost the attention of most children. On the other hand, when you're too brief, they'll ask for more information if they need it.

Your kids will understand you a lot better if you're specific and you get right to the point:

- ✔ Don't ramble on and on.
- ✔ Don't go into long explanations.
- ✔ Say exactly what you mean.

Children don't have to listen to you (if they have their way). You can't force, bribe, beg, or plead enough to get them to listen. They don't care if you're in the middle of a sentence. They'll walk away if they get bored or are just tired of listening. Good communication between you and your children is the foundation for a long, happy, and growing relationship. If your children aren't listening to you, you've lost that foundation to build upon.

Don't yell

Yelling is the worst way to communicate. Let me say that louder in case you didn't get it:

YELLING IS THE WORST WAY TO COMMUNICATE.

Here's a guarantee. When you yell at your kids, they're not listening to a thing you're saying. All they're doing is sitting there teary-eyed and upset because you're yelling — or they're getting angry themselves. Your point is lost, they're upset, you're upset. *Nothing* has been accomplished.

If you yell, you won't get your message across. So if you reach the point where you're about to yell at someone, stop and leave the room. Just for a second. Take a few deep breaths, get your composure back, and approach the situation again.

You're trying to be a role model and teacher. Yelling isn't a trait you want to pass on to your kids. (It'll come back and haunt you as your kids get older and their hormones get all stirred up.) This yelling stuff happens with kids when you least expect it. You'll say something ever so calmly and innocently, and — all of a sudden — your sweet, lovable child turns into Damien the Devil Child who will start yelling. Remember to set a good example by being a *good* role model yourself.

Explain What Is To Be Expected (or "how to avoid those ugly grocery-store incidents")

Outbursts in grocery stores and other temper tantrums can be reduced by a simple communication method: Explain to your kids what you expect of them. Tell them how they are to behave.

Kids like to know what's going on just as much as you do; they like to be prepared and informed. You must set the ground rules before you do something. Use this strategy when you can, and you'll see things go smoother with your kids. For example:

"Tommy, we're going into the toy store to buy your sister a birthday present. We're not buying you a present. You can look around. You can tell me what you like. But we're not buying you anything today. Today is for your sister. Do you understand?"

But don't be surprised if your child protests, whines, or still comes up to you with a toy explaining that he's always wanted this special Batman with the attachable BatWings and — if you get it today — he'll never ask for anything again.

This tip about explaining works only if you don't give in to the whining and the throwing of major fits. Your kids won't believe you the next time if you tell them they can't buy anything — and then you give in and get them that *one little toy*. Your buckling under the pressure only leads to more tantrums since, obviously, they work.

- ✔ Let them prepare whatever things they need. This is important. Their preparation may only mean tucking Barbie in her Malibu Barbie house before she leaves. It may mean searching for ten minutes for a toy to bring along. Whatever it is, give them time to do their thing before you leave — and they won't feel rushed.

- ✔ Look them in the eyes when you get to where you're going (making sure you have their attention) and tell them how they are to behave. Be precise and clear about what you mean. You don't need to go into long explanations unless they ask for more information. But don't expect miracles. Children do have short attention spans, and this process takes time. Advanced preparation can make a world of difference.

- ✔ Never assume your kids know what it is that you want. When you stop talking and start assuming, you get into trouble. For example, suppose that you're going to your cousin's wedding. Tell your kids what a wedding is (briefly), and what it's going to be like. Then tell them they're to sit quietly and watch. No talking or getting up is allowed. They need to get a drink and go to the bathroom *before* the wedding starts so they won't have to do it during the ceremony.

Giving instruction beforehand is a lot easier than trying to set the rules while you are already involved in your activity. You end up doing a lot of "Shhh-you-need-to-be-quiet" or "No-you-can't-have-anything." Instead, you'll be giving a few reminders of the rules you have already gone over. Explaining things to children in advance works really well, too, especially when you're in a hurry: "We're going to the store for just a few minutes. Don't ask for anything." It will take a while for them to believe that you really mean what you said, so they may go ahead and ask for something. Don't give in, and eventually they'll get the idea.

Advanced planning works only if you don't give in to whining and change your mind about the rules. Once you set rules but don't stick by them, you're in serious trouble. Your kids will always push you, whine, and throw fits if you go back on your word (a parental behavior also known as *not being consistent*).

Teaching the Basic Communication Skills

Everyone loves a good communicator. Look at someone who's charismatic — without a doubt an excellent communicator. Look at top executives, and you'll find enthusiastic communicators. These are the kind of people you admire, and the kind you want your children to grow up to be like.

The problem is that communication skills must be taught. This is your job. And communication, like everything else, has rules. The rules are simple, and if you currently don't use these rules, now is the time to learn them:

- ✔ Use correct English.
- ✔ Look children in the eyes.
- ✔ Speak slowly and clearly.
- ✔ Let children express themselves.
- ✔ Set an example.
- ✔ Allow disagreements.
- ✔ Listen and hear.

Kids who have good communications skills do better in school. They make friends easier. And they grow up to be more confident people.

Use correct English (don't use baby talk!)

The first mistake a new parent makes is wanting to talk *baby talk* to a baby. Babies use baby talk. It sounds real cute to everyone else. But if you ever expect children to speak properly, you have to speak well. When you speak babyish, they assume that's the way adults talk, too.

Baby talk is not *how* you speak, but what you say. Go ahead and speak softly and with a variety of interesting tones — but watch your *baby words*.

If you say, "Does baby want his blankey?" your children will call a blanket a *blankey*. That's neat for a while. But when you see a five-year-old walking around calling a blanket a *blankey,* it's not cute anymore.

It's not fair to your kids to teach them to talk one way only to change it later. It's just as easy for you to say *bottle* as it is to say *baba*. Your children will say *baba* when they first talk. You should follow that up by saying, "Yes, *bottle*." Say *bottle* a few times slowly. They'll eventually catch on. English is hard enough. Don't make it any harder than it already is.

It's not just new parents who succumb to baby talk. Grandparents do it — along with brothers and sisters, strangers in the mall, and just about anyone you encounter. You should gently correct the offending words by restating them so that your child gets the idea. For example, if your Aunt Margie says, "Aren't those the cutest itty bitty tootsies you've ever seen?" simply reply, "Yes, those are the cutest little toes I've ever seen."

English as it is speaked

"Him was des da cutiest iddyy bitty precious lovey lamb,
An him is jus da sweetes iddy bitty singie, yes him am.
Wis his cunnin ittle tootsies,
An him sayin goo goo goo,
Him iz muzzies ittle lambie boysie,

Oochie chochie coo."

To this the baby listens by the hour and day and week,
And yet his mother wonders why he never learns to speak.

Author: Unknown — as told to me by Grandma Marcia Gookin

Look children in the eyes

Looking people in the eyes establishes a sense of confidence and trust. We look at babies in the eyes all the time. I don't know anyone who avoids looking a baby in the eyes. It just can't be done.

Start looking your kids in the eyes when you talk to them; do this from the moment your baby is born. As they get older and more mobile, it's harder to get them to look you in the eyes because they're too busy watching the cat spit up hair balls.

Younger children automatically look at you when they start trying to communicate. Look back at them. (Talk to them and look them in the eyes!) But as your kids get older, eye contact is lost. You'll eventually have to ask them to look at you when you're communicating. If there's eye-to-eye contact, everyone is paying attention.

When your kids start talking to you and telling you stories about things that happen to them, take the time to stop what you're doing and listen. Pay attention! This is the best way to teach eye contact. It also shows your children that you're interested and that you think what they're saying is important.

Speak slowly and clearly

Your kids will talk a lot like you do. If that's a disturbing thought, now is the time to make some changes. Do you speak too fast, ramble on and on about nothing, or sound like you have mush in your mouth? Then don't be surprised when your kids do, too.

There are only two ways to teach kids to speak well:

- ✔ Speak slowly and clearly yourself. They'll pick it up and eventually do the same.
- ✔ Tell kids to slow down when they get overexcited and start talking too fast.

Don't make it sound like you're scolding them. Just let them know you could understand them better if they slowed down a little. Once they've slowed down, they'll naturally begin to speak more clearly. For example, you might say, "I'm sorry, Sarah, but I can't understand you when you talk so fast. Please slow down."

Let children express themselves

"There are some days that all I want is for my kids to be quiet and now you're telling me to encourage them to express themselves? You've got to be kidding!"

It's true. Having your kids express themselves is a wonderful way to teach them to communicate. When you express happiness, anger, disappointment, confusion, or whatever, you have to formulate your thoughts and then try to say what you feel. It's not easy to do. There are many adults who haven't been able to learn this feat. If you encourage your kids to communicate, they grow up not only to be better communicators, but they also learn to express their feelings.

If you know that you've done something to make your children mad — like not giving them a second bowl of ice cream — *ask* them if they're mad. As they're sitting there pouting, they may say, "No." Tell them that it's okay to tell you if they're mad and that you won't be angry. Encourage them to tell you how they feel.

If you start training your youngsters how to open up to you, it will be easier for them to communicate their fears and frustrations by the time they have to go to school. This moment is where many of their feelings will pop up and need to be discussed.

Set an example

The best way to teach anyone is by example — which means you have to follow the same rules you set for your kids. In addition, you have to remember to be a good listener; don't interrupt a child, and don't finish his sentences for him. (even if you know what he's going to say.) You'll have the urge to hurry him up when he's telling a story because it may seem to take forever. (Kids don't get the idea of what "make it brief" means.) If you think having your child tell you about his day can be long and drawn out, ask him to tell you a joke!

Setting a good example may mean making changes in the way you communicate. Read the following and see how many of these apply to you. These changes aren't really going to be as painful as you may think.

As you read these, try to think of better ways for your children to express themselves. Give them words that may be better suited for them to use. They may be using words or phrases they've picked up from somewhere (like friends or the evil television) and may not be aware that what they're saying is inappropriate for their age or the situation.

✔ **No cursing, damn it!**

Don't use a word you don't want your kids to learn. If you do, they're sure to take it to school and share it with all their friends. Then you'll have all the parents calling you to thank you for helping their children to expand their vocabulary in such a colorful fashion.

If you hear your children saying something that you feel is inappropriate, even if it's something like "shut up," let them know that there are better words that they can use — and that you would appreciate it if they didn't use that expression again. Tell them to say "be quiet," instead. Don't ignore children if they use bad language. They may interpret this silence as you not caring. And don't overreact by yelling or getting mad. This may be the reaction they were hoping for.

✔ **No sarcasm.**

Sarcasm is very contagious and can be extremely hurtful to others — and don't act like you didn't know it, either.

If your children are too young to understand sarcasm, you won't make any sense when you use it. If they do understand sarcasm, they may be hurt by it. Sarcasm is an unnecessary form of communication.

✔ **No yelling.**

Talking louder doesn't make things more understandable or clearer. If you don't understand, I'LL TALK LOUDER, OK?

Your job is to communicate your ideas to your children in a calm manner. Yelling lets them know that you've lost control of yourself. And they're not listening. They're just watching your face turn red and get all distorted.

✔ **No arguing.**

It takes two or more to argue; don't be a part of it. If you and your kids have a disagreement, resolve it calmly. Stay calm. Don't argue. Don't even act like you're going to argue because it won't solve a thing. ARE YOU LISTENING TO ME? IT WON'T SOLVE ANYTHING!

If you find that your conversation is on the brink of an argument, calm yourself down and remind your kids that they, too, need to calm down.

If you have to yell at your kids, you're not close enough to them. — Virgil Hardin

Don't lie

It's possible that you may be asked a question for which you don't know the answer. It's OK to admit that you don't know something. Never lie to your children or make up an answer to a question that you don't know (it's the same as lying). Simply tell your children that you don't know — but that maybe you can find the answer out together. Then follow up with that and find out the answer. Your kids won't think less of you because you were able to admit that you didn't know something.

The *smartest* people in the world are able to say they don't know something. The *dumbest* people in the world are the ones who think they know everything.

Allow Disagreements

The first response you may have is "kids naturally want to disagree. They're kids. That's what they do." This may be true for a lot of kids, even most. But your role as a parent is *not* to discourage disagreements. If your children disagree with you, it doesn't have to mean they're arguing — which is how many parents interpret disagreements.

When you encourage your kids to express their differing points of view, you are doing the following:

✔ **helping your children to explain their feelings**

As I mentioned in the preceding section, verbalizing your feelings is a great practice for perfecting communication skills.

✔ **encouraging discussions**

Believe it or not — and please accept this in the best way possible — you're not always going to be right. Sometimes your kids can bring up a point of view you may not have thought of. It could happen.

✔ **allowing your children to be heard**

There's such a great feeling in the ability to express yourself. Your children will also appreciate the ability to express their feelings and know that their opinions have been heard.

✔ **teaching fairness**

It's only fair to allow people to voice their opinions. With this approach, though, your children will also learn that just because they voiced their side of the story or their opinion, they won't always get what they want. And sometimes they might have a good argument for why they need to spend the night with Aunt Kathy.

Thank your children for participating in the discussion. Let them know that you've heard their point of view and you appreciate their input. Still, don't be afraid to veto their request. Parents have the final decision. But explain your decision. "You've obviously thought out why you should be able to spend the night with Aunt Kathy, and I appreciate your input. However, Aunt Kathy is having guests, so she's not going to be able to have you come over tonight. How about if we arrange it for another time?"

Listen and Hear

Listening and hearing are not the same. Both are extremely important but overlooked at the same time. Being a good listener means not interrupting your children and not finishing their sentences for them — even if you know what

A few of the traditional answers to commonly asked (yet unanswerable) questions

Q: Why is the sky blue?

A: It has something to do with chromatic filtering.

Q: What's chromatic filtering?

A: It's the stuff that makes the sky blue.

Q: Why can't I stick my elbow in my ear?

A: Because it would get stuck.

Q: Where do babies come from?

A: Mommies.

Q: Where do the mommies get them?

A: Daddy helps Mommy make the baby in her tummy.

Q: How?

A: Want some candy?

Q: Where does the sun go at night?

A: It settles into the ocean, where it cools.

And if all else fails, you can always satisfy them with:

A: Because *God* made it that way.

However, and in all seriousness, please don't be ashamed to say, "I don't know" to your children. It's much better to say, "I don't know" than to always sound like a punch line.

they're going to say. You'll have the urge to hurry them up when they're telling a story, because it may seem to take forever. (Kids don't get the idea of what "make it brief" means.) If you think having your children tell you about their day can be long and drawn out, ask them to tell you a joke!

Hearing is different than listening. You can be hearing what your children are saying, but you may not be listening. Hearing means that the noise is hitting your eardrum. Listening means that you understand what they're saying, or even what they're not saying, but are really meaning.

Do You Have a Question?

Your goal as a good parent (who is able to communicate well) is to be approachable by your children. You want your children to be comfortable enough to ask you complicated or awkward questions.

You can answer awkward questions effectively by following four rules:

1. Rephrase the question.

Make sure you understand exactly what they're asking. The more you understand what they're trying to know, the easier it'll be for you to answer.

— "Why does Uncle Richard like to wear Aunt Robin's dresses?"

— "You want to know *why* Uncle Richard likes to wear Aunt Robin's dresses?"

2. Keep your response simple.

Your children don't want a textbook answer.

— "Where do babies come from?"

— "From Mommies."

If you answer their questions and they skip off happily, you answered as much as they needed to know at that time. If they continue asking for more information, you may have to get into more detail and drag out the visual aids.

3. Try to respond as quickly as possible.

If you're unable to answer at the time, follow up later. You don't want your children to feel that you're unwilling to answer their questions.

— "What is sex?"

— "Well dear, *sex* is an interesting topic. How about we sit down after dinner and talk about it?"

Then remember to sit down with your children later.

4. Be observant.

If your children seem to be bothered by something or if they only ask vague questions (but never want to go into detail), sit down and talk. There may be something bothering them that they are having problems talking about — or perhaps they are confused about something and don't quite know what to ask.

— "Daddy, do you *love* me?"

— "Well, of course I love you. Why do you ask? Is something bothering you? You know you can talk to me about anything."

An unusual child is one who asks his parents questions they can answer.
— E. C. McKenzie

Make time to talk

You're busy and so are your kids. But during all the hustle and bustle of your lives, you need to *make* the time to sit and talk to your kids. It's not always possible to *squeeze* in this extremely important time. If you don't make this time, you may find that both you and your kids are using the moment right before bedtime to try to cram in the day's events. You need something better.

Alternate Forms of Communication

Tired of telling your kids *every* morning to make their beds and brush their teeth? As a parent, you hope they'd understand that they have to do this every morning regardless if you've told them or not. How is it possible kids can remember that three days ago you promised to buy them Fruity Pebbles cereal, but they can't remember to brush their teeth? Maybe it's time to change the way you're telling them.

A good way to get kids to do things that they don't like to do is to make it as fun as possible. Tell them what you want them to do with notes, charts, and pictures.

If you can't get your kids to remember to make their beds every morning, make a chart that lists their daily chores. After they've done their chores, let them put a sticker beside each chore they've finished. Give them an award for the completed chart. If the chart is complete by whenever (set a time), they can do something special, like watch a favorite video. Or promise to play a game with them. If they don't complete their chart, don't let them do whatever you set as their reward. Be consistent. Don't give in to whining or big Bambi-eyes filled with tears. This strategy works only if your kids know you're serious.

Good Morning!

CHORES	Mon.	Tues.	Wed.	Thurs.	Fri.	Sat.	Sun.
Make your bed	☺						
Put pajamas away	☺						
Brush your teeth	☺						
Get school work done							
Feed dog/cat	☺						
Kiss parents good-bye							

Writing notes to your kids is a great way to praise them for a job well done — or simply to show them that you love them. A note in their lunch box can say it all:

You did a great job
making your bed
this morning!
Thank you so much.
We love you,
   Mom & Dad

Your lesson for the day

Before you go anywhere, tell your kids what you're doing, where you're going, and how they're to behave. Set up the rules beforehand. Explain what's to be expected from your kids.

Chapter 3
Being a Consistent Parent

*T*he Parenting Game is played on this huge game board. But there are no squares! Your kids can just run wherever they want. In fact, it's the rule they play by: run amok. Your job as parent is to steer them, guiding as if there *were* little squares to move across. When you start doing that stuff, you had better keep it up. That's called being consistent.

Consistency requires a lot. Kids will power-up the charm to get you to break. They'll smile. They'll cry. They'll toss tantrums like the pizza man flipping a pie. But you mustn't waver. The result will be well-behaved children, not brats. (All of your kids' future teachers will appreciate that fact. As will your neighbors, family, and friends.) Basically, anyone who meets your kids will be pretty grateful to you.

The ground rules for consistency

Before you can practice your never-ending goal of being a consistent parent, you have to set the rules and boundaries for your kids. This approach makes perfect sense to anyone who cares about their children. Boundaries include things such as:

✔ where your children are allowed to play

✔ what kind of behavior is allowed

✔ what your children can play with

You get the idea. After you've set these rules (and you've made sure they're realistic), you consistently enforce them.

Consistency requires you to be as ignorant today as you were a year ago. — Bernard Berenson

Where your children are allowed to play

For babies, these areas are very limited. You can't allow your children to play in the bathroom one day, and then decide the next day that it's too dangerous to be in there (which it is).

As your children get older, you can slowly start expanding the territory. This territory depends largely on your house, yard, and neighborhood. If you live in the heart of New York city, your territory is different from people who live out in the sticks of North Idaho.

What kind of behavior is allowed

Behavior you need to keep an eye on is anything that is harmful to others, like hitting and throwing toys, as well as any behavior that is harmful to your children. For example, temper tantrums aren't always bad — unless your child starts banging his head against the floor. (This activity needs to be stopped and never allowed again!)

What your children can play with

Everything your children see is a potential toy. Buttons, coins, balloons, candy. You name it, and it has *toy* potential. Now, out of the things just mentioned, which ones are dangerous for small children to play with? All of them. Babies and toddlers have an annoying habit of putting everything in their mouths, regardless of the taste. Buttons, coins, balloons, and candy are all things babies typically choke on. (Read Chapter 29, "Ten Choking Hazards.")

You don't allow playing with the stereo one day, and then get mad the next day when you catch a child resetting your treble and bass knobs. You don't allow hitting one day, and then turn your back the next day. You should always handle these situations so that children know what they *can* do and what they *can't* do.

Be very critical about your decisions as to what your children can play with. For more information about safety and house rules, refer to Chapter 9, "Making a Safer Lifestyle."

Consistency Is the Art of Being an Unbending Jerk

Nobody suspects that gravity is evil. It's just there. (It's constant. It never gives up.) And it proves that to you all the time. Drop that brick on your toe, and, well, it's gravity again telling you to be more careful next time. Fall out a window? Hey, gravity pulls you down every time. Gravity won't kill you; it's the sudden stop that does.

As parents, you must be as consistent as gravity. *Never yield.* This policy is tough, and I'm sure gravity has a hard time of it, too. But gravity is always there, giving its gentle pull to keep us all on the ground.

If you've never been hated by your child, you've never been a parent. — Bette Davis

Make your words the law

Gravity is a law, but there is no punishment for breaking it because everyone is obedient. (Though floating off into the vacuum of space is *very* threatening.) So gravity's reward for being consistent is that no one breaks its law. As a parent, if you practice being consistent, it will be its own reward as well. There are two simple rules:

1. Think before you say something.

It's hard to be consistent when you say something goofy or something you don't mean. As long as you've taken the time to consider your words, you only need to avoid the major weapon your child has to battle your consistency: *persistence.* (And Chapter 4 teaches you how to follow through after being consistent.)

Yes, it's hard to think before dishing out some pleasant threat while you're stuck in traffic with a car full of three wild and untamed children. It's just much easier to scream. If that sounds like a situation you've been (or will be) in, refer to Chapter 5, "The Art of Keeping Your Cool."

Consistency also applies to your general nature. Most people have mood swings; you know, *off days* where nothing seems to go right. As adults, we usually let other people's moody days roll off of our back. Kids, however, will take your bad moods personally. Living with a schizophrenic can't be fun, so don't make your kids feel like they're living with one.

2. **Make your rules realistic.**

You can't be consistent on a rule that is set before it was really thought through — or on a rule that you would like to set, but which just doesn't jive with having kids around.

For example, you may want to establish the rule that all toys are kept in your children's rooms. But reality sets in, and you realize that it's an impossible rule to enforce because your kids spend all their free time in the family room. So, re-think your rule. Maybe the rule should be that all toys are to be picked up before anyone goes to bed. (That may be more of a realistic rule, anyway.)

Stick to your words or suffer the sad consequences

When you make the rules, make them stick. An hour's punishment is an hour long. That's 60 minutes, or 3,600 seconds (and a whole lot of nano seconds). The instant you give in the punishment becomes less effective, and your kids have won.

— "Johnny, why don't you tell the parents what their kids have won?"

— "Well, Jack, for the rest of their lives, the kids will be little jerks! Brats! That's right, they know the unbreakable laws of their parents can be broken. And if it can be done *once,* it can be done *again.* And if it can be done at home, it can be done at school, at work, for the rest of their lives! That's the grand prize for playing and losing the consistency round of *The Parenting Game!*"

Obviously, you don't want your kids to win this round. Therefore, be consistent. Let your word be the law: Think before you make the law. Make the law realistic. Then stick to it, even at the price of being a creep. Remember, no one has been a parent who hasn't felt a child's hate (at least for a little while).

Goofy rules set by anal-retentive parents

- Candy will be eaten neatly.
- There will be no drooling on the furniture.
- Poopy diapers are not allowed to overflow.
- Children will always be in bed and asleep by 7:00 p.m.
- Children will clean all the food off their plates.

When your kids know that you're not going to stick to your word, you're in a parent death wish. Your children will be running your life (which is more painful than bikini waxing). That's the definition of a spoiled child — not one who has too many toys.

Please don't raise your kids to be brats. America will thank you for it.

Cuteness and Persistence: the Art of Breaking Your Consistency

It's very easy to thrust your jaw forward, point your chin to the sun, and announce to the heavens that you'll be consistent from this point forward. And you probably mean it. But you should count on two weapons in a child's arsenal against you: cuteness and persistence.

Don't discount these weapons. They're mighty nuclear missiles compared to your vow with your Creator to be consistent. History has shown that kids use these tools, so you must strengthen your resolve. To do that, become familiar with the ways of the *enemy*.

"I'm too precious for your feeble attempt at consistency."

The first several months of your children's lives you spend telling them how utterly cute they are. They're angels. They're cuddly. They know this, and store the knowledge for future use, at a time when they can also use their countenances to pour on the charm. "Watch me light up Mommy like a Christmas tree." This is a learned behavior taught by us as parents, and children can put it to good use.

When the time comes to be firm and consistent, you think before you speak. You say what you mean. (It's the law, right?) But then comes the charmer. Out pops the boo-boo lip. Eyes swell with tears. Emotional pain contorts the face. "How could you do such a thing to me when I live to love you?"

This is emotional warfare! It has a purpose, primarily to make you give in. To make you break with being consistent. This is the point where you can't give in.

Don't give in! No matter what!

Remember, you thought of the law first. You set out to be consistent, so keep with it. Don't change your mind.

This is really a game your kids are playing, a game called "I'm going to get my way." It's not, "I'm cute, and you emotionally wounded me." That's just not true. Your kids rely on you to be consistent. Don't let them down even though it looks like just the opposite. If you give in, not only do you lose, but so does the charmer.

Loving a child doesn't mean giving in to all his whims; to love him is to bring out the best in him, to teach him to love what is difficult. — Nadia Boulanger

"Give me persistence and I'll carve Mt. Rushmore with a spoon."

Inconsistent parents are the perfect foil. You tell your child he's behaved badly and there'll be no dessert. Then the imp decides to clean his room or do some other chore you've been nagging him for and — lo — a sweet-faced angel asks you for dessert. Don't waver! You're answer is still "No."

Persistence is the art of doing something over and over, maybe with subtle changes between, but still over and over. Ever wonder why kids ask again and again when you say "No"? Because there may be some remote chance you'll change you mind. Why? Because, maybe, just perhaps, there was a time you *did* change your mind in the past. That's the payoff of persistent effort.

You must be constant! Don't let the persistence wear you thin. You must win this game because your kids win when you give in. If you break down, everyone loses: You lose because they know how to get to you, and they lose because they *need* your consistency to help keep them from developing brathood.

Your kids will continue testing you, but they won't spend as much time doing it when they realize you don't go back on your word or succumb to whining and temper tantrums. After all, why bother when it doesn't work?

Building Walls around Your Children

Building walls for your children is important. I'm not talking about walls like Edgar Allan Poe's in *The Cask of Amontillado*. No one who loves their children would do that — build brick walls around them in their basement. (Poe was sick!) Instead, these walls are mental barriers erected to keep your kids safe and you sane.

You build the walls by setting rules. The rules are designed to keep your children safe and happy. For example, there are rules against climbing on things and throwing, as well as rules on how to behave around grandma, how to act in the store, and how to treat siblings. These rules form walls around your children. But your kids will *constantly* push against the walls. They'll always test you, and they do this for two reasons:

1. **They need to know where the walls are.**

   This knowledge makes them feel secure. Therefore, you must erect the walls and keep your kids within them if you want secure kids.

2. **They push because they need to grow.**

   Your children can't always have the rule not to play outside unsupervised. Eventually they'll outgrow that rule — as they'll also outgrow rules on nap times and what they're allowed to play with.

Eventually you'll move the walls outward. Don't lower the walls! The kids need them there. But move them out, set a later bed time, change the *off-limits* rules. And be consistent about it. Maybe even announce a change and say why: "You've done such a good job of turning off the TV after watching it, we think you're old enough and responsible enough to use the VCR by yourself now."

Never interpret your kids' pushing against the walls as a reason for taking the walls down. Kids push but they rely on your consistency. You must be consistent and keep those walls up for them to be secure, happy people. They get some sadistic type of pleasure testing you, but they really do like for you to set their boundaries and have you enforce them.

Your lesson for the day

As your children get older and more responsible, the more you can let the walls out and allow them to do more things. But even then, they'll still push.

The 5th Wave

By Rich Tennant

"DON'T TOUCH ANYTHING. DON'T PICK ANYTHING OFF THE FLOOR AND EAT IT. DON'T PLAY WITH YOUR EARS. DON'T FOOL AROUND WITH BILLY MAGUIRE'S RETAINER. DON'T GRAB ANYONE'S HAIR. DON'T FORGET TO SAY PLEASE AND THANK YOU. DON'T PICK YOUR NOSE, TALK LOUD OR PLAY WITH TOO MANY TOYS. AND HAVE A WONDERFUL TIME."

Chapter 4
Follow Through

"I'm going to give you to the count of three, and then you'll really be in trouble."

"Don't make me have to come after you."

"If you do that one more time, you'll be sorry."

Do these statements sound familiar? Maybe your parents didn't use any of them on you, but you've heard them. These are threats of sorts. They're meant to *scare* kids into proper behavior. Do they work? Not really. As an adult, if you had someone as big and tall as we are to our kids threaten you like this, wouldn't you listen? Then what is it that kids know that we don't? Could it be that they've heard these threats before and realized that nothing's going to happen? That's why this chapter is on *follow-through,* which is related in a weird way to *consistency.*

"Follow Through with What?"

Follow-through has two parts:

✔ When you tell your children you're going to do something, be it good or bad, you do it.
✔ When you punish or discipline your children, you follow through with the discipline, and then you follow up on the discipline to ensure they understood why they were disciplined.

"I said I would do it, and I'm going to."

Children need to know that if you say you're going to do something, you do it. It lets them know that they can trust what you say — and that you're a reliable person. This works for both good and bad situations.

When you promise to get your children a treat at the store if they clean their room, it gives them something to work toward. They know you're going to buy them that treat. When, on the other hand, you tell your children that if they start hitting each other, they'll have their toys taken away for the rest of the night, they'll understand you mean that, too.

Promising to do something (whether it be good or bad) and never doing it, makes you look like a flake, even to your kids. Your children need to trust and believe what you say.

"Now, did you learn anything from this?"

Follow-through after punishment and discipline consists of three different but related situations. To be completely effective, you should follow each one of these steps:

1. When you see your children doing something wrong, stop the action or behavior. Don't turn your head and pretend you didn't see it.

2. After you've set a punishment, you follow up by enforcing the punishment.

3. You then follow up to make sure your children understood why they were punished for what they did. Punishment is not effective if your children don't learn anything from it.

It's extremely ineffective if you punish your children and they have no idea why they're being punished. Never assume that what your children just did is obviously wrong to them. (They may be oblivious that they did *anything* wrong.)

Discipline and punishment should be used as a form of education. You discipline your children so they learn right from wrong. You punish them for the same reason. Refer to Chapter 24, "Punishment and Discipline."

[Parents] must get across the idea that "I love you always, but sometimes I do not love your behavior." — Amy Vanderbilt

"Are you ready to try follow-through?"

You find your son taking the claw end of the hammer and ripping chunks of wood out of your deck. You tell him that he knows better and — as a punishment — he can't watch television for a week. The follow-up action is to forbid him to watch television. If the next day he comes home from school and switches on *Batman* (and you let him watch it), you've failed. You didn't follow through. You're not being reliable. You're flaking out. So now your son thinks that since he basically got away with the hammer deal, maybe he can try the hammer out on your new car. That should be *tons* of fun.

Your kids are better behaved if they know that when you say you're going to do something, you do it. You don't give false warnings and you don't make wimpy threats that you know you aren't going to make happen.

I've Followed Through, Now My Life Is Easy!

Your life will become a heavenly bliss when your kids get to the point where they understand when you say you're going to do something, you do it. You don't make threats and you don't give twenty warnings.

You'll stop chasing your kids after the same violations if they know that you follow through with the punishment that you say you're going to give.

Understand that training your kids to follow your direction takes time. It's a learning process for them. It may take several times of punishing your children for doing something you've told them not to do before they get the idea that it's just not worth it. Then again, your children may catch on quickly. A lot has to do with that *stubbornness* gene that kids tend to inherit from their parents.

It's your children's job to test you. Don't be surprised if your children will try to get away with something that you thought was understood they *weren't supposed to do*. It's just their way of making your life a little more interesting.

Watch Your Mouth!

Too many parents enjoy hearing themselves say things like, "Ginger, if you don't stop kicking the back of my chair, I'm going to rip your legs off." Do you think the parents really mean it? Hopefully not. So if you don't believe it, your child won't either. Your child learns to stop believing threats. I'm not at all saying that you should start ripping your children's legs off. Be careful what you say. Make sure that you do what you say you're going to do and you mean what you say. Parents like to hear themselves make goofy threats. It actually sounds kind of funny, and the kids probably laugh at the very thought. But you know they aren't taking you seriously.

Unrealistic threats

- ✔ If you don't start cleaning your room, you'll be grounded for a year!

- ✔ If you don't get your homework done, I'll never let you out of your room!

- ✔ I'll beat you to a bloody pulp.

- ✔ If you don't behave, we'll never take you outside again.

- ✔ I'll never buy you another toy for as long as you live.

- ✔ Eat everything on your plate, or I'll never feed you again.

Threats are hard to follow through with because they're usually unrealistic and impossible to enforce. If you threaten your child that you'll never take him back to a restaurant, that means you'll never get to go back to that restaurant unless you get a babysitter. Is that what you *really* meant to say?

Timeliness — It's Oh-So-Important

Kids' memories are fairly short, so when you say you're going to do something, you have to act on it quickly. Don't put off discipline or punishment until another day. It's OK to allow yourself some time to gather your thoughts, perhaps even to calm down some and get the thought out of your head of sending your kids to military school.

Don't put off punishment. Your kids will have forgotten what happened if it takes a week after they've thrown the trash off the balcony (and not picked it up) for you to decide to do something about it.

The purpose of follow-through is so that your kids can rely on what you say. They also learn that there are consequences for their actions. If you threaten to punish them for something and you don't do it, you might as well not have said *anything* in the first place.

Your lesson for the day

Following through with your child is hard to do. But like any good business deal, if you follow through with what you've done, it pays off in the end.

Chapter 5

The Art of Keeping Your Cool

. . . .

In This Chapter

▶ Yes, you have an "inner coolness"

▶ The Deaf Syndrome

▶ Having a patient child

▶ Sometimes it's just too hard to be patient

. . . .

*Y*ou may think you're a patient person. People who take 36 items to the 15-item-limit line in the grocery store don't really bother you. The airhead working at the Espresso booth doesn't annoy you when she won't get off the phone to her boyfriend long enough to take your order. You can live through that, too. You've even managed to get through rush hour in 100-degree temperature without an air conditioner and not flip anyone off. You're a real champ when it comes to *patience.* Then you have kids. . .

It would be great if there were an Evelyn Wood course on getting patience and getting it fast. You know, some course that you could take at night and then — all of a sudden — have this wonderful skill that you would be so proud to show off to your friends. Boy, wouldn't they be envious.

Finding Your Inner "Coolness"

You may have had patience. So you thought. But how are you going to act when you find your three-year-old daughter, who has just emptied a whole bottle of Joy perfume over herself and smeared lipstick (not the inexpensive *Cover Girl* kind, but the expensive *Borghese* kind) completely over her face, your walls, and maybe even the cat who got in her way, only so that she can be pretty like Mommy? Do you:

1. Lose all the color from your face, whisk your daughter up, and throw her into the bathtub?

2. Say, "Don't you look pretty. How about we get you all cleaned up? The next time you play dress up, why don't you ask me and I'll help you"?

3. Look at your daughter, heave a sigh, and then turn around and leave?

If you're sitting there scratching your head, the answer is number two.

Number one is for those parents who don't have any patience. They failed to see the humor in the situation. Number three is a lost case. These people are obviously at their wit's end and don't even want to deal with the situation. Parents who chose number two are dealing with their daughter in a calm, relaxed way — at the same time getting the point across that their daughter ought not do this again without supervision.

Being impatient means you will eventually do something foolish. — old Japanese proverb

Not having patience may stem somewhat from your own upbringing. Your parents may not have had much patience, so you weren't able to learn from them. Although your inner "coolness" is there just waiting to come out, maybe it can't because of things you're overlooking, such as:

✔ your attitude

✔ how you feel

✔ high expectations

✔ feeling rushed or hurried

Your attitude may need fine tuning

Having patience all begins with your attitude. If you're a perfectionist, now is the time to get over it. Not until your kids are grown and out of the house will everything be sane, clean, and in order (at least not all at once). If you have the attitude that it's all going to be OK — and you can deal with it for about 18 years — you're ahead of the game.

Wisdom is learning what to overlook. — Will James

Don't take things too seriously. Allow kids to be kids and do the goofy things that they're supposed to do. This means they're going to make messes, drop and break things, spill, topple, destroy, kill, mutilate . . . you know, be kids. The key here is not to go ballistic when these things happen. If you accept the fact that these things will happen, you won't lose your patience when they do.

Your thought for the day: I'm not going to be in a hurry today. I'm going to remain calm and relaxed. Whatever spills can be cleaned. Whatever breaks can be replaced or glued. I won't take out my anger or frustrations on my kids because I love them.

"Why don't I have more patience?"

You'll lose your patience because you're over-tired, over-stressed, have the feeling of being over-worked without any help, and don't have enough time for yourself. If you *fix* these areas, you're more likely to have patience with the little things kids can do to push your stress buttons.

Fixing these areas means you go to bed earlier. Being stressed and tired is not worth staying up late to watch David Letterman.

If your family comes home and leaves all the work to you while they then go off and do their own thing, ask them to help you. Remind them that you didn't have kids to do all the parenting yourself and you want some help. They, in turn, will stand and scratch their head and say, "Well . . . what do ya mean?" That's when you sit down and divvy out chores and tasks to those in your family. If so far your family is only your spouse — or even a roomate if you're a single parent — put together chores that will take some of the work schedule off you.

Read Chapter 19, "Guidelines for Co-Parenting (The Two-Party System)." This chapter will give you information about how to make the most out of having a partner to help you.

Lower those expectations

You may also lose patience because your expectations for your kids are too high. You can't expect your five-year-old to sit quietly through all your favorite parts of *An Affair To Remember*, nor can you expect your one-year-old to remember to stay out of the toilet paper even though you've told him at least 50 times. He may really love toilet paper, and you may have to tell him another 50 times (along with taking the toilet paper away and moving him out of the room where the toilet paper is).

Then again, maybe that same five-year-old always sits quietly while watching *Sesame Street*. And maybe you've only had to tell your one-year-old to leave the litter box alone three times before he got the idea.

Don't expect your kids to listen to you the same in all situations, and don't expect miracles from them. Parenting is a lot easier when you stop setting expectations that are too high on your kids and you take them at face value.

Don't take devilish actions personally. When you tell your toddler not to do something and he does it anyway, he's not disobeying you to make you mad. He's either young enough that his stubbornness outweighs anything you could possibly say, or he's just testing his boundaries — pushing on the *walls* (as mentioned in Chapter 3). Realize that this behavior is very typical, is to be expected, and shouldn't be taken personally.

Even though you have kids you probably love more than anything else, it's extremely important that you have some time to pamper yourself. It's easier to have patience with your kids if you feel good about yourself.

Read Chapter 19, "Guidelines for Co-Parenting (The Two-Party System)," for more information about relieving your workload and taking care of yourself. It's amazing how much more patience you have when you actually feel human.

"I need more time!"

Patience runs short when time runs short. Being late can drive some people insane, and they take everyone with them. If you're this way, you can solve the problem by giving yourself lots of time to do things and to get to places. Do as much advanced planning as possible.

Don't wait until the last minute to do anything. Always think ahead and plan your time out. Trying to hurry your kids can be disastrous. If you tell them, "We've got to hurry," that phrase automatically puts them in a time lock, and they're sure to go even slower.

If you know that your family has something special to do in the morning, do most of the preparations at night so there is little left to do by morning. It's easier to be calm and relaxed if you aren't hurried.

"I Can't Hear You."

Kids develop *The Deaf Syndrome.* That's when you talk and they act like they don't hear you. Some people would call it ignoring. Why is this behavior mentioned in a section on patience? Because the first time this happens — when you realize that your child who not long ago was crawling on your lap to have you read a story — is flat out ignoring you, you'll go crazy.

This is the time when it's acceptable to lose your patience. I bet you thought I was going to say to breathe or meditate and get over it, didn't you? No. Ignoring is a bad habit and somehow your children will learn to do this. Don't let them. Resist yelling, but once you do get their attention, let them know how rude it is to ignore someone.

Recognize the differences between *being a kid* and *rude behavior.* Have patience with kid stuff. Don't tolerate rudeness or disobedience.

Don't laugh

Don't laugh at your children if they get really upset over something you may think is silly. It's not silly to them, and no one likes to be laughed at.

For example: Your daughter is trying to make her bed, but can't seem to control the blankets. She's sitting in the middle of her bed crying, with the blankets piled all around. It's a funny-looking sight, but your child is obviously very frustrated. The last thing she needs is for you to come in and laugh at her. She won't see the humor in it at all.

Developing Patience in Your Child

There aren't any shortcuts when it comes to teaching your children to have patience. There are going to be several times in their lives when really important things, like not being able to get a round toy in a square hole, is going to put them into a screaming rage.

These are difficult situations. You want them to learn that they have to work things out for themselves, but you also don't want them getting so frustrated that they quit playing with their project (or whatever it is) that has made them upset.

Watch carefully. If it's your toddler who's getting upset and is on the verge of picking up a toy and throwing it across the room, come in and very calmly help him. Reassure him that nothing is worth getting upset about.

If it's your six-year-old child who's getting upset, let him try to work it out. If he comes to you for help, talk him through his problems, but still let him work on the project so that in the end he will have been the one to complete it .

Lack of patience and frustration is linked heavily to kiddyhood. Your calm and reassuring manner is the best way to teach your child that no matter what happens, things can be solved calmly and with a little bit of patience.

"I Failed!"

Beaver Cleaver's mom was the queen of patience. No matter how goofy Beaver was, his mom was there, never raising her voice, never seemingly annoyed. She was great! She also had to be that way only thirty minutes a week. Anyone can be patient for that long. Even if we had *the Beaver* for our son.

Of all wild animals, the boy is the most unmanageable. — Plato

Good days to have patience

- When your spouse changes the diarrhea-filled diaper on your white Battenburg comforter.

- When your two-year-old has taken the time and effort to carefully peel an edge off the wallpaper in order to more easily rip off a big sheet.

- When your one-year-old has dug in the drawer, found an old metal cookie cutter, and left it on the floor for you to step on barefooted.

- When someone has left the bathroom door open and you find your toddler taking the toilet paper and unrolling the whole toilet paper roll into the toilet.

- When your toddler takes the pint of ice cream from the grocery bag set on the floor — and you find it three days later behind the house plant in the dinning room.

- When everyone under the age of five in the house has decided what great fun it would be to throw anything down the laundry chute.

In real life, you'll lose your patience. It's human nature, sort of like getting zits. (It happens to everyone.) How you handle the situation afterwards is what's really important. When you find yourself losing your cool, apologize to your family. Let them know the point that you were trying to make . . . but that you should have made this point without losing control of yourself. When you let your kids know that you lost your patience and that you're sorry for doing so, you're letting them know that sometimes even parents make mistakes — but you're sorry and you'll try hard not to lose your patience again. It is possible to get your point across to your children while at the same time letting them know that parents aren't perfect.

One common way that you as a parent lose patience is when you see your children involved in something that you think is taking too long. Avoid jumping in and trying to help them if they seem happy to work at their project at their own speed. By jumping in you'll undermine their confidence and — in the end — you'll be doing more harm than good.

Don't give your children a chore to do without the understanding that it probably won't get done as quickly as you would like. That's OK. Let your children accomplish the task in their time. Don't allow piddling (the technical term for standing around and not doing anything), but don't jump in and finish the task if they are doing everything right . . . just a little slowly.

Your lesson for the day

Patience is a skill, a talent, a blessing. Whatever you want to call it, it's something that will be tested over and over and over again. Just take each situation slowly, take deep breaths, and hide all your sharp objects.

Chapter 6
Behavior Management

· ·

In This Chapter

▶ Learning about behavior management

▶ The power of praise

▶ The strong effects of giving lots of attention

▶ How to keep idle hands busy

▶ The importance of keeping a safe and happy house

▶ Laughter is the best medicine

· ·

*E*ver hear the term *terrible twos*? Who hasn't, right? Those poor two-year-olds have had a bad rap. It's not enough that they've spent the last two years learning to talk so they can yell right in the middle of cousin Tracy's wedding, "Mommy, I went poop!" They've also learned to walk in front of cars in the parking lot, run from us at bedtime — and their manual dexterity is great. (They practice it all the time as they peel off all the labels on your canned goods.) That's a lot to learn in two years, and here we go calling them *terrible*. The nerve!

Two year olds aren't really that bad. Kids *at any age* can seem difficult if they aren't managed the right way. They're out of control. This chapter is all about how to manage your kids so they don't get to the point where you want to call them *terrible*.

Behavior Management (or the Manipulation Game)

Behavior management is actually manipulating your children's time and behavior so that they don't have the time — or need — to get into situations that make us want to label them *terrible*. If you're an over-sensitive parent who thinks it's just awful to want to manipulate your children, look the word up. It means to guide, direct, or handle.

So the thought of manipulating your children isn't so bad when you realize that all you're doing is guiding or directing the things that they do so they stay out of trouble. The way you guide your children is by doing the following:

✔ Give praise.

✔ Give lots of attention.

✔ Keep idle hands busy.

✔ Keep a safe and happy house.

✔ Don't forget to laugh.

Train a child in the way he should go: and when he is old, he will not depart from it. — Proverbs

Give praise

Offer your children *lots* of praise. Praise means giving hugs, kisses, pats on the back and on the head, and saying things like, "Wow, look what you did" or "That's wonderful" when your children have done something good.

When you praise your children, you're giving them positive feedback for what they've just done. They, in turn, will want to do more things to make you happy. Kids love to hear how good they are, that you're proud of them, or that you think they're special. Don't hold out on giving these comments to your kids — you need to be their best cheerleaders:

"Simon, Simon, he's our man, if anyone can break it, Simon can!"

When you praise your children for picking up their toys, or taking something to the trash, they'll quickly learn to do these things again to get that same positive attention from you. Say "Thank you" or "Good for you" whenever you can. When your child brings you a dead spider he found on the floor, smile big, give him a hug, and thank him. He needs to know that you appreciate his efforts.

Praise, however, is like eating M&Ms. If you ate the one-pound bag of M&Ms all in one sitting, several times a day, you'd get sick. Too much of a good thing. But if you spread that bag out over a period of time and just ate one M&M every now and then, you wouldn't get sick. Same thing with giving out praise. You don't want to overdo it because both you and your child would *get sick* (sort of). But if you dole it out like one M&M every little bit, it'll just make you feel warm and glowing all over, just like M&Ms do.

It's possible to give your child *unrealistic* praise. Be realistic. If your daughter shows you her finger painting from school, let her know what a great job she did and that you're proud of her. Go a step further and put the finger painting on the wall. There's no need to say or do more. Don't feel compelled to say it's the best finger painting you've ever seen and that it should be displayed in a museum or framed in gold. Your kids are bright and will recognize insincerity when they hear it.

Give lots of attention

Kids love attention, and they'll get it anyway they can. If they can't get your attention by doing good things, they'll get it by doing things they know are wrong. If the only time you acknowledge that your kids are around is when they do something wrong, they'll continue to do wrong things. To a child, negative attention is better than no attention. This is very important, so let me say it again: *Negative attention is better than no attention.*

Give a little love to a child, and you get a great deal back. — John Ruskin

Spending time with your kids is the best way to give them your attention. No matter if you stay at home or work outside the home, you can *still* give quality time to your kids. Quality time doesn't mean the whole family sitting for four hours watching TV. It means turning the TV off (Oh Lordy, anything but *that!*) and playing games together, reading books, going for walks, toilet papering your neighbor's tree — anything!

Giving kids your attention means listening to them when they talk. I don't mean half-way listening and saying "uh huh" like we do to our spouses when they're talking about their day at work. I mean sitting down, looking children in the eye, and listening. Ask questions. Be interested. It shows that you're paying attention even if your question turns to, "So you say you painted the cat blue?"

Raising kids is not the time to be selfish with your time. You can be selfish later on when they're grown and having kids of their own.

If you feel guilty about not being able to spend enough time with your kids, resist trying to *buy* their attention. You don't have to have every weekend a Disneyland-kind-of-day. And you don't have to continually buy them gifts as a means of letting them know you love them. Time. Time is what they want most from you. You can't buy it anywhere, and Kmart doesn't discount it during their blue-light special.

Don't wait until it's too late

Nothing should be more important than your kids. There's not going to be any other time in your life when someone's only joy is spending time with you. Don't blow it. Don't be a parent who looks back in life and whose only regret is not having spent enough time with the kids. A day will come when your kids are going to have their own set of friends, their own interests, and their own schedules. If you don't make time for them now, they may not make time for you later.

Keep idle hands busy

Kids will look for something to do if you don't provide some sort of entertainment. This doesn't mean you have to put on the Las Vegas showgirl feathers (although your kids would probably enjoy *that*). It also doesn't mean you have to fall off the scale on the other end and never allow them the time to be quiet and get creative with their own play. However, if you don't keep kids busy most of the time, they may choose to color on the wall, string toilet paper all over the bathroom, or pull all the towels out of the cabinet. And, as experience shows, it's really hard to put toilet paper back on the roll!

Your kids, no matter what age, are on some type of schedule. They get up, eat breakfast, eat lunch, eat dinner. What do they do the rest of the time? Fill up some of the empty spots in their schedules with activities. Have them help you do something around the house or get them involved in a project. This is how day care workers are able to keep so many kids under control — they fill up the day with activities.

The idea behind this topic is that if your children are kept busy, they can't get into trouble. Keeping busy doesn't mean that you have to enroll your children into every conceivable activity. It means keeping them active enough that they don't have the time, or need, to look for activities to keep boredom from setting in.

Good projects for kids (which is also helping around the house) are putting silverware away — except for the butcher knives, of course — sorting laundry, wiping cupboards, and picking up toys. Remember to praise their efforts. These activities need to be done when you're in the room with your child. You not only need to monitor their work to teach them good work habits, but it also satisfies the requirement of spending time with your children.

Keep a small basket of toys in each room of the house. When you go to do laundry, your children will have a basket of toys to play with. *Try* to keep these toys in this room. That way they'll be somewhat new when you and your children come back to do more laundry — and they won't get bored with them.

Keep a safe and happy house

A safe house is a happy house. This sounds extremely corny, but it's true. The more you do to childproof your house, the less time you spend following your kids around putting back porcelain figurines or sweeping plant dirt up off the floor. You'll realize that it's easier to have door locks on your cupboards than it is to follow your toddler around all day taking canned soup away.

Childproof your home the day you bring your baby home from the hospital. Don't wait until he's sticking a toy into an electrical outlet before you decide to put plastic caps on the sockets. You never know when your baby will be able to roll over to the staircase — until one day he does and is practicing a balancing act on the top stair.

Keeping your house childproof, such as removing glass objects or picture frames that are too low, will keep your child out of mischief. If it's not there to break or mutilate, the little one won't get into trouble.

Read Chapter 9, "Making a Safer Lifestyle," for more information about childproofing your home.

Don't forget to laugh

The best way to manage your kids is through humor. Approaching situations jokingly, or making everyday tasks fun, can turn otherwise uncomfortable confrontations into enjoyable situations.

Instead of saying, "Why isn't your room clean?"(which sounds very threatening and demanding), try saying, "You know, I thought you had carpeting in your room. Why don't you pick up your toys so that I can see your floor again?" Remember to add a "Thank you" to the end.

Another Way to Say It	
What you do say	*What you could say*
Just eat those peas!	I bet you can't eat just 12 peas! No kid has ever eaten that many. You might set the record.
Didn't I tell you to make your bed?	Let me time you to see how long it actually does take you to make your bed.
You left your shoes out. Get them picked up now!	Oh my gosh! Your shoes must have walked right out of your room. Why don't you help them back to the closet where they belong.

When you use humor, you still get your point across, but it comes across a lot better than demanding things from your kids. No one likes to be barked at every time they're being asked to do something. Your kids will be more receptive to your requests if they come across as friendly and non-threatening.

If you're a parent, it's guaranteed that you'll develop those unwanted "character" lines by all the laughing your kids induce. Don't stop the laughing just because things don't seem so funny anymore. If your kids have a messy room or forget chores, it doesn't mean you have to turn into *the Grinch*.

Chores can be fun. Make picking up laundry into a game of toss into the laundry basket. Turn a day of picking up toys into a race to see who can pick up the most toys the quickest.

Your lesson for the day

The only way to effectively manage your children is to pay attention and spend time with them. You can't do this by being a weekend parent, by being oblivious to what your kids are up to, or by not making your kids the most important things in your life.

Part II
Getting to the Nitty Gritty

"I FIND IT EASIER TO SAY 'NO', IF I IMAGINE THEM SAYING, 'MOMMY, CAN I HAVE THE LATEST OVER-HYPED, OVER-PRICED, COMMERCIAL EXPLOITATION OF AN OBNOXIOUSLY ADORABLE CARTOON CHARACTER.'"

In this part...

Certain parenting issues have plagued the world for centuries. Did Genghis Khan have trouble getting his son, Ogadai Khan, to bed (especially with a name like that)? Did Agrippina struggle to get wee Emperor Nero out of the bath before he looked too much like a prune? And did Mrs. Curie have trouble keeping darling Marie from pulling everything out of the cupboards?

The great parents of the world have anguished over these issues for ages. Have faith, you're not the first. And you're not alone.

Chapter 7
Raising Your Child

· ·

In This Chapter

▶ The importance of treating your child like a person

▶ Talking to your kids with respect

▶ The power of positive communication

▶ Do you interact with your child?

▶ Giving your kids time reduces your stress level

▶ Parenting means you and your mate working together

▶ Making moral fiber a part of your life

· ·

*I*n the movie *Raising Arizona,* Holly Hunter tells Nicholas Cage, "If you love me, you'll get me a child." And so he does. Of course, he has to steal one for her, but that's beside the point. Once they have their beautiful little boy, they set him down and look at each other. Holly Hunter breaks out in tears and says, "I love him so much." After that point, they're a little unsure about what to do with this child they both love so much.

That's the dilemma this chapter is about. Here are more guidelines and some general things to practice once you have that child you're destined to love "so much!"

Treat Your Child Like a Person

Don't misinterpret this section's title, "Treat Your Child Like a Person," to mean "Treat Your Child Like an Adult." Those are two different things all together. The difference between the two are that adults make life-long decisions. Not necessarily good decisions, but they make them. Your kids may not be able to decide what to wear to the park. They do, however, deserve the respect that all people deserve.

To treat your child like a person means to treat your child with respect. Don't take advantage of children or embarrass them because they can't fight back. (You wouldn't even think of it, right?)

Consider this scenario: A man and women are going to the grocery store. The man tells the women he has to go to the bathroom. She says, "OK," and he goes. No big deal.

Now change the players: A mother and her son are going to the store, and the son says he has to go to the bathroom. The mother grabs the boy by the arm and jerks him while at the same time saying, "I told you to go to the bathroom before we left. Can't you hold it?" The boy, with tears in his eyes, says, "No Mom. I really have to go." So the mother yanks her son to the bathroom, all the while saying, "I can't believe you do this to me."

Ever see that happen? It's embarrassing and humiliating to the child. Can you imagine this woman saying to her husband, "John, I told you to go to the bathroom before we left. Are you *sure* you have to go? Can't you *hold it* until we get home?"

Most parents don't realize they're humiliating their kids. It just happens because parents either lose patience or just don't think about what they're doing. It's easier to overlook children's feelings if they aren't capable of saying, "Hey, knock it off, you're embarrassing me!"

Taking the time to understand and care for another person is a true sign of love. — wise old lady

Another embarrassment and potential humiliating situation for children is making them perform their little "tricks" or talents when they don't want to. When you make your children perform before others (like playing the piano) when they don't want to, you risk ruining their enjoyment of that talent. Their talent may be a personal thing that they enjoy doing privately — but not for an audience.

If you do get your kids to perform their tricks, understand the difference between laughing *at* them and laughing *with* them. No one likes to be laughed at.

Talk to Them (and about Them) with Respect

Your children should be the most special things you have. They're like a precious stone that should be treated with care and shown with great pride. Even if your three-year-old dumps juice all over the floor, remember that he's special. He dumped that juice with such pride and precision, even a diamond cutter would be envious. How else could someone dump juice and not only get it on the floor, but *also* in your purse, drawer, and the chair across the room? There's no need to go into an explanation to your friends about how clumsy your son is.

Too many parents are comfortable bad-mouthing their children. You're supposed to be your children's greatest supporter, their cheering squad. This can't be done if you're always pointing out their shortcomings. After all, they've managed to keep their mouth shut about how you can't pull out of the driveway without knocking over the garbage cans.

Your children are very bright. They catch on to more than you realize. Imagine how crushed you would be if you heard your best friend talking about your big butt, your inability to drink without spilling it on your shirt, or your body making mysterious noises in public.

Your children share the same feelings you do about being embarrassed. They like to know that when you talk about them, you bring up the good things they do and not the bad. This practice may sound like bragging on your children. So what if it is. You have something to be very proud of, and it's OK to let other people know that you think your children are *terrific.*

Children are likely to live up to what you believe in them. — Lady Bird Johnson

Use Positive Communications (or What Most of Us Call "Happy Talk")

The best way to let your kids know you think they're special is to treat them special. Do this by the way you talk to them. Don't talk down to them in a superior way, don't be condescending, don't use foul language, and don't yell.

Your communication style should be positive, up, and cheerful. Sort of like Mr. Rogers. Mr. Rogers is cool. He never says anything bad about anyone, he always says nice things about the people he meets, and he looks at life in a positive manner. He doesn't even yell at his train friend when he's late. Mr. Rogers uses *positive communication.*

Your kids will use your style of talking. If you speak in negative tones (calling everything *stupid* or *dumb*), so will your children. If you think positively, you'll use positive words — and your kids will do the same.

Read more about communication skills in Chapter 2.

Children have never been very good at listening to their elders, but they have never failed to imitate them. — James Baldwin

Interact with Your Children

Like your communication with your children, interacting should be fun and positive.

Recognize the difference between being in the same room with your kids and interacting with them. The difference is when you interact with your children, you become a part of their lives; you participate in their conversation and their playing. Too many families think that if they all sit in front of the television together, they're doing the *family togetherness thing.* It doesn't work that way. You can't be interacting with each other if you're sitting in front of the TV mesmerized by the latest basketball-shoe commercial.

Your goal as a family should be to schedule your life so that you have as much time as possible to interact with your children. This means making choices. You can either work late every night — or you can choose to go home and spend time with your family. You can opt to have everyone grab snacks all evening, or you can all work together to make dinner, sit down and eat together, and then all clean up together. You can decide to watch TV after dinner — or you can do something that everyone in the family can have fun doing together, like playing a game. Leave your activities open to things that encourage communication between you and your family.

Don't fall into the dreaded pit of thinking that your job, making money, is more important than spending time with your family. If you were to ask your kids what they would like most — money, or to spend more time with you — *time* would be the answer.

As your kids get older and start to have outside interests like sports or clubs, you may have to actually schedule a *Family Night.* This night should be where everyone commits to staying home and spending the evening together. Make it a rule that there are no friends allowed over, no telephone calls, no working late, and no plopping in front of the TV all night.

Letting your kids choose what nights to have the TV on and what nights to have "No TV Night" will help eliminate TV wars. — Denise DeLozier

Television robs you of time with your family

The most interaction you get from spending all your time in front of the TV is when you ask each other who has the bag of chips. Since it's unrealistic to ask people to go without their television (because, after all, it is a form of entertainment), *limit the amount of TV you watch.* Keep to shows that you and your kids are able to discuss afterwards, and watch it only for special occasions. Plan your TV watching. Never fall under the lure of let's-see-what's-on-next or watch TV while you're waiting for your show to come on.

Is TV evil? There have been studies on declining values and the disintegrating family, drawing this conclusion or that. Yet everything ties into the introduction of TV into American life. TV probably isn't evil. However, it can rob you of valuable time you can spend with your family. Don't let it do that to you. Control your TV and your TV viewing habits. Remember, the thing has an OFF button.

Give Kids Time

Your kids don't know, and won't know for several thousand years, what the concept of time is. In kindergarten, they'll start learning what yesterday, today, and tomorrow mean — but that knowledge really won't *mean* a lot. And certainly the phrase, "You have 15 *minutes* to brush your teeth and get in bed" means zilch. You might as well say "You have 15 *minogranits* to brush your teeth and get in bed."

If you want to keep your stress levels to a minimum, allow your kids lots of time to prepare for things. Buckets of time. Oodles of time. If they have one hour to get dressed, make their bed, and brush their teeth, you'd think that was enough. Generally it is. But, you never know when they have to engage in battle with ten invisible Putties, duel with the Joker, or re-dress all their Barbie dolls.

To keep your sanity, practice these steps:

- ✔ Give your kids only a few chores at a time rather than a long list of things to do. (You may have to give only one chore if you're dealing with a two or three year old).

- ✔ When you give your kids a chore, let them know how much time they have to finish it. Be realistic: Give them a little extra time. Don't assume that, if it takes you five minutes to sweep the porch, it'll take them five minutes. Since kids are oblivious to what *ten minutes* means, for example, show them a clock and let them know what the clock will look like when their job is to be done.

- ✔ Check on your kids periodically to make sure nothing is getting in their way of finishing their chore (you know, land mines, three-eyed monsters, the Princess of the Galaxy, and so on).

> ✔ Give them a countdown every ten to fifteen minutes. This intervention helps to teach them the concept of time. Also, they're not surprised when you walk in and say, "Time's up."
>
> ✔ When they've finished their chores, have them come back and give them something else to do. This doesn't leave room for the "But I forgot" line that kids dish out so easily (and which is probably the truth).

Share With Your Mate

Unless things have changed radically since this book went to press, the women are the ones who get pregnant, who go through labor and delivery, and who breastfeed. That's the way it happened in our house. If it happened differently in your house, we'd be interested in hearing about it. But it's not just one person's job to do all the parenting. Both parents need to be involved in *The Parenting Game*.

Both parents need to know how to change diapers (yes, even the explosive, stinky ones), clean up puke stains, discipline, put the kids to bed, and do all the other joys and chores of parenting. Not only will you miss out on a lot of fun and quality time with your kids if you don't help with the kiddy chores, but you're really going to irritate your mate if you don't help — and make him or her do all the work.

Read Chapter 19 for more information about the roles and relationship you and your co-parent should have during parenting.

Darn good reasons why things take so long for your children

✔ The stair monster grabbed their feet and wouldn't let them walk.

✔ Someone *hid* their toothbrush in the drawer (next to the toothpaste), and now they can't find it.

✔ Skipper couldn't possibly wear that outfit to bed.

✔ Someone maliciously put their pajamas in the drawer with their other pajamas. They aren't on the floor where they left them.

✔ The light was too bright, and they had to get ready with their eyes shut.

✔ You didn't say "Right now."

✔ They had to arrange all their stuffed animals up in a tidy little row so that they could watch.

✔ Their _____ hurts.
      (fill in the blank)

✔ They're hungry now.

Put Moral Fiber into Your Day

I've got to warn you, we're going to talk about religion here. The purpose is not to shove any specific type of religion down your throat (because really, there are so many cool ones out there). The only point of this section is to bring this issue to the table and have you consider it as a part of raising your child. Much like the fact you have to consider how to handle other topics that your child will raise, such as sex, divorce, death, and eating cookies for breakfast. It's just a fact of life.

When do you tell your children they should be kind to everyone? Hopefully before they've punched the neighbor kid in the stomach. How do you relay the message that they should honor and respect their mother and father? Your actions should be teaching these things — but is that always enough? Sometimes it's more effective to bring in an outside source when teaching things as important as moral issues. These lessons are best taught by bringing a spiritual aspect into your child's life.

Children who go to Sunday school are seldom found in court. — Reverend John Coppernoll

At home, you should be teaching lessons about honesty, making good decisions, being kind to others. When you go to your church or place of worship, these lessons are also taught, but in the form of, "this is the problem this guy had and this is how he handled it." This example is helpful to your children because they not only learn that their problems are real (and other people have them), but it also gives them a path to follow when these problems occur again.

Religion, no matter what religion it is, shouldn't be scary or unapproachable for children. In fact, children are the ones who usually have the greatest faith and openness about religion. They are also the ones who will bring up religious topics for you to answer.

The best way to teach kindness, love, and honesty is to be that way yourself (oh yes, it's the set-a-good-example theme again). Teach your children the importance of being fair and honest. Let them know that it's always best to do the right thing. Cheating is bad; telling the truth gets rewards and makes other people trust you.

If there is anything we wish to change in the child, we should first examine it and see whether it's not something that could better be changed in ourselves. — Carl Jung

Somewhat good reasons to go to church

✔ You get to wear nice clothes.

✔ It keeps your kids occupied for a while.

✔ You get to go into a large room and sing off-key with other people who are also singing off-key.

✔ It sets up the day to go out for lunch (no cooking).

✔ Free coffee (and even donuts at the nicer places).

✔ God likes it — what more can we say?

Going to your local house of worship is another way that you as a family can spend time together. You'll learn that sometimes things taught by Mom and Dad aren't taken to heart as much as if they're taught by someone else. As a parent, we need all the enforcement we can get to teach right from wrong. It's great to be able to ask your child, "Now Jordan, do you think Jesus stuck his tongue out at his mother?"

Many children have invisible friends that they make up so that they can have someone to talk and play with. Having someone like God as an invisible friend couldn't be a better choice. He's tons better than Pee Wee Herman.

Religion is a foundation. It's there for your children to build their lives upon. This foundation can always be there no matter what kind of problems your children will have as they grow up. Don't underestimate the power of being able to answer the question, "Where do babies come from?" with, "From God."

Your lesson for the day

Your children are going to rely on everything you do and say to make them the kind of people they grow up to be — not to put any pressure on you or anything.

Chapter 8
Your New Job — Teacher

You're in luck! You're getting a teaching position without doing the college thing, state-board tests, or the PTA (not until later). The only drawback is that you work seven days a week, no vacations, no sick days, and no weekly paycheck. You got this job the day you became a parent. Your students are your children. Your job description includes — but is not limited to — teaching English, Math, Science, Social Behavior, Gym, Health, and Hygiene. And the list goes on.

Your evaluation period comes every day. Look at your kids. How do they behave? What kind of people are they turning out to be? Do they seem well-balanced, or are they leaning more toward your Uncle Richard's side of the family?

Good or bad, you can look to yourself as part of the reason why.

When Do You Teach?

Your kids are constantly learning. You start teaching them the day they're born. They watch your smile, your actions, the way you talk and walk. Their goal is to do what you do. It's like a lifetime game of *follow the leader* — and you're the leader.

You'll be teaching your kids every day of their lives. Even when you're old and gray, you'll probably be giving your kids advice about how they should be raising their kids (or maybe you'll just give them a copy of this book). Of course, at that time, they won't appreciate the lessons as much.

If it's scary to think that your kids are going to try the things that you do, you need to take a close look at your lifestyle. If your three-year-old spills his crayon box, puts his hands on his hips, and yells, "Damn it!" — think before you get mad. Where do you think he learned that? He had to get it from someone. Maybe you'll find the culprit in your mirror.

Set a Good Example

The easiest and most effective way to teach is by example. Even as adults, we learn better by seeing other people do whatever it is that we want to learn. Can you imagine learning how to paint pictures without first watching someone else paint?

You are the bows from which your children are as living arrows sent forth. — Kahlil Gibran

Once your kids see you do something, they'll practice what they've learned. They see you walk, and then they'll slowly start out trying to walk. They hear you talk, and then they'll start babbling. They'll see you smoke, and then they'll head for the Bic lighter.

When your kids first learn to speak, they're imitating the words you say. Even when they say *Dada,* it's their try at *Daddy.* Hopefully, when they say *Baba,* that isn't short for *Bud Light.*

A friend relayed a story of her and her daughter who were driving down the highway when this man quickly cut them off and drove away. The daughter, seeing that her mother was mad, said, "Mom, why don't you just flip him off like you always do?"

Don't compare

Don't be tempted to teach your children by comparing their behavior to that of their siblings or to that of yourself. You need to keep this warning in mind when you set expectations for your children. Take each child separately and accept them for who they are. It really doesn't matter that one child has taken longer to walk, or talk, or ride a bike. Each child has a personal timetable.

Avoid Making a Spoiled Brat

We, as parents, do not maliciously do things to harm our children (at least we're not supposed to). So be aware of these things listed so that you don't turn your precious darling into a spoiled brat.

✔ **Don't buy love.**

Do you give your children everything they ask for? Some parents try to compensate for the fact that they aren't with their kids as much as they would like to be, so they give their kids everything they want. If you want to make it up to your kids that you aren't able to spend as much time with them, take a day off, or come home early and play games. Your child will get more enjoyment from an afternoon of sitting on the floor playing games and eating popcorn than from any toy you can buy.

✔ **Reward work.**

Let your kids earn the extra stuff they want by doing extra chores for you. They'll appreciate their possessions more if they've had to work for them.

✔ **Watch yourself.**

How do you act? Is your behavior less than perfect? If you criticize others, act hard to please when someone wants to do something for you, return or exchange gifts often, put too much importance on the monetary value of something, you are acting poorly and are setting a bad example for your child.

Read the book *The Berenstain Bears Get The Gimmies* to your children. It's a good lesson on kids (or bears) who ask for something every time they go to the store. Written by Stan and Jan Berenstain (Random House).

Good habits

You've put it off long enough. Now is the time to start developing *good* habits and get rid of those bad habits. Don't even think about saying that you don't have any bad habits. We *all* have bad habits. Admittedly, some are worse than others.

You can't have the attitude, "I'm going to pick my nose if I want. I'll teach my kids not to do it. They'll know better." Alas, it doesn't work that way. You are your kids' heroes. You are their role models. Whatever you do, your kids will want to do it, too. (If you think that your bad habits aren't going to affect your kids, you probably still think the earth is flat!)

How sharper than a serpent's tooth it is to have a thankless child! — Shakespeare

Only worth reading if you want a lesson on bad habits

Bad habits include smoking, getting drunk, taking drugs, yelling to get your point across, drinking out of the milk carton, cursing, lying, cheating, littering, crossing the road on a red light, farting in public, picking your nose, belching out loud, talking with food in your mouth, interrupting, ignoring, forgetting your mother on Mother's Day. These, of course, are just to name a *few*.

Please and thank you (alias: manners)

Don't underestimate the importance of good manners. You know that guy who flipped you off on the highway this morning? He didn't have good manners (or maybe it was the friend I mentioned earlier). You don't want your kids to grow up to be one of those finger flipping, road hogging, inconsiderate drivers who are plaguing the highways and byways of our lives.

Your children will grow up to be kinder and more considerate of others if you teach them how to be so when they're young. Again, you do this by setting a good example. You must always say *please* and *thank you* to your kids. Even if you are saying, "Please get your bicycle off my foot" or "Thank you for the dead slug."

Don't forget good table manners, also. We all tend to get a little too relaxed at the dinner table when it comes to proper behavior. Maybe you think it's funny when Daddy balances a spoon on the end of his nose or one of the kids makes a hat out of his napkin and wears it on his head all during dinner. If you don't mind this kind of monkeying around, even when you're out to dinner, ignore this advice. If you're like me and don't think it's appropriate to do this stuff in public, don't allow it at home.

Kids have a hard enough time remembering household rules. They have an even harder time remembering rules for *dinner at home* and rules for *dinner out* if the rules aren't the same. Some general table manners include no gross jokes, no elbows on the table, no throwing food, no leaning back with the chair, no talking with food in your mouth — and definitely no loud farting or belching.

In some cultures it's acceptable, even encouraged, to belch after a meal. However, don't let someone's excuse about practicing multiculturalism sway you. If belching isn't allowed in your culture, don't allow it at the table. And if you do burp (and who doesn't?), say "Excuse me." If you laugh, you've created a family precedent, and your kids will belch and laugh about it the first time they have dinner at a friend's house.

Good manners to teach are not to interrupt people while they talk, and not to shove your way in front of others to always be first (two things kids are *infamous* for doing). Teach your children how to write thank-you notes, make get-well cards for sick relatives, say *please* and *thank you,* acknowledge when someone is talking, say *good-bye* to someone who is leaving, share cookies with a friend, and always give their parents the green M&Ms.

Many children's books are designed to teach children about manners. I strongly recommend that you take the time to read these stories to you children. Examples of books on manners are *Manners* by Aliki (Scholastic Inc.), *Perfect Pigs* by Marc Brown and Stephen Krensky (The Trumpet Club), Richard Scarry's *Please & Thank-You Book* (Random House), and *The Berenstain Bears Forget Their Manners* by Stan and Jan Berenstain (Random House).

Boring safety and emergency information (but read it anyway)

Remember the movie *Kindergarten Cop*? Arnold Schwartzenegger asks how many kids were born in Astoria. Everyone in the class raises his or her hand. Then he asks how many kids were born outside of Astoria. Again, everyone raises their hands. What's the lesson here? As a parent, it's your job to teach your kids some basic information. This includes having them do the following:

- ✔ Memorize their complete name and phone number. (If they can remember their address, teach that, too.)
- ✔ Memorize the complete name of their parents or guardians.
- ✔ Memorize the phone number of a neighbor or family member in case there's an emergency and you can't be reached.
- ✔ Know what 911 is, what it means (and the phone number for 911 is nine-one-one), and what constitutes an emergency.
- ✔ Know who a stranger is and what to do if a stranger tries to get them in their car.
- ✔ Know who to go to in case they get lost in public places like shopping malls, fairs or carnivals, movie theaters, or parks.

It's an unfortunate fact of life, but there are people out there who steal children. To protect your children from this awful situation, invest in a home fingerprinting kit. It contains forms for information on your children as well as the supplies to do your own fingerprinting.

You and your children should have a private password that only you and your family knows. If someone tries to pick up your children, but doesn't know the password, tell your children not to go with this person. If you don't know how your children should respond to strangers or getting lost in public places, go to your local police station and get public safety information.

Read *Never Talk To Strangers* by Irma Joyce to your kids. It's a fun book about who is a stranger.

Teaching Honesty and Responsibility

Your new teaching job keeps getting harder and harder. To teach honesty and responsibility takes a lot of time and patience. It's not something like teaching your kids how to tie their shoes where they basically get the concept down after a few lessons. You'll have to keep hammering away at these lessons for a long time.

Can we be honest?

You teach honesty by encouraging your kids to tell the truth and to let you know what's on their minds. Having your children let you know what's on their minds shouldn't be a frightening thought.

If you've taken away a toy because your child was throwing it, you know he's going to be mad. Ask him how he feels. Let him know that it's OK to tell you if he's mad, and that you won't be angry. Then ask him why he's mad. This strategy teaches your kids that they can talk to you honestly without you getting upset or yelling. Your part in this business is that you have to be prepared for this kind of input from your children.

A second way to encourage honesty is to avoid confrontations where it would be easy for your child to lie. Instead of saying, "Debra, did you color on the wall?" say "Debra, you know you're not suppose to color on the wall." Avoid direct confrontation when you already know the answer. Asking her if she colored on the walls, when you saw her do it, sets your child up to lie. Don't put your kids in situations where it's easier to fib than to face up to the truth. Even as an adult, if someone asks if you ate the last chocolate chip cookie, you get a little nervous — like maybe you did something wrong. Learn, however, to stick out your chest and proudly announce, "Yes! I ate the last cookie, and I must be honest, it was the best cookie out of the whole package."

Now, if Debra really didn't color on the wall, she can easily say, "But Mom, I didn't color on the wall, it was Dad!" Figures.

WORDS OF WISDOM

Pretty much all the honest truth telling there is in the world today is done by children. — Oliver Wendell Holmes

The third (and most important) way to teach honesty is to be honest yourself. Don't ever lie to your children. You're setting an example. If you lie to your children, they'll think that it's OK to lie and do the same. But if your children lie to you, you'll get mad. You can't have double standards.

It's easy to think that you would never lie to your children. Be careful about the unintentional lies: "I'll be back in just a few minutes" — and you're gone for several hours. These kind of *white lies* will teach your kids not to trust you.

Traditional White Lies	
White lie	*Truth*
"It's just medicine. It tastes good!"	It tastes like lighter fluid.
"This won't hurt."	Gestapo-approved torture tactic.
"I just have to grab one thing from the store."	Two hours later, you own the store.
"We're going to Aunt Mildred's. We won't stay long."	Any time at Aunt Mildred's is long.

Correct answers to the traditional white lies:

1. "The medicine helps to make you feel better."

2. The best thing is not to say anything about pain. If you can't get away with that strategy, say, "This may not feel so good."

3. Either grab your one thing and leave or say, "I have some shopping to do. I don't know how long this is going to take."

4. "We're going to Aunt Mildred's. We'll leave by 11:30." Show your children on the clock what 11:30 looks like if they don't know.

Kidding and teasing can be fun. Everyone does it and thinks that it's a hoot. But be careful not to overdo the kidding with your kids. They don't have the knowledge and experience to determine what's a joke and what's not, so they take everything you say to heart. If your kids get to the point where they follow everything you say with, "Really?", perhaps you ought to hold off on some of the joking until your kids start believing what you say without questioning it.

Let's be responsible boys and girls

Teaching your children responsibility starts out with small tasks. When your children are old enough to understand simple commands, start giving them a job. I don't mean sending your two-year-old out for a paper route, but simple tasks. Ask them to give the book to Grandma, take the paper to the trash, and put the spoon in the drawer. After they've completed the job, let them know what a terrific job they did. Give them lots of praise — and, of course, hugs and kisses. Your children will beam when they realize that they've completed a task that made you happy.

As your kids get older, start adding to their responsibilities. Teach them how to make their bed and put their dirty clothes in the hamper. You're not only developing their sense of responsibility, but you're also starting good habits and teaching them a valuable lesson on how important it is for everyone to help clean up around the house.

The important part of teaching chores to your children is to *do* the chores with them until they understand how you want the chores done. After they've learned how to do their chores, follow up to make sure they don't start slacking off. They'll need your constant supervision for a long time — even though they may think they don't need it.

Make tasks and responsibilities fun. Your kids will enjoy doing them more if you turn setting the table into a game, or picking up clothes into a race. When you give your children responsibilities, avoid the let-me-help-you-with-that syndrome. Your children need to learn how to handle small tasks and may not want you to help.

Sometime your younger kids may be too preoccupied with something to want to stop to help you. That's OK. You can't force a two-year-old to do something if he doesn't want to (short of picking him up and physically moving him). And you really *don't* want to use force. Having responsibilities should be fun. As your kids get older, you can start using gentle persuasion when they decide they can't break away from Superman Saving the World.

Be aware that your kids may go through a stage where they don't want to handle their responsibilities. Don't let them whine their way out of their jobs (and whine they will). And don't let them put it off until later. This behavior starts them down that road to procrastination.

Steps to teach chores

1. Do the chore with your children. Explain each step and why it's necessary.

2. Go through the chores with your children, but only observe. Have your children do it all by themselves. If they need your help, that's a sign they aren't ready to do the chores by themselves.

3. When your children can do the chores by themselves without your help, leave them alone and let them do their chore. After they're done, have them show you what they've done. This practice not only gives you a chance to observe their work to make sure they did it right, but it also gives you the chance to praise their work.

4. Reduce the amount of time you have to observe their work. They'll slowly become more independent and responsible, and you'll be comforted to know that they can consistently do their chores correctly.

Build Independence, Self-Confidence, and Self-Esteem

Some adults go to expensive seminars and faraway camps to help them *find themselves.* They go to build their self-confidence and self-esteem. They dance around fires beating tambourines and eating bean sprouts. Then they feel *empowered* (or something) — until they get the bill.

Building this kind of character into your children should be done before they have to go away to camp. It's a long process. It's taking every day and giving your children little responsibilities. Add on to their responsibilities and praise them when they do it. When they say they *can't,* let them know they *can* do anything — if they just try. It doesn't have to be done perfectly.

Independence and self-confidence begin when you let your children do things for themselves that you would normally do for them. Allowing them to order their own food at a restaurant, or telling the doctor how they feel, are good ways to build their confidence. They can also start getting their own bowls of cereal, calling friends to confirm birthday parties, picking out their own clothes for the day, and making decisions about what movie the family should go out and see together (or where they should eat for dinner). It's best to start these decision-making steps by giving your children options to choose from. For example, let your children know the two movies you'd like to see, and let them choose the one you all go to. Your children will also have to learn that making these decisions is a special event — and that it's not up to them to make *all* the family decisions.

All the *positive* things you do and say to your kids is the best way to develop their confidence and self esteem. If you believe in their abilities, and you let them know you believe in them, they'll believe, too.

All of this *praise* stuff may sound ridiculous to you. That's because, as adults, we don't always get told how special we are and that we're doing a good job at something. We're basically confident (except for that small group of people off at camp dancing around fires and eating sprouts). Your kids aren't adults. Be careful not to tear down your children's self-confidence by always pointing out weaknesses instead of focusing on strengths:

> *Michelangelo, what a nice painting you did on the Sistine Chapel. But you know, you really didn't clean your brushes out very well. I think they're ruined now!*

They need to know that what they're doing is wonderful, and that you think they're special:

> *Goodness Virgil, look at that fence you built. That is a terrific fence. You should be so proud of yourself. Hey Shirley, come over here and look at this great fence.*

Whenever your children use the word *can't,* tell them there is no such word. *Try* or *do*, there is no *can't.*

Last but Not Least: Respecting Others

I can't say this enough: Kids learn by example. If you don't show your kids they need to act respectfully to those around them, they won't. They won't understand that it's rude to interrupt people or to ignore someone who is talking. They need to learn to be a good listener, to be polite and kind to people, and to be helpful at all times. OK, this sounds like a Boy Scout creed, but it's true.

The biggest brats around are those kids who don't do any of the things just mentioned. They talk back to their parents — or to any adult, for that matter. They aren't loving to their siblings, and they don't play fair with their friends.

Ways to teach respect

- Set a good example yourself.
- Have your children do volunteer work.
- Encourage the relationship between your children and their grandparents.
- Go to your local house of worship.
- Develop a good relationship between you and your children.
- Enroll your children in a sport or club.
- Buy children's books that emphasize respecting others.

Kids learn respect not only by watching you and how you interact with others, but also by receiving gentle reminders. You have to teach them how to behave. If they start to interrupt you, ask them to wait until you're finished speaking. If someone else is talking and your child is obviously not paying attention, put your child on your lap, hold his hands, and tell him he needs to listen to the person talking.

A moment of self-reflection: Could this be you?

If you're someone who doesn't let others finish their thoughts before you jump into the conversation, stop it! Your friends have neglected to tell you how annoying it is. Not only is it annoying, but it's rude — and you don't want your kids to do the same thing.

Your lesson for the day

Being a parent means being on display. Sort of like living in a glass house. Be nice!

Chapter 9
Making a Safer Lifestyle

In This Chapter
▶ How well do you know your child?
▶ The Do's and Don'ts of safety
▶ Unsuspected dangers

*T*his is the lifestyle of not necessarily the rich and the famous, but about you. You've no doubt worked hard to make your home warm and comfortable — and, of course, tastefully decorated. You'd think Martha Stewart herself decorated your house with all its beautiful little knick-knacks and little baskets of potpourri strategically placed with things made of old jelly jars (and who'd guess those Christmas snowmen were once lint balls?). Be it ever so humble . . .

Your house may be in the Show of Homes, but how safe is it for your kids? You may have the coolest car in the neighborhood with flames painted on the side and big fuzzy dice hanging from the rear-view mirror, but is it equipped for a safe ride for your children? And are you prepared to take your kids on an outing and have the event as safe as possible? This chapter covers procedures to make your home and your immediate environment safe. Safety is a vital thing, especially if you have wee ones wandering about.

You'll find many of these safety lists repeated in convenient forms in Appendix A.

Know Your Children

There are some *givens* for all children. Babies will put anything in their mouths, regardless if it's a piece of dirt, a screw, a penny, or even dry paint chips. Taste and size aren't important. If you have stairs, they'll want to crawl either up or down them. If you have cabinets, they'll want to open them and take whatever is in them out. Apparently, this kind of fun is right up there with kids as taking a cruise or winning money is for adults.

Not all kids like to do the same thing. Some kids are climbers and some aren't. Some kids like to pick at things (like wallpaper), and other kids let small things like that go unnoticed.

The *better* you know your kids, the easier it is to foresee any potential problems and do something about them before something happens. If your child is a climber, for example, make sure all the chairs to tables are pushed in, stairs have gates on them, and drawers are always shut (they can be used as stairs). And don't leave furniture near open windows. (If your child likes the dog and follows her everywhere, watch out for pet doors, which could just as easily be renamed *kiddy doors.*)

Do your older children leave doors open for your younger ones to pass through? Do they leave their Lego set out, or the Ninja Turtle action figures with the one thousand tiny parts, so that your baby can start eating the pieces like an appetizer? Make sure your older children are well versed on house rules to keep the little ones safe.

Safety Procedures (the Do's and Don'ts)

Don't ever underestimate what your kids can do. They'll crawl, walk, reach, snatch, grab, jump, and run sooner than you would expect. And they aren't even nice enough to forewarn you of their new-found talents. All of the sudden, out of nowhere, they'll stand up tall, reach over the coffee table, and spill your hot cup of tea — before you even know it.

To be extra safe, take it for granted that the day you bring your little ones home, they have amazing talents and can do everything anyone else can do. They're just waiting for the right moment to spring them on you.

The best thing to do is to take each room and look at it from a child's point of view. Go ahead and sit on the floor to see what a child sees. Try to be as critical of the room as you can. Is there anything that could hurt a child, or anything that he can get into or put into his mouth that he shouldn't?

When something does happen to your children, you're not going to have the time to open a book and start reading about stopping a lip from bleeding or treating a burn. Learn basic first aid now. Then you'll be prepared for the worst — if it ever does happen.

General household safety

Look at your house in a general sort of way. Overall, how equipped is your house for safety? Look at the following list and see how well your house rates. If you don't have any of the stuff listed, get out that checkbook and go shopping! (Use the checkbox list in Appendix A.)

- ✔ smoke detectors
- ✔ fire extinguishers
- ✔ escape ladders
- ✔ carbon-monoxide detectors

   These are especially needed in the mechanical room or wherever the furnace is located. Unlike smoke, carbon monoxide is colorless and odorless, so you can't detect it unless you have a special carbon-monoxide detector.

Get fire safety information from your local fire department. They provide information on family fire drills (which you should plan and practice), how to protect your home from fire hazards, and what to do in case of a fire. Don't forget to check the batteries in your smoke detectors.

Make it a practice to test your smoke detector batteries once a month. Do it the same time you pay your rent or mortgage — some time that you'll remember.

The bedroom (it's more than a sleeping place, it's an adventure)

Start with your baby's bedroom. This room can be scary if you think about it. Bedtime is the only time your child is going to be alone. You almost want to be microscopic when looking at this room. Remember, tiny fingers can peel, dig, and pry more than you might think. Start with your crib. It should be from a known manufacturer, such as Simmons, Child Craft, or Furil Baby. (Use the checkbox list in Appendix A to help you keep track of bedroom safety.)

- ✔ **Don't let babies sleep with plastic covers on their mattresses.**

   Unlike the tags on pillows that say *Do Not Remove*, you're supposed to remove plastic.

✔ **Babies should never sleep on adult waterbeds (which can cause hypothermia), cushions, bean-bag chairs, adult comforters, or pillows.**

These surfaces are too soft for babies who are too young to move themselves around. Babies can easily smother.

✔ **Never, under any circumstances, walk away from or turn your back on a baby who is on the changing table.**

Even if there is a safety strap. A baby can roll over and fall off — a baby as young as four weeks old can do this!

✔ **Don't use home-made cribs or antiques.**

They aren't tested for safety. If the bars on the cribs are too far apart (more than 2 inches), your baby's head could get caught between them, and he can strangle trying to get free. (And remember to remove the plastic from the mattress.)

✔ **Keep bedding simple.**

A sheet, blanket, and bumper pads are enough. Newborns can't move around, and they can either get overheated — which is thought to be associated with the cause of SIDS (Sudden Infants Death Syndrome) — or they can suffocate.

✔ **Don't use pillows.**

Babies don't need pillows and may suffocate.

✔ **Get rid of bumper pads when your children are old enough to pull up.**

A baby can stand on the pads and get more leverage to try to jump out of the crib. Like any POW, it's a baby's job to attempt escape.

✔ **Remove any toys strung across the crib when your children are old enough to pull up.**

There is the risk of strangulation if a child gets hold of this kind of crib toy.

✔ **Don't put cribs or toddler beds near blinds, drapes, or wall hangings with cords that hang down.**

Cords can get wrapped around your child's neck. Watch out for wallpaper or borders. Little fingers like to pick at these tempting papers so that they can rip them off the wall with much more ease than what it took to put them there. The danger comes when a baby decides to eat the wallpaper.

✔ **Put plastic covers on all the electrical sockets, and plastic boxes over the cords that are already plugged in.**

You can find these things at any store that carries baby stuff, like Target, Kmart, Sears, or Wal-Mart.

✔ **Make sure the toys in the room are appropriate for the age of your children.**

Young babies shouldn't have toys or games that have small pieces. They wouldn't play with them, anyway. They'd just eat the parts. Also be wary of ribbons on dolls or stuffed animals. These can be pulled off, popped into the mouth and swallowed.

✔ **Wash and dry all toys on a regular basis.**

They collect dirt and dust (not to mention baby drool, dried snot, slimy cracker juice) and will eventually end up in your child's mouth.

✔ **Don't put toy chests or children's furniture near windows.**

If your windows are fairly low, your child can crawl up on the furniture and fall out the window.

✔ **Use toy chests made of light material, like plastic, with a lid that either comes off or hinges and stays up.**

Babies get hurt by trying to get toys out of a toy chest and having the lid fall on their heads.

✔ **Make sure purses and fanny packs are out of reach.**

They usually contain small coins, medications, or other small objects that you don't want your children playing with.

Children's accessories (junk for the little ones)

Your kids, like you, will have their own stash of personal belongings. Things that they need to keep them happy. Your job is to continually inspect this *stuff* to make sure that none of it begins to break, crack, tear — or do anything that could potentially hurt your child. (The checkbox list in Appendix A can help you keep track of dangerous situations.)

✔ **Check toys for missing parts.**

(Besides frequently washing them to get rid of the dried-on gunk and germs that your children will inevitably sneeze onto them.) When plastic toys break, they leave sharp edges that can cause scrapes and cuts. Throw those toys away.

✔ **Check pacifiers to see if the plastic nipple is still in good shape.**

If it becomes too old, it will crack and break. Throw the old pacifiers away.

✔ **Wash pacifiers often.**

Wash them just like you would a bottle and nipples, to get rid of germs and dirt that will collect.

✔ **Never tie a pacifier around your children's necks, or "rubber band it" around their heads to keep it in their mouths.**

Don't use these pacifier tethers when they are sleeping.

✔ **Remove crib mobiles when your children are old enough to pull up on hands and knees.**

Your baby will try to reach for the mobile and, if successful, pull it down and shove everything possible into his mouth. The mobile's cords can also wrap around a child's neck.

✔ **Don't put your children to bed with toys in the crib.**

A baby can roll over on one and get hurt.

✔ **Don't use a baby carrier or a baby swing as a car seat or as a seat when riding bicycles.**

Cars and bicycles have special seats for you to use.

✔ **Follow all manufacturers' directions for assembly when using a baby swing.**

Also, use the belts and straps when a child is in the swing. Never let older or heavier children play in the swing. Not only could they break it, but they could also fall from the swing and hurt themselves.

✔ **Don't put high chairs too close to walls, counters, or tables.**

Children will use their feet to push against these things to knock over their chair. Also, don't get them too close to hanging objects that they can pull on, and don't let them stand up in their chairs.

✔ **Use your strollers with all the safety equipment they come with.**

Always use the seat belts in the strollers, and lock the wheels when you're not pushing the stroller. This precaution prevents the stroller from rolling away. Remember Robin Williams in the movie *Hook*? His mother didn't lock the wheels on his stroller, and he ended up rolling away. Look what happened to him: He became Peter Pan.

✔ **Watch out for little fingers when setting up the stroller or folding it.**

Fingers can get pinched!

✔ **Don't hang heavy bags, purses, or diaper bags from the handle of the stroller.**

The weight of these bags can pull the stroller over.

✔ **Don't use a baby walker.**

In 1993, 25,000 children between the ages of 5 and 15 months were treated in hospital emergency rooms because of walkers. Most of the injuries were caused by children falling down stairs in these walkers.

Living/family room

Because this is the room where you and your family spend most of your time, you need to take extra precautions to make this room safe. (Use the list in Appendix A to check your safety precautions.)

✔ **Put plastic covers on all the electrical sockets, and plastic boxes over the cords that are already plugged in.**

These covers make it impossible to plug or unplug cords.

✔ **Put gates on all the stairs going up or down.**

You don't want to find out that your baby has learned to crawl up the stairs by seeing him teetering on the top step.

✔ **Take portable gates to place in the doorway of staircases if you're traveling to someone's home.**

Remember to ask permission before you start setting up your gates.

✔ **Put breakable items either away for a while — or in a higher place.**

At least until your child is old enough to learn what's OK to touch and what's *not* OK.

✔ **Don't leave babies and young toddlers unattended on furniture.**

The moment you do, they'll fall off. It doesn't matter how many pillows or blankets you use to place around them, the day will come when they figure out how to get over those obstacles. (You'll find out their new trick when you hear a thud — and a scream — and you find them on the floor.)

✔ **Scrape, sand, and repaint all old paint areas.**

Old paint may contain lead, which is poisonous. It's pretty much a given that once children are tall enough to reach a window, they'll suck or chew on the window sill. Remember to do all this work without your children in the same room. This is toxic stuff, and your kids shouldn't be around it. In fact, to be really safe, you should wear a mask yourself.

✔ **Have furnaces, fireplaces, and gas barbecue grills checked for carbon monoxide leaks.**

This poisonous gas, which you can't see or smell, can not only make you very ill, but can also kill you if it is breathed for too long. Also, don't use charcoal grills indoors (it's the gas thing again), and get rid of the charcoal. You don't want your kids playing with this stuff.

✔ **Clean air filters from heaters and air conditioners once a month.**

This practice will keep your air cleaner and reduce the amount of germs flying around.

✔ **Don't keep your car running in the garage.**

Not only will your car spew out carbon monoxide, which will make you sick (and it kills!) if you're in the garage with the car, but the fumes will also go into your home if your garage is attached to the house.

✔ **Keep blind or drapery cords tied up, out of the reach of children.**

If the cords are looped at the bottom, cut the loop, and tie the ends around the top of the blind so your kids can't reach them.

The kitchen

You'll be trying to cook dinner and there your kids are, perched on your toes begging to be picked up or wanting something to eat. Kitchens, however, are one of the most dangerous places for your kids to hang out.

The kitchen is full of wonder with lots of shiny toys (like butcher knives), neat knobs that turn machines on, and — if you're a wild cook — lots of goodies to nibble on from the floor. Protect your children from this Fun House (and use the checkbox list in Appendix A to be sure you are).

✔ **Put locks on all your cabinets.**

You don't want your kids juggling your china, sucking on a knife, or gargling with Liquid Plumber.

✔ **Use the back burners when cooking on the stove.**

Little fingers can reach up and grab hot pans and pull them down.

✔ **Keep drawers locked.**

Eating utensils, knives, and even the stuff in the "junk" drawer can all be dangerous to kids.

✔ **Keep the small kids out of the way when cooking.**

If they're too small to help prepare dinner, put them in a high chair or at a table to color or play with a toy. If they're big enough to help, put them to work. Beginning chores for your youngsters are setting the table, filling water glasses, and putting condiments on the table.

✔ **Lock up or throw away plastic bags.**

This includes shopping bags, garbage bags, plastic wrap, plastic sandwich bags, plastic dry cleaning bags, or plastic film of any kind (like toy wrappings).

✔ **Keep alcoholic beverages away from children.**

Their little systems can't handle alcohol, and they could get alcohol poisoning.

✔ **Keep chairs away from counters.**

You don't want to find out that your little one can crawl by finding him sitting on top of the counter.

✔ **Keep important phone numbers on a list, displayed, and by the phone.**

These numbers should include the Poison Control Center's number (look in your phone book for your region's number), fire, police, (911 if it's in your area), and a couple of neighbors' phone numbers.

✔ **Keep *Syrup of Ipecac* in your medicine cabinet.**

But don't use it unless you are instructed to by a physician or someone at the Poison Control Center. Syrup of Ipecac is used to induce vomiting, which is what you want your children to do if they take something poisonous. It's the quickest way to get whatever they took out of their system. But remember to only use this stuff *if* you are instructed to do so by your physician or the Poison Control Center. *Never* use this stuff on your own.

The bathroom (otherwise known as the potty room)

Bathrooms are another room that kids should not use as a playroom. It only takes one inch of water for someone to drown in, and your toilet has more than one inch of water in it. When your kids are old enough to pull themselves up, they'll go to the toilet and reach in to play with the pretty water. A baby who is old enough to reach into the toilet is old enough to fall in and drown. (Use the checkbox list for bathroom safety in Appendix A.)

✔ **Keep bathrooms blocked off with gates or install safety locks high enough so your children can't reach them.**

✔ **Keep lids to toilets closed.**

✔ **Keep shower doors closed.**

✔ **Never leave water standing in sinks, bathtubs, or buckets used for cleaning.**

Little people are attracted to standing water. It's an open invitation to them to come and play with it.

✔ **Keep cleaners, perfumes, deodorants, and any other *foofoo* stuff locked up and out of baby's reach.**

You kids will start to imitate your morning hygiene ritual (if they see you doing it) and will want to play with all the stuff you play with.

✔ **Always keep medicines in the medicine cabinet and away from children.**

Most adult medicines can kill a child.

> ✔ Use child-resistant packaging for anything and everything you use.
>
> ✔ Keep small appliances (like blow-dryers, curling irons, electric razors, and irons) unplugged and put away.

Read Chapter 11, "The Joys and Perils of Bathtime."

Water safety

Water is such a scary thing when children are around it. Keep these safety tips in mind:

> ✔ **Always supervise your children when they are around water of any type.**
>
> This means water that is in a bucket, a child's pool, or even big water puddles from rain.
>
> ✔ **Use swimming-pool safety.**
>
> Your pool should have a four-sided, five-foot fence around it with a self-closing, self-latching gate.
>
> ✔ **Wait until your children are at least three years old before starting them in a swimming program.**
>
> The American Academy of Pediatrics advises against infant swimming programs. They claim that babies can get parasitic infections from swimming pools. Babies can also swallow too much water, which leads to water intoxication. They also believe that parents develop a false sense of security thinking their infants can swim.

The saddest thing to hear is a parent who has lost a child to drowning say, "I was gone for just a minute."

Traveling: car-seat safety

Everyone in your family should wear a seat belt. If you're in a car accident and only your kids are in seat belts, you could just as easily hurt them by flying around the car if you're not buckled in. You may think that you're an excellent driver as did Dustin Hoffman in *The Rain Man*, and you may be. But you can't vouch for everyone else on the road. If you want to *gamble,* go to Vegas (but use the checkbox list in Appendix A before you hit the road).

Chapter 20, "Social Skills to Be Proud Of," covers traveling with your child. Yes, it is possible to travel with children.

There are several types of car seats: those that face forward, those that face backwards, infant car seats, and toddler car seats.

✔ **Always, always, always use a car seat when traveling.**

Even if you're going a short distance, take the time to put your kids in car seats. Besides, it's the law!

✔ **Use only the type of car seat that is age- and weight-appropriate for your children.**

Don't stick your six-month-old into a toddler seat. It won't give enough support.

✔ **Fasten the car seat down with the seat belt.**

If your child is in his seat but it's not fastened down, he instantly becomes a large projectile: Something that could easily fly around the car and either go out a window or smack you in the back of your head. Either way, it's not a pretty sight.

✔ **Always use the car seat's safety belt.**

Car seats are not meant to be glorified booster chairs. If you don't use the safety belt to hold down your child, the seat is useless.

✔ **Read the directions on the car seat and FOLLOW THEM!**

If you have a rear-facing car seat, face the car seat only to the rear. Never face it forward. Manufacturers make these clarifications for a reason.

✔ **Don't put rear-facing car seats in the front seat where there is an air bag.**

Either have the air bag disabled or put your child in the back seat. The force of an expanding air bag is too strong for a car seat.

✔ **Children weighing under 20 pounds should always be facing the rear.**

Up until that weight, they don't have enough head control to be facing the front. Their head will bobble around like a rag doll.

The safest place for your baby is in the middle of the back seat. In a car seat, of course.

Your child *must* be in a car seat — it's the law. If your kids are in the car without a car seat, you are breaking the law.

Putting Your Child in Danger

One of the biggest reasons kids get hurt is by accidents: Some of the falling down and bumps and bruises can't be helped. But kids also choke, get burned, and get cut for unnecessary reasons (as if there were good reasons to get choked, burned, and cut). You can take measures to prevent some of these accidents. (The checkbox list in Appendix A should help you keep track of your measures.)

Burning

- ✔ **Put your coffee cup in the middle of tables or counters.**

    Just when kids get old enough to grab over the edge of coffee tables or counters, they'll go for that steaming cup of coffee or tea. And don't use tablecloths or doilies that can be pulled so that the coffee comes tumbling down.

- ✔ **Don't hold your children when you're holding a cup of hot liquid.**

    Sure as you do, they'll stick their hand in it. Please don't assume they know better, because they don't.

- ✔ **Use your back burners to cook when possible.**

    Also, buy a stove guard that doesn't let little fingers touch hot pans. You can also buy guards to go over the burner knobs so toddlers can't turn stoves on.

- ✔ **Turn pot handles toward the rear of the stove.**

- ✔ **Keep kids away from floor furnaces or area heaters.**

- ✔ **Hide your disposable lighters, or don't use them.**

    Many fires start by children playing with disposable lighters.

- ✔ **Don't let your children use the microwave oven.**

    They get burned by hot food or steam that comes from bags of popcorn or dishes that have lids or plastic on them.

- ✔ **Never hold your children while you're cooking.**

    Grease can pop up on children, or they can reach down and grab something cooking before you can stop them.

Keep an Aloe Vera plant at home to relieve pain from minor burns. Cut a small piece off the plant, peel back the top layer, and squeeze or rub the gooey middle onto the burn.

Choking

Kids will put the darndest things in their mouths. They can find the tiniest microscopic item just so they can gag and choke and scare the *bejeezus* out of you.

Kids choke the most on the following items. (So mark them on Appendix A's checkbox list if you need to be reminded to keep them away from kids.)

- ✔ grapes
- ✔ hard candies
- ✔ deflated or bursted balloon pieces
- ✔ coins
- ✔ raw vegetables cut in circles
- ✔ buttons

- ✔ nuts
- ✔ popcorn
- ✔ pins
- ✔ small toys and toy parts
- ✔ hot dogs cut in circles
- ✔ plastic bags

Playing

Playing should mean fun, good times, yippeee, let your hair down, be wild and free, go for it, let it all hang out. For adults, maybe. For kids, playing can be just as dangerous as walking a tightrope. If they're not careful, it can be very dangerous.

Kids' play should be restricted to children's games and activities (and kept away from adult activities). This is why you don't see a nine-year-old playing craps in Vegas.

Don't put your kids in possible dangerous places or areas thinking that you'll keep a close eye on them. Kids can squirm around and move quicker than you can react. This is why places like the top of the Empire State Building have signs that say not to set kids on the wall. Too many kids have gotten too good a look of the view (if you know what I mean).

- ✔ **Don't let your kids ride on the lawn mower with you.**
- ✔ **Don't let your kids ride in the back of pickups.**
- ✔ **Don't leave your kids on the edge of a swimming pool thinking they'll sit there quietly.**
- ✔ **Don't let your kids ride on recreational equipment (such as four-wheelers, motorcycles, jet skis, wave-runners) if they are below the recommended age limit.**

Get real. How often do kids sit quietly anywhere (unless they're doing something they shouldn't).Too many accidents are caused by parents doing things, not knowing how dangerous it is.

Homemade toys that are fun for kids are cardboard boxes and Tupperware with wooden spoons to bang on. Unsafe toys are anything with plastic bags or cellophane wrappers. Plastic and cellophane can be choked on easily. Kids also like to put bags on their heads for pretend hats. Plastic bags over the head cause suffocation.

Personal habits

If you're going to take the time and effort to make your home safe, you also need to look at any personal habits that may be harmful to your child.

Smoking

No matter how much you try to justify your habit of smoking, it's a bad habit that will not only eventually kill you, but (while you're busy making yourself sick) you will also be making your children sick.

Second-hand smoke is bad for your children, and has been linked to premature babies, low-birth weight babies, SIDS (Sudden Infant Death Syndrome), learning disabilities, an increased risk of asthma, pneumonia, and other medical problems. Even if you try to rationalize your smoking by saying that you only smoke outside, you have to realize that your children aren't stupid. They'll eventually realize what you're doing. Remember the earlier chapters on setting good examples? Smoking anywhere, inside or outside the house, is still a bad example.

Research has also found that pregnant people who are around smoke are also exposing their unborn baby to the same smoke.

Drinking

Just two things. Don't get drunk around your children, and don't leave alcohol laying around so that your kids can get into it. Drinking around your children is teaching them that you think drinking is acceptable. If you must drink, do so responsibly.

Guns

If you're going to have guns around the house, keep them unloaded and put away so that your kids can't play with them. There are too many shooting accidents to justify having a loaded gun in the house. And please, don't try saying, "Oh, my kids know better than to play with the guns" or "I have them hidden so that the kids can't find them." Both these excuses have been used by parents of children who have *died* because of guns.

Drugs

What can I say? Don't use illegal drugs — ever. Even if you use drugs privately, where your children won't see you using them, drugs will still slow your mind and reaction time, which are two things that you need to have when you are a parent. If you use drugs in front of your children, you're teaching them that it's okay — and then you've gone and ruined *their* life, as well.

Your lesson for the day

Even if you go out and buy every safety gadget available, put locks on everything, gates on all stairs, and clothe your children in rubber suits, they'll still get hurt. Nothing you can buy does as much good as parents who are attentive to their children.

Chapter 10
Understanding Food and Nutrition

. . . .

In This Chapter

▶ Starting your kids on solids

▶ How to avoid raising a picky eater

▶ The truth behind a balanced diet

▶ Food guidelines

. . . .

*F*ood and nutrition are not the same thing. Food is what you *want* to eat, nutritious food is what you *should* eat. Actually they're both subcategories of things-we-put-in-our-mouths. For a baby, that includes just about anything. As we grow older, we grow pickier. And yet, while everything you put in your mouth and swallow can be considered food, it may not be nutritious. As a parent, it's your role to decide what's food and what's nutrition — and how much of each your children need.

They All Go Through It

Your children are going to go through several stages during their lives. Besides the mood swings during puberty, nothing will be more disturbing than the changes they'll have with their eating habits.

This fluctuation is disturbing to parents because these eating changes can be rather dramatic. One day you'll think your children have a hollow leg — and you'll be tempted to hide the family pets so they don't get eaten as well. The next day, your kids may not be interested in food at all.

Trust your children. They know how much they need to eat. If they push the bottle or spoon away, or don't clean their plates, trust that they've had enough to eat. If they keep asking for more food, by all means shovel it in. As long as you're giving healthy foods, they should be allowed to eat as much as they want. They'll stop when they're finished (or you run out of food, whichever comes first). Healthy food does not include Chee-tos, M&Ms, Hershey kisses, or jelly beans. (Darn!)

A balanced diet is having ketchup on your hamburger. — Jordan Gookin

Your children are unique. They'll grow at a different rate than other children. Their eating habits will also probably not match any food chart you've read. Changes in eating habits not only include the amount your children will want to eat, but also the times. Don't be surprised when they're not hungry at dinner time — but thirty minutes later they complain that they're starving. To be really convincing, they may even show you their rib cages for special effects.

For breastfeeding and bottlefeeding information, read Chapter 15.

Is It Time for Solids Yet? (Babies)

Doctors used to advise parents to start kids on solid foods when they were four months old. Then they said to wait until they were six months old (prompted by the makers of formula products). If you ask a dozen doctors what they think, you'll probably get a dozen different answers.

Here's the scoop. Start your baby on solids anywhere between four to six months. Your doctor may recommend solids anywhere between these ages, depending on:

- if your baby's birth weight has doubled

- if your baby stops gaining weight

- if your baby is gaining too much weight (formula is high in calories and may be putting excess weight on your baby)

- if your baby wants to eat frequently (more than 40 ounces of formula a day) and doesn't seem satisfied

- if your baby is interested in the food you're eating

- if your baby keeps pointing to pictures of steak and potatoes

Your doctor may suggest waiting on solids if your baby is gaining weight at a normal pace, or if there is history of allergies in your family. Starting a baby on solids too soon may cause food allergies later on.

Once your baby has shown you signs that he's ready to eat the good stuff (solids), proceed slowly and follow these guidelines:

Pick a good time

You don't want to try to start feeding your baby solids if he's too hungry to try out this new *gooey-stuff-on-a-spoon* thing. Feed him a little from the bottle or breast — so he knows you're not planning on starving him — then proceed with some food.

Pick a good place

Your baby should be sitting upright. That means either in an infant seat or sitting on your lap. If you lay him down and try to feed him, he may spend most of his time gagging and choking. (You don't want this to happen!) When he's old enough to sit up on his own, you can make that big move to the high chair.

Peanut butter and jelly is a food that will go with anything — like your chair, piano keys, pet. — dear Aunt Margie

Start off feeding your baby rice cereal

Iron-fortified baby cereal is the best for most babies. Rice cereal is easier to digest than other cereals (this *doesn't* mean Rice Crispies). Offer cereal twice a day: at breakfast and then again at dinner. Make the rice cereal thin at the beginning. Your baby has to learn to move the food around in his mouth and then down his throat. You'll spend some time putting the same spoonful of rice back into his mouth before he gets the idea of how to eat. As you find more of the food is staying in his mouth — and you're not shoveling the same food in again and again — make the cereal thicker. But don't put baby cereal in bottles. Your baby has to learn to *eat* the cereal. He already knows how to drink.

Start off slowly

Your baby's going to think you've lost your mind when you start with the solid food, and he's going to have to get used to the idea that not all food comes in liquid form. Put a small dab of food on the spoon, slowly put it in your baby's mouth, and then watch him make a funny face and spit the food out. Wipe up the food, and try again. Don't give up hope if your baby doesn't seem to like new food. Spitting the food out doesn't necessarily mean he doesn't like it. It's just a reaction to something new in his mouth. If you keep putting the food in, and he makes a horrible face and spits it out, he may not like the food. Keep trying. Eventually he'll grow accustomed to the taste (or texture) and eat it.

Introduce new foods

After your baby gets the idea of how to eat (which means you're only shoveling the same bite of food in once or twice) and he doesn't have any allergic reactions to the cereal, slowly start introducing vegetables and fruit into the diet. Give your baby vegetables for a month or so before you introduce fruits. If he starts off eating fruits, he may turn his nose up at vegetables. Fruits are naturally sweet and more appealing to your little one than vegetables — which mankind pretty much agrees are bland.

Introduce new foods (including baby cereal) one week at a time. This strategy will give your child's body a chance to react to the food, if it's going to at all.

No Picky Eaters Here! (Toddlers)

Your kids are going to turn their noses up to some of the foods you offer. Depending on your children (because they're all different), they may refuse everything you put in front of them — or they may rarely sneer at food. Toddlers are especially good at being picky eaters.

Here are some things you can do to avoid raising a picky eater:

- ✔ Introduce a wide variety of foods.
- ✔ Don't give up on a food after one try.
- ✔ Leave warfare out of mealtime.

Lots of neat foods

Give your kids a wide variety of foods at a young age. This variety will give them an opportunity to experiment with food and find more things that they like. It also makes them more open to different foods.

Japanese, Thai, Indian, and organic are all foods that have lots of textures, colors, and tastes. In addition, they are good sources of vitamins. You may not like miso soup, but your one-year-old may love it.

Food reaction

If your child develops a rash, diarrhea, vomiting, or excessive gas after eating a new food, take him off the food and call your doctor. These symptoms may reveal an allergic reaction to this new food. The doctor will most likely advise you to stop giving the food, but to try it again in six months. Your child's body may be ready to handle the food at that time. Read the section, "Food Do's and Don'ts" at the end of this chapter for more food safety information.

By the way, we're talking about one-star Thai food here. And with the Japanese and Indian food, avoid the spicy stuff. That green stuff — *wasabe* — is too much for babies. And Indian food should be made less spicy. You do this by ordering the non-spicy food that is available. Indian and Thai restaurants are good about letting you know what you are going to be able to handle (spice wise) and when you're going to need a fire extinguisher.

 ✔ Take more time at the grocery store and actually look at all the different types of food instead of always reaching for your regular items. Take the time to experiment with new flavors or textures. Food can be great fun.

Keep trying

If your kids snub carrots, don't give them a Milky Way candy bar as a replacement. Just give them another vegetable. Offer the carrots again in a week or so (allowing for an *off* night for carrots). If they still don't like the carrots, wait. Offer carrots again in another six months. The kids may have a different attitude about them at that time. If six months down the road they still look at the carrots like you set a plate of worms in front of them, try again in another six months. It's your job to distinguish between, "Yuck! These things can't be in the same food chain that humans eat" as opposed to, "I don't think I'm in the mood to eat carrots tonight." The first situation is where you want to introduce the food later — as in six months or so. The second is where your child is just being a kid and is trying to exert the decision-making process over *something*. Put the carrots back on your child's plate the next time you choose to fix them. Your little one may have a different attitude this time around.

Don't give up offering the food without a little bit of coaxing. With younger kids, you can't con them into eating. The open-wide-for-the-airplane tricks don't really work if you have children who have definite opinions about what you're trying to put in their mouths. If they don't like the taste, the food comes out. This is where the six-month wait comes in. As they get older, you can encourage them to at least try the food. Here's a good rule that many families have: You don't have to like it, but you at least have to try it. The kids may find out that the corned beef hash you set in front of them doesn't taste like Alpo — even though it looks like it does.

Don't let your prejudices about food stop you from giving them to your children. Even though you may detest brussels sprouts, your kids may love them.

Remember, these are small people you're dealing with. Just like you, they're not going to like everything you put in front of them. As adults, we learn to be polite and eat the green glob of *goo* rather than be rude. Kids don't care. If they don't think they're going to like it, they don't mind letting everyone know.

■ ✔ Chocolate is not one of the major food groups.

No fighting

Dinner shouldn't be a battle zone between you and your children. There shouldn't be a winner and a loser. It's food — not a power struggle of the wills.

As we grow up, our taste buds develop, and food has more of a flavor than when we're younger. To little kids, a lot of the food we offer doesn't really have much of a flavor. That's why kids love *sweets* so much. The flavor is strong, and they can taste it. Peas? You might as well give them some wet cardboard to chew on.

Wait until your kids are old enough to hold their emotions before you insist that they eat a bite or two of food they don't like. Dinner shouldn't be a time of crying and temper tantrums. There are plenty of different kinds of nutritious food to offer. You don't need to force your two-year-old to eat something he obviously doesn't like.

If your kids start throwing temper tantrums and want to eat only sweets for dinner, make them leave the dinner table. They'll eat when they're hungry.

French restaurants do such a wonderful job presenting the meal. You know it's going to be great food just because it *looks* so good. You could be eating tar, but that's OK because it's presented well. If you have a child who tends to reject food, make the food look fun. Cut sandwiches into shapes, arrange the corn in the shape of a heart, or serve it in a plastic toy (washing the toy first, of course). Do whatever you can think of to make meals more fun.

Kids have an interesting way of testing food. Don't be surprised if your kids put the food in their mouths and then take it out. It's not necessarily a sign that they don't like the food — it may mean that they're testing the food for flavor and texture.

The "Balanced" Diet: Concerns for All Ages

According to the nutrition experts, in order to have a balanced diet, we should be eating the following:

- ✔ At least one serving of vitamin A foods each day, such as apricots, canta-loupe, carrots, spinach, and sweet potatoes.

- ✔ At least one serving of vitamin C foods each day, such as oranges, grape-fruit, and tomatoes.

- ✔ At least one serving of high-fiber foods, such as apples, bananas, figs, plums, pears, strawberries, peas, potatoes, and spinach.

- ✔ A cruciferous vegetable several times a week, such as broccoli, cauli-flower, brussels sprouts, and cabbage.

Based on this list, how well do you do? You can stop laughing now. I know it's hard to accomplish this on a daily basis — especially when your kids go through their growing spurts and don't seem to want to eat anything.

You're also supposed to be giving your family five servings of fruits and veg-etables a day. Again, this is hard to do. If you can't get all these foods in on a daily basis, try to look at your eating schedule as every *48 hours.* Try to get these foods in by every two days. It's better than not getting them in at all.

It's easier to work these foods into your family's diet by substitution: Replace chips, crackers, cookies, and ice cream with fruits and vegetables. It's just as easy to grab a banana as it is a graham cracker.

Your children will learn their good eating habits not only from what you feed them, but also by what they observe. You need to have good eating habits, as do older siblings. If baby sees her older sister eating chocolate Pop Tarts for breakfast, she'll want to eat them, too.

Avoid processed foods. They're high in salt, sugars, and fat. These foods hide in cans, bottles, and plastic bags. To be sure, check the label for sugar, salt, fat content, and any chemical name you don't recognize. Get in the habit of reading labels. If there's anything on the label you can't pronounce, don't put it in your mouth. How about this for lunch:

```
Ferrous Sulfate, Thiamine Mononitrate, Riboflavin, Sauterne
Wine, Calcuim Caseinate, Soy Protein Isolate, Monosodium
Glutamate, Lactic Acid and Yeast Extract.
```

This is off the label of a can of soup. Umm, umm, good! Food manufacturers have made it easy for us to have quick and easy meals. They haven't, however, done much to make the food good for us.

Chocolate chips are not considered part of a complete balanced breakfast.

Diets for Children

Richard Simmons, Jenny Craig, Weight Watchers, Susan Powter, and all the other lose-weight-my-way programs are all designed for certain people: those who are overweight or those who have eating disorders. None of these programs are for your children.

Unless specified by your doctor, the only "diet" your children should be on is a normal, healthy, eating-the-right-kind-of-foods diet. Don't count the calories or fat grams for children. Just keep them away from sugars, fast foods (grease), junk food (crackers, chips, candy), and a lot of processed meats (like hot dogs and bologna), and they'll be fine. This may sound impossible, but if you make the effort, you'll at least cut the intake of these foods down considerably.

Hot dogs and other lunch meat products contain nitrates. Bad, bad, bad. Nasty nitrates, nasty.

As your children grow, they may seem chunkier at times, and then they'll slim down. It's normal. If you're concerned that your children are too thin or too heavy, talk to your doctor. But don't put your baby on a low-fat or no-fat diet. Babies need the fat to develop a healthy body and brain.

If your children are over two years old, you can start cutting some of the fat out of the diet. Buy low-fat milk or low-fat yogurt. But don't go on a strict *no-fat* diet with your kids.

Don't fall into the trap that many people do when it comes to fat in their diet. They have the idea if they buy *no-fat* chips, or *no-fat* ice cream, they're doing fine. Chips and ice cream are still considered junk food — they don't do anything for your body. Your kids especially don't need them.

A lot of foods advertised as low-fat are also high in sugar. There is no benefit here. Keep your kids on a naturally low-fat diet by giving them plenty of fruits and vegetables. It's the best solution to the diet dilemma.

Snacking

Your children's bodies are not able to eat enough during one meal to last until the next. So let them snack! Work in those fruits and vegetables for snacks. The word *snack* doesn't have to imply junk food.

Plan to feed your children three meals a day, with two to three snacks a day. These snacks are needed to help balance their diet and give them the energy to terrorize their siblings and jump on beds.

Children after the age of 12 months often decide they don't like three meals a day. Some children will only take one meal per day, and then be happy with several small meals or snacks during the day. Don't worry. This behavior is normal. Just make sure the small meals or snacks are healthy foods.

If you don't like the idea of cooking for a child who will just take two bites and then run off, give small portions on the plate and refrigerate the rest (this is where that $300 worth of Tupperware you bought at a garage sale comes in). When the kid's ready to eat again, give the rest of the meal.

The Basics of Kiddy Food

According to the American Cancer Society, the growing cancer rate in America right now is in children. This is partially caused by all the processed meats and sodium nitrates — which is the stuff they put in lunch meats, hot dogs, and most other processed meats.

We're getting to be fast-food families. We spend too much time at McDonald's (although your kids may claim that McDonald's is *better than food*) and are eating foods that are high in fat (the bad fat they cook French fries in). Limit fried burgers, French fries, and buttery popcorn from movie theaters. Start giving out raw fruit and vegetables instead.

Food Quiz: Is it good or is it bad?

✔ **Dehydrated fruit:** Good! Dehydrated only means the liquid has been sucked from it (sort of). Kids like dehydrated fruit because it's poppable food, like candy, and it fools them into thinking that they're eating something that's not good for them.

✔ **Reese's Peanut Butter Cup:** Bad! Yes, peanut butter is a good source of protein, but when you sandwich it with rich, creamy chocolate, it negates the goodness.

✔ **Smoothies:** Good! Surprised? Smoothies are typically a mixture of fruit put in a blender with crushed iced. Sometimes plain yogurt is added as an extra bonus. Your kids will think they're having a shake.

✔ **Banana Split:** Bad! I know this comes as a surprise for you who have justified eating banana splits all your life. It doesn't matter that it has a banana (fruit requirement), or that ice cream is made out of milk. The bad news is that banana splits are high in *sugar*. Bet you didn't know that (because you've suppressed reality from your brain).

If your child tends to have mood swings or gets cranky easily, it may be caused by his blood sugar going up and down. Diet is the reason for this. Foods that are high in carbohydrates and sugar are one of the reasons we all tend to be moody, tired, and easily upset. Foods that are high in carbohydrates and sugar are presweetend cereals, crackers, cookies, cake, and ice cream (basically all the good stuff that makes life worth living).

Moodiness, crankiness, or hyperactive behavior can also be caused by food allergies. Allergies to food don't always involve breaking out in little red bumps all over one's body. Allergies can also alter behavior. For example, your docile, sweet child may be fine all morning until lunch. After your child eats a peanut butter and jelly sandwich, you may find yourself peeling the kid off the wall. This kind of behavior could be a reaction to the bread, the peanut butter, or the jelly. If you suspect that your child is allergic to some sort of food, you can try your own *at-home* test. Take your child off all processed foods, sugars, and anything with food coloring. Your child will then be on a protein, fruit, and vegetable diet. See how your child does. If he doesn't seem to have any problems, slowly start adding foods, one by one, to the diet to see how he does. If this seems like a long process, you may just want to take your child to the doctor and let an expert know of your concerns. The doctor can give your child a series of tests to look for any food allergies.

Kids, like adults, need water. Start them out as babies with a sip of water after they've finished eating. This practice not only helps them to get used to drinking water, but it also washes out their mouth — which is the first stage of proper dental care. As they get older, have a water bottle around for when they need a quick drink to quench their thirst. Being a kid is hard work.

Babies who are breastfed or bottlefed can develop a bacteria in their mouths called *thrush* if their mouths are not washed out after they eat. Thrush looks like white, caked-on milk, and it can be transferred to your breast if you're breastfeeding (this is painful, so be aware).

Food Do's And Don'ts

Kids have their own special needs when it comes to food. If you're not careful, food can not only be a source of nutrition, but it can also be a health and safety hazard.

> ✔ **Feed your baby with a baby-size spoon.**
>
> Preferably the ones that are covered with rubber. You'll have less food coming out because the bite sizes are smaller — like your baby's mouth. The rubber on the spoons prevents your baby's gums from getting hurt.

✔ **Keep food in small, bite sizes.**

About the size of your thumbnail for your kids. Kids choke easily.

✔ **Peel foods like apples, pears, and plums.**

The skins get stuck in those little swallowing pipes.

✔ **Cut pulpy fruit like oranges and grapefruits into small pieces.**

They are also easy to choke on. And watch your kids carefully.

✔ **Buy baby fruit juices in the baby food department of your store.**

If you choose to use the canned or frozen juice that the whole family uses, dilute the juice by half with water. If you give your baby this juice without diluting it, it may cause diarrhea. It's stronger than *baby juice* found in the baby-food section of the grocery store.

✔ **Buy only juices that are 100 percent juice.**

Read the labels. There is a difference between fruit juice with 100 percent juice and fruit *drink* (which may actually contain no juice at all). Don't buy juice that has added sugar or fructose.

✔ **Keep kids in a high chair or at a table when it's time to eat.**

Running around and trying to eat at the same time increases the chance for choking. Besides, keeping your kids confined during meals keeps your house cleaner. There's nothing worse than sitting on a chair and finding its arms coated in peanut butter and jelly.

✔ **Keep a stash of raw vegetables in your refrigerator for snacks.**

If your kids start out eating raw peas, carrots, or celery for a snack, they won't know what they're missing. Unless some neighbor kid corrupts them for you and sneaks them chocolate behind your back. Ummmm, chocolate.

✔ **Keep outings to McDonald's and other fast foods for only very special occasions.**

The hamburger and French fries that they sell are high in salt, carbohydrates, and bad fat (not the good fat that we need for healthy bodies, but the fat that makes us *fat*).

✔ **If you want to give your kids sweets, limit the amount they have.**

Don't give them hard candies (it's the choking thing again) and avoid sweets with caffeine, like chocolate and soft drinks. Sugar isn't what necessarily makes kids hyperactive, it's the caffeine (this is currently a big debate, and the effect varies from child to child). It's also believed the thing that makes kids hyperactive — like putting a hummingbird on uppers — is not sugar, but the activity around which it's given. For example, a birthday party.

Giving a kid a Coke is equivalent to an adult drinking four cups of coffee.

✔ **Look for baby food that doesn't have any added sugars or salts.**

Read the labels. Some baby food manufacturers still add sugar. You *don't* want to use these.

✔ **Always wash the fruits and vegetables you get from the grocery store.**

Grocery store produce is covered with pesticides, which aren't healthy for you or your kids. If it's possible, buy organic fruits and vegetables, which are grown without pesticides. Go to a farmer's market or grow your own (which may be unrealistic for a lot of people, but it's an idea).

✔ **Don't give your kids citrus fruits or citrus fruit drinks until after they are one year old.**

Citrus is too acidic for their little bodies. Your kids may react by vomiting, nausea, or having acidic poops that will burn their bottoms.

✔ **Don't feed your child honey until after the age of one year.**

Honey contains a bacteria that makes babies sick. Read labels, especially those in yogurt. Food manufacturers are now adding honey to their ingredients as a "good" sugar.

✔ **Don't always use your microwave to warm food.**

Microwaves heat food unevenly and can cause burns in sensitive little kid mouths. If you do use your microwave, stir the food and taste it to make sure it's not too hot.

✔ **Don't force your kids to clean their plates when eating.**

Forcing a child to eat everything that is set in front of them is leading them down the road to be an overeater.

✔ **Don't add salt, sugar, or artificial sweeteners to your children's food.**

Your children don't need it. All you're doing is seasoning the food to the way you like it. Children are used to the natural taste of foods and don't have the bad habits that we have of overseasoning . . . yet.

The best way to teach your kids how to eat is by example. You should be eating the right way. Your kids deserve to have you around for a long time, so be nice boys and girls and eat more protein and fresh vegetables — and give up the Ding Dongs. You'll feel better!

How microwave ovens cook food (as if you cared)

There are a lot of urban myths about microwave ovens, and we really don't have time to list them all here (though it would be fun). One of the most common myths is that microwave ovens cook from the inside out. This is horsepucky.

Microwaves cook food because microwaves love water. What the microwave oven does is to "excite" the water molecules inside whatever's in the oven. Therefore most food cooks because the water inside of it gets hot. This is why coffee warms up so well — but also why you can't make toast and why turkey dries out. It also explains how something warmed up can be "spotty"; a bottle of milk may be tepid or cool in parts, boiling in other parts.

If you're going to heat food in a microwave, put it in a proper, microwave oven-approved container and cover it with some plastic wrap. That wrap will keep in the steam produced by the microwave-excited water molecules. (Be careful when removing the plastic wrap, since steam can burn.) If you dare to warm up a bottle, be sure to shake it well before testing it.

Your lesson for the day

A good, balanced diet is the foundation for a long, healthy life. Don't take that away from your kids by throwing quick fixes and fast food at them. They deserve to have a well-balanced meal at least every now and then.

The 5th Wave
By Rich Tennant
YOUR CHILD'S FANTASY RESTAURANT
©RICHTENNANT
I'LL START WITH THE BOLOGNA AND COCOA PUFFS FRUIT ROLL UPS AND A BOWL OF FRENCH JELLY SOUP. FOR AN ENTREE I'LL HAVE SPAGHETTIOS WITH PEANUT BUTTER AND A SIDE OF CHOCOLATE HOT DOGS.
VERY GOOD SIR.

Chapter 11

The Joys and Perils of Bathtime

....

In This Chapter

▶ Bathing newborns, infants, and toddlers

▶ Giving your kids a safe bathtime

▶ Washing and drying everywhere — even if it's hidden

▶ The truth behind using lotions and powders

....

*B*aths have been around for a long time. The ancient Romans — who knew baths — discovered the concept of public baths: men and women all bathing together. These baths were the center of the Roman social life and a place to relax and have fun. And where you could see your neighbors naked.

This chapter covers bathtime because there's a lot to bathing. Ask the Romans. They went through great efforts to make the baths elaborate, soaking themselves in oils and making a big *to do* of it. Things haven't changed much for present-day parents. Baths are still a big event in households. But instead of worrying about elaborate oils, you just try to keep the number of toys floating around in the tub to a minimum.

Do I Really Need a Bath?

Most kids love taking baths. When they reach a certain age (like around five years old), you just let them loose in the water. Cleaning themselves may be secondary; the bath is the thing. But no matter what age, bathing is an important — if not social — event.

Your children lose weight every time they take a bath. — Shirley Hardin

Bathing babies

It's not necessary to give babies a bath three or four times a day, even though it may look like they need one after every meal.

Newborns don't even get a real bath until their umbilical cord stub falls off. Sponge them off with a wash cloth until this time and then give them a bath every other day. Use a cloth to wash their faces, hands, bottoms, and necks on the days they don't get a full bath (their necks are where the drooling milk goes to hide so that it can start to really smell bad at a later time).

If you give too many baths, that soft baby skin that we all wish we could still have will turn dry. And then your baby will develop dry patches of skin.

Don't give babies a bath — especially newborn — right after they eat. Movement in the bath can cause babies to spit up.

Bathing infants

Infants should get a bath once a day (or at least every other day if that's all you can manage). Don't be shy about using a wash cloth to wash their faces and hands often during the day, too (like after meals). They'll fight you on the face washing, but remember, you're the boss, so get it done.

Babies are considered infants anywhere between three months and one year. At three months, they're really not newborns anymore. They've been around and start to show off their cool personalities. Whatever the age they start walking — or toddling — is when they get that term of endearment: toddler.

Bathing newborns

Newborns typically don't like baths. Being stripped naked and put into water makes them uncomfortable. To help them feel a little more secure, try the following:

✔ Keep your body as close to your baby as possible. This is why a newborn tub in a kitchen sink comes in handy. The bath is at your level so you don't have to be a contortionist to stay close to your baby.

✔ Keep a warm wash cloth on your baby's stomach. This approach makes babies feel like they have something on and aren't naked to the world.

✔ Keep the room warm where you are bathing your baby. Babies chill easily.

✔ Talk to your baby in a soft, comforting manner. Your voice will help calm a nervous baby.

It usually doesn't take a long time for a newborn to get used to — and eventually like — bathtime.

Bathing toddlers

Toddlers and older kids should have a bath once per day or at least every other day. There are occasions when an extra hosing off is in order, and that's OK. Just make sure that your kids' hands and faces are clean during the day, even if the rest of them may be a little questionable.

✔ Kids lick their hands and rub their faces all the time. If they have outside dirt — or who-knows-what — on their hands and stick a finger in their mouths or eyes (or worse yet, in *your* mouth), they can get sick from the germs and get diseases like worms.

This is what you win if you don't keep 'em clean

Bathing is not only a means to have a cute, sweet-smelling child — or an excuse to play in water. Although bathing is a good course to keep down diaper rashes and yeast infections, its main purpose is to wash away the germs that fly around, are picked up, wiped up, and smeared on our children. It's yucky stuff. The simple process of washing hands and faces can keep down infections that are easily spread to everyone.

Most infections are spread by the hands — a small percentage by coughs:

✔ Toddlers are especially good at passing infections because they have a habit of touching or sticking everything into their mouths.

✔ Most diarrhea — and hepatitis — are caused by poop (which is 50 percent bacteria) getting on hands and being spread. Wash those hands after using the bathroom or changing diapers. Watch that your child doesn't reach down and get dirty hands when you change those messy diapers.

✔ The most common source of respiratory infections are caused by the spread of nose, mouth, and eye discharges (like runny nose, eye infections, coughing). These discharges are spread by dirty hands.

✔ Contaminated objects, such as hats, combs, and brushes, can spread yucky stuff like ringworms or lice.

✔ Eye infections can be caused by your children rubbing their eyes with hands covered with dirt (which can contain more than you'd care to know) or runny-nose stuff.

A Safe Bath Is a Happy Bath

Baths can be dangerous if you don't prepare properly. Keep these things in mind when it's time to give your kids a bath:

✔ safety first

✔ supplies at hand

✔ holding baby

Safety first

Bathing your kids is one of the true joys of life. There's nothing more fun than seeing your kids, piled in a tub with as many toys as possible, trying to dodge you as you attempt to wash their hair. But bathing can also be dangerous — and should never be taken lightly. Always be on your toes during bathtime.

Start the bath carefully

Turn on the cold water first, and then gradually add the hot water until the water is the temperature that you want. When you want to turn off the water, turn off the hot water first, and then the cold water.

Check the water temperature

The bathwater should be a little warmer than room temperature. Always test the water before you put your child in by sticking your hand in the water and moving it around the tub looking for uneven water temperatures. Water temperatures change and can cause *hot spots* in the bath water. Also, either you or child can accidentally knock one of the faucets, causing the water to become hotter or colder.

The water from your hot water tank should be no hotter than 120 degrees. If it's too hot, either turn it down yourself, or call a plumber and have it changed for an outrageous fee.

Keep kids seated

As your kids get older, bathtime play gets more rigorous — and they get to the point where they want to stand up to grab a toy, or just to walk around. Don't let them. Make it a steadfast rule that light play in the tub is fun, but they are never allowed to stand up or walk around in the tub. It's too easy for them to fall and hurt themselves on the slick tub surface. If your bathtub doesn't have a non-skid surface, invest in those ever-so-fashionable bath mats or rubber stencils that stick to the bottom of tubs. There are some really cute ones that your kids will love to try to peel up.

Watch these mats and stick-ons carefully. If you see that they're beginning to turn black, peel them up, throw them out, and buy some new ones. This black stuff is mold caused by the water being trapped under the rubber.

Keep water levels low

Kids always want the bathwater high so they can *swim*. It's not really necessary (and for babies, it's dangerous). If the water is too high, they'll have a hard time keeping anchored down — and they'll float. Yes, float. They'll start to float — because they weighs less than the water — then fall over. See the danger in this? If you have high water for your older kids, all they do is kick and splash and make a mess.

Never leave kids alone

It only takes one inch of water in which to drown.

You have to keep a constant eye on your kids. Never leave them alone. The comments of parents whose children have drowned are all the same, "I only left him alone for a few minutes." It only takes a minute.

We're programmed to answer bells. If the phone rings, we run to it. If someone rings the doorbell, we run to the door. You can do one of two things. Either ignore the door or the phone, or install an intercom system throughout the house and carry a cordless phone with you wherever you go. Whatever you decide, *don't ever* leave the bathroom with your kids in there alone. Take them with you when you leave.

Don't let them drink the water

I don't know why kids do this, but if you don't watch closely, they'll drink the bathwater. Since kids are infamous for peeing in bathwater, drinking it is anything but a healthy idea.

Before you fill a tub with water, start the water running, and then set your child in the bath before you close the drain. This strategy allows them a few minutes to pee in the bath. After *they're* drained, plug the tub's drain. That way your child isn't sitting in a bath of pee water.

When you let your child sit in a tub with running water, keep one hand in the water flow until the tub is filled. If there is a change in water temperature, you want to be the first one to know.

Supplies at hand

Keep all your bathing supplies close at hand — they should all be within arm's reach. You don't want to leave your kids alone to go on a hunt to look for their bath supplies. Before you start the bath, do a quick inventory so that you know everything is right where you need it.

Another possibility is to have a bath basket. Get a large basket and put everything in it that you could possibly need. It should have the basics like the things in the following list. This way, if you decide to give an impromptu bath in the kitchen, just grab the basket and go.

- bath soap
- shampoo
- wash cloths
- towels
- lotion
- powder
- Vaseline
- baking soda
- comb or brush
- diaper-rash ointment
- baby thermometer
- liquid acetaminophen

Don't forget the fun spplies of bathtime. Great bath toys are plastic cups, boats, rubber animals — evn dolls and action figures. Keep toys that are too small or have a lot of sharp points out of the water. You don't want little bottoms sitting on these things.

If you have to give your kids liquid acetaminophen, you may want to do so while they're taking a bath. This stuff is usually very sticky, and — kids being kids — they'll drip it on themselves. But, if they're already in the tub, just hose them off. Instant clean!

If your child is running a temperature, pour a little baking soda into the tub (enough to make the water look a little cloudy). Baking soda is a natural ingredient that helps lower temperatures.

Holding baby

You should always have one hand on your baby when he bathes. He'll squirm, topple over easily, and — if you pour water over his face — he'll stiffen his little body and fall backward. If you aren't holding him well, he'll bonk his head.

There are these wondrous things you can buy that are supposed to help hold up your baby while you bathe him. Save your money. Just do a good job supporting him with your arms and hands.

Don't Overlook Those Overlooked Body Parts

Being a baby is the only time when we think that having extra folds of skin is cute. As we get older, it loses its charm.

Since babies have these extra folds, you need to pull them back and wash the skin that's between the folds. Just because we usually don't see these areas doesn't mean they don't get dirty. Rashes develop here if you don't clean and dry these areas on a regular basis. Keep in mind that these body parts aren't limited to babies. Your children, no matter what their ages, still have to scrub these areas like they're going into surgery. Babies are typically the ones that have the extra folds — but not always. Look at your Great Grandma Mattie. There's a woman with folds!

Washing the secret hiding places

Behind the ears — Food and milk sneak behind the ears and wait to turn sour. Don't even try to guess how it gets here. The fact is that it does, and kids get crusty behind the ears if you don't scrub back there.

Feet — Yes, your kids' feet can smell just as bad as anyone else's in your family. Their little toes like to hang on to the fuzzies that socks leave behind, so don't forget to wash between the toes, too.

Penis — Gently pull back the overlapping skin of the penis and wash with soap and water. Smegma (it's like skin residue) collects around the penis if it's not washed and rinsed thoroughly. This advice is only for circumcised boys. If your child is uncircumcised, clean around the outer and exposed areas, but don't try to pull back the foreskin of the penis.

Vagina — Open the lips of the vagina and, very carefully, wash the area with soap and water. Remember to wash from front to back so as not to spread germs. Just like little boys, little girls collect smegma, and it needs to be cleaned.

Butt — (otherwise known as bottom, tush, heinie) Even if your baby has been sitting in a tub of water for two hours, if you don't take soap and water and wash the bottom (and the little hole the poop comes from), the poop will continue to stick to your baby, and you'll end up wiping it off with one of your pretty towels.

Lower back — When your baby has one of those explosive bowel movements, it sometimes goes up the back (poop, like water, takes the path of least resistance). Even though you may do your best to get to that area when you change a diaper, you won't always be able to do a good job. After all, it is kind of hard to get to.

Hidden crack areas — The prime target for diaper rash is the inside crack of legs near your baby's genitals. This area usually has a lot of fold to it, and it gets wet and warm — the breeding grounds for diaper rash and yeast infections. Pull back these folds and wash the area. Explosive diapers hide extra poop here, too.

Drying the secret hiding places

Drying thoroughly is just as important as the wash job. When you leave folds of skin wet, rashes and yeast infections develop. This, of course, is *not* a good thing.

After baths, lift the folds of skin in between cracks of legs near the genitals, under necks, under arms, behind knees, and around wrists and ankles. Some babies who are extra chunky (umm, like peanut butter) look like they're wearing rubber bands around their wrists and ankles. Those are just hiding places for water.

Baths are a great way to relieve stuffy noses. Set your child in the bath and pour warm water over his head (a little at a time). Wipe the snot away as it comes out of your child's nose. Make sure you support your child's back well — when you pour water over a baby's head, he'll leans back (trying to get out of the way of the water) and will topple over if you don't have a hand behind his back.

Lotions, Potions, and Powders

The smell of a child can't be duplicated. Depending on when you take a deep, loving whiff, it can be a clean, natural smell — or that of soured milk, strained peas, or an old baseball glove with a hint of peanut butter.

Lathering with lotions

Parents are almost obsessed with the lotions and powders designed to make our wee babes smell better, be softer, and look better than they naturally are. Lotions and powders have a purpose, but you should use them sparingly.

Lotions are designed to make baby skin soft. The only time it isn't soft is when you give too many baths, or during the wintertime when heaters take the moisture from the air. If you feel your child's skin and it feels naturally soft, don't bother with the lotion.

Bathtime pleasures

Hopefully you'll have a child who loves to take baths. But take this warning: Just because your child's in the bathtub doesn't mean that you're not fair game for getting a few suds on you, too. I suggest you get fully dressed in your *parenting* clothes, which, of course, is anything that you don't mind getting wet. Enjoy your bathtimes, and keep that camera close at hand. You can't pass up the opportunity for all those Kodak moments that occur during bathing. Besides, you need a great picture to show your child's first true love!

Don't put lotion an your children during hot weather. Lotions clog the pores. This warning is especially important for babies since they don't drip sweat like adults do to cool themselves. They can feel extra hot if you apply lotions.

Read Chapter 23 for more information on children and the heat.

Putzing with powders

Powders are designed to soften and cool the skin — and absorb dampness. They're good to use on warm days to help keep your baby cool. However, overuse of powders, like anything else, is bad. I've seen parents pour bottles of powder on little bottoms. I'm not sure if they think they're going to absorb all the pee or what, but it's too much. If you use too much powder, it will absorb the urine, and if not washed away thoroughly, may cause infection.

Powder is good for backs, under arms, behind knees, necks, and stomachs. Use sparingly, and only if the situation calls for it. Before you apply powder to your baby, first sprinkle the powder into your hand, and then apply it to your baby. This way, you won't have powder flying all over the place.

When you powder your baby, it's like love.

Fun with potions

Bubble baths are a fun way to make bathtime a little more interesting. However, use bubble baths sparingly. They aren't to be used for every bath. Some kids may be sensitive to bubble baths and develop bladder infections, not to mention the fact that the soap can dry out delicate skin if used too much.

Your lesson for the day

Use extreme caution when giving your kids baths. You've been taking a bath for years (hopefully), so it seems like a harmless act. However, unforeseen dangers lurk and you have to be very aware and observant.

Chapter 12

The Joys and Perils of Bedtime

- -

In This Chapter

▶ Newborn's sleeping schedule

▶ Working with a bedtime plan

▶ How to end a sleeping habit that you shouldn't have started

▶ Keeping your kids in bed

▶ What to do when your kids wake up in the middle of the night

▶ The ever-dreaded nap

▶ The family bed controversy

- -

Honey, the baby woke up, it's your turn to get him. Honey? I know you're not asleep, I can tell by the way you're breathing. . . .

*1*t's 3:00 in the morning and your night owl wants to play. So now what? Getting kids to bed and keeping them there is the topic of many a conversation among parents. You've tried straps. You've tried eating therapies. You've read this book and that. You're about to consider heavy duty staples and a stun gun. What's left?

This chapter covers bedtime rules and rituals, safety tips, and the truth behind all that advice you've read or have been told about getting your children to bed.

Putting Newborns To Sleep: No Big Deal

If only all kids would sleep as easily and soundly as a newborn, our lives as parents would be near perfect. Of course, keeping them asleep for any amount of time is the trick.

There are no tricks for getting a newborn to sleep because you don't need any. Just feed them and there they go off to La La Land. Or they may be sitting in their rocker, car seat, or infant seat, and they naturally fall asleep. Then there's always the case where you just lay them down when you know they're getting sleepy. This, of course, excludes babies with colic. Nothing short of a parting-of-the-waters-type miracle works on colicky babies.

Whatever ritual or habit you start with your newborn to get him to sleep is the same ritual or habit he'll come to expect as he gets older. With this in mind, don't start any habits that you'll have to break later on.

Start your child's lifetime sleeping habits off right. Lay your baby down in his bed when it's time for him to sleep — this means after your child has eaten, and when you see him starting to doze off in his swing or infant seat.

As your child gets older, he'll understand that lying in his bed means sleep time, and you won't be saddled with the ritual of rocking him, patting him on the back, or any other thing you've done thinking that it will help him to go to sleep.

The older your children get, the less they'll sleep, and the more their personalities will come out. Then they start exerting their will — and everything is messy from then on. Be grateful for your newborn — they typically don't need help falling asleep.

Strategic Bedtime Plans

There's a Golden Rule when putting your children to bed, regardless of their age: They must be sleepy. Trying to put them to bed if they're not tired is a fruitless effort. Your kids may more than likely fight bedtime anyway. (Excluding newborns. They live to sleep.)

Old habits die hard

Sleeping habits you may unintentionally get into are rocking your baby, patting him on the back, playing music, and driving your baby around until he falls asleep. These habits you may develop are sincere attempts to comfort your baby. All new parents cherish the times when they can cuddle their little babe who then falls asleep in their arms. Doing this every now and then is great. Just don't make it a habit that your child will grow to rely on to fall asleep.

Before you actually try to put your children to bed, work up to bedtime. This is the time you help your kids feel sleepy. You can accomplish this by following these steps:

1. Play with your child — a lot of activity.

2. Offer your child a snack (optional).

3. Give your child a bath (optional).

4. Have a quiet time to calm your child down.

5. Put your child to bed, turn off the light, and leave.

A fun book to read to your kids about getting them in bed is *Just Go To Bed,* by Mercer Mayer (Western Publishing Company).

Activity time

First, chase your toddler around the house or yard; crawl around the house with the baby. Do things that encourage them to run, crawl, or scoot. This physical activity is not only good for them, but it'll also make them more ready for bed. Basically you're trying to wear them out.

Snack time

Now it's time for a snack. If you feed your kids before they go to bed, they're more likely to sleep longer and not wake up in the middle of the night wanting steak and potatoes. This is an optional stage because some kids won't need a snack before going to bed. That's perfectly OK. This snack time also starts the process of calming them down.

Good evening snacks are warm bowls of soup or a warm grilled-cheese sandwich. Feeding them something with *substance* will give them a full, comfy feeling — which of course helps to make them feel sleepy.

Bathtime

Next, give them a warm bath. No exciting play during this bath. It should be a calm, relaxing time — so you don't want to start a water fight that'll get them pumped up and ready to go some more. Warm water makes us sleepy which again, is our purpose here. See? Warm water = sleepy kids.

Quiet time

After playing, snacking, and bathing comes the quiet time. You've worn them out. Now you have to let them know that they're really tired and they want to go to bed. During all this night-time preparation, turn off the television, put on some soothing music (or just have it quiet), and grab a good book to read to your kids. When your kids are old enough to start paying attention to the fact that there's a television, they'll start watching it and becoming involved in what's going on. If there's an action, shoot-em-up movie, or Mutant Power Ninja something or another on, your kids may get excited and want to start play fighting like they are on TV. Again, this activity defeats your purpose of wanting to calm them down for bedtime.

Sit down with your kids and read a story. If they're too young to sit and really listen, just go through the book and point out the pictures, or make up your own story as you go along. Your toddler will like to point out various things on the pages, like a tree or a dog.

It's important that you give your kids enough time to quiet down. This time depends on your children. For some, it may only be 15 minutes. For others, it may be an hour. This is why the snack time and bathtime should also be a calming phase for your kids.

Bedtime

After you've done all of your preparation, tuck them into bed, kiss them goodnight, turn on the night light, *and leave*. It's that simple.

You don't think so?

Getting your kids to bed should be this easy, although it may not for a lot of parents. Sleeping problems begin with the bad habits you develop with your newborn. These are habits that *you* start, and then they rely on those habits. For example, sleeping problems occur when parents decide that they don't want to rock their two-year-old to sleep any more and that same two-year-old says, "Hey, what do ya think you're doing? Don't you dare think that you're going to get out of doing this anymore. I like it."

Putting your kids to bed because you're exhausted just doesn't work. They're the ones who have to be tired.

For some reason, kids think all sorts of fun happens after we put them to bed, and they want to stay up and participate. You know, after the kids go to sleep we break out the candy and cookies, run around the house, and jump on the beds — all the fun things that we won't let them do.

Once your kids are used to your evening ritual, they'll fall asleep more easily than they would if they were all wound up, pumped full of sugar and action adventure shows running through their heads. This ritual needs to be followed every night. Don't feel bad if you find it's too late for the bath or story. You've probably done something else to fill in that time anyway. But try to keep to your schedule as much as possible.

"I've Already Started Something I Shouldn't Have. Now What?"

Famous Parenting Experts have advised parents on how to put their children to bed — which includes letting them cry, ignoring them, shutting the bedroom door and holding it closed so that your child can't escape the bedroom (honest-to-God I'm not making this up). I can't say that I agree with these methods. I don't ever advocate ignoring your children.

If your children have already become accustomed to being put to sleep by some ritual, now is the time to start making those changes.

Follow the same rules of preparing your children for bed that are in the previous section, "Strategic Bedtime Plans." Then, when it's time for them to go to sleep, kiss them goodnight and leave the room. They may or may not fuss for a while.

This is important here. *Listen carefully.* Are they fussing (whining, whimpering) or are they screaming bloody murder? There's a difference. Stay outside the door and listen to the fussing. They may stop after a few minutes. Fussing only means that your child is really not happy with the situation but can live with it for a while. Screaming bloody murder means you need to go in and help out a little.

Assume that your child is screaming pretty loudly. Go in and comfort your child, and then leave again. (Comforting means laying your child back down, stroking his hair for a few minutes. Don't pick him up because he'll be *really* mad when you put him down again.) Wait a little longer before you go in the next time. Gradually add to the time that you wait before you go in.

You will probably need to take the time to wean your child from your sleeping ritual by combining it with leaving while he's still awake. For example, if you've developed the habit of patting your child on the back while he falls asleep, gradually reduce the time that you pat. Be prepared to go back into the room and pat some more if he cries, but then leave after a few minutes. Gradually increase the time that you're gone, and decrease the amount of time you stay in the room. This weaning process isn't going to happen overnight. You've developed a habit that your child likes — and this kid is not going to part with it very willingly.

A different kind of weaning

We take the time to wean our children off of breastfeeding, bottle-feeding, and diapers. I think we can be compassionate enough to wean our children off of any bad habits that we've started with them in their sleeping. I also don't see the need to set a world record in getting our children to sleep on their own within a matter of a few days.

I would take more time to wean my children so that they learn to sleep on their own rather than sit and listen to them cry for 45 minutes while I stand outside the door crying, too.

And what if a child goes to bed just fine, but pops back awake at 3:00 a.m. *every single night?* See the section "He's Waking Up, He's Waking Up!" at the end of this chapter.

Letting your child cry himself to sleep is not necessarily a bad thing. There's crying, and then there's that blood-curdling screaming. Work with your child by listening to him and gradually taking away the *crutch* that he's used to get himself to sleep.

Bedtime

Babies fall into schedules rather nicely. Always allow room for changes in these schedules. As they grow, their naps gets shorter and they sleep longer during the night. Basically, as much as we hate it, they grow up. They're heading for that day when they won't need naps.

It's easier to get your older kids to bed if they have a set schedule. These schedules will slowly change over time, so you'll have to be aware and sensitive of these changes as they happen.

Establish a bedtime for your kids. Remember, this is your *kids'* bedtime. It's the time when they act like they need to go to bed. This isn't the time when *you* would like them to go to bed. Those are usually two different times. This also isn't the time that you think they ought to go to bed because that's the time you went to bed when you were a kid. Your children have their own clocks to go by. And, if you have more than one child, be aware that each of your children may have an individual bedtime, depending on the age.

You have to be very observant of your children to determine what their needs are. You should pay attention to how long their naps are and how long they sleep through the night. When you're aware of this, it's easier to predict when they need to go to bed.

SIDS

Babies from newborns up until one year of age are the target victim for *Sudden Infant Death Syndrome* (SIDS: the sudden death of an infant who has had no serious illnesses and no apparent cause of death). This event is also known as crib death because it occurs when the baby is sleeping.

SIDS occurs mostly among males, those babies born with low-birth weights, and premature babies.

Putting your baby to bed properly is critical. Follow these guidelines:

- Lay babies on their side when they sleep. Do not lay them on their backs or stomachs. The current belief on SIDS (although doctors confess they're not real sure of the cause) is that babies who sleep face down breathe their own air and suffocate. There is also the theory that SIDS is caused by babies getting too hot when they lay on their stomachs. Their bodies over-react and their systems shut down, so they just stop breathing. Whatever the cause, doctors all agree that SIDS is related to babies sleeping on their stomachs.

- Don't put extra bedding in the crib such as lamb skins, pillows, or thick comforters. Again, your baby could get overheated, or get caught up in the bedding and suffocate. Keep bedding simple. All you need is a sheet, bumper pads, and a thin cotton blanket.

- Don't overdress babies. Keep the pajamas simple and without a lot of layers. You don't want your baby to get overheated.

If you lay babies on their backs, they may spit up and choke. Newborns aren't able to roll over to spit out so they'll just choke, possibly even to death. To keep babies propped up on their sides, roll a blanket or towel up into a long wiener shape and put one behind and one in front of them. This will keep them from either falling backward or forward.

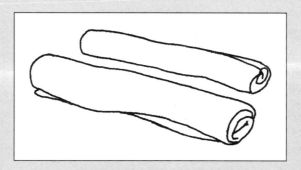

If you find that your children do not want to go to bed until midnight, you can adjust their schedule. Cut their naps shorter, or get them up in the morning rather than let them sleep in. Or you may have to do a combination of both. Doing this will adjust their sleeping habits so that they are more in line with what is reasonable.

When All Else Fails

Putting your children to bed every night and keeping them there isn't always going to go smoothly. If every night seems to be a struggle, look at your night-time ritual and see if you or your children are doing something that makes going to bed even harder.

✔ **Are they really tired, or do you just feel they should go to bed?**

There's a big difference. Maybe it's time to adjust bedtime. You could be putting them to bed too early.

✔ **Are they getting too many sweets before bed?**

Think twice about ice cream, cookies, cake, Jell-O, soda, and crackers. Try a bowl of soup instead of a bowl of ice cream. Or are they eating something they may be allergic to, causing them to be hyperactive?

✔ **Are they getting too much stimulation right before bed?**

If you and your kids are rough-housing and then you abruptly stop and say, "OK, time for bed," they may be too wound up to go to sleep. Television can also be a source of too much stimulation. You should have a quiet time before bed to calm everyone down.

✔ **Is there too much noise outside the bedroom?**

Some kids, no matter how much you try *not* to tiptoe around them, are very sensitive to noise.

✔ **Does your child have a fear he's not talking about?**

Perhaps you shouldn't have mentioned your fear of the closet monster when you were a kid. That may be your child's biggest fear now.

✔ **How's the room temperature?**

Kids have a harder time going to sleep if they're not comfortable — just like grownups.

Read the section "Strategic Bedtime Plans" at the beginning of this chapter. It covers a night-time ritual to prepare your kids for bed.

"He's Waking Up, He's Waking Up!"

Many times kids sound like they're awake when they really aren't fully awake. Don't be tempted to run in to comfort your children. All you really would be doing is waking them up. They'll go back to sleep on their own.

Stand outside the bedroom door or just peek in. If they're still in bed, all is well. If they're standing in their room crying, that means something different.

If a child actually gets up, walks out of his room, walks into your room, and then taps you on the shoulder, you know he's definitely awake. Persistence on your part is the key here. Don't be tempted to stay up and play (remember, you'd be starting a nasty habit). Take him to go potty, give him a drink, and then escort him back to bed. If he gets right up, take him again. Don't give in no matter how tired you are. He has to learn that 3:00 in the morning is not a time to get up and watch TV. It's a time for sleep.

There may be several nights of crying and whining, but *you'll* stop soon enough. Remember Chapter 3, "Being a Consistent Parent." This is one of those times where you'll have to consistently take your kids to bed. Not to worry, though. They'll eventually grow out of it. I mean, how many 17-year-olds do you know who are still waking up at night wanting their parents to take them potty and get them a drink of water?

- If your children routinely wake up and just wants something to drink, leave a cup of water by the kid's bed.

- When your children do wake up, try not to pick them up or have them walk. This gives the false hope that they get to get up and play for a while — which you know not to be true. It will also wake them up more. You don't want you children to go from a drowsy, "I'm thirsty" state to a "Now I'm really awake, let's play!"

- You may need to check a baby's diaper if the little one wakes up for no apparent reason. Try to do so without exposing the whole bottom to the chilly night air. That alone could wake your baby up even more.

Naps (Those Things Adults Long For)

Your children will want to nap anywhere from several times a day to once a day. It really depends on your child. Some kids are nappers, some aren't. Newborns nap all the time. By the time your children reach three or four, they may be taking only one nap a day, or simply lying down with a book to rest. Some kids may want a nap until they're five or six. Some kids start fighting naps at age two. You'll have to determine what your children need as they grow up.

Schedules

Babies to toddler ages usually will take a morning and afternoon nap. The time will vary from child to child.

Don't worry about the amount of sleep your children are getting. They'll sleep as much as they need to. Although, if the afternoon naps are getting longer and your children are going to bed later and later at night, you may want to start waking them up from their afternoon naps. You don't want to have to stay up until midnight because your toddlers' nap was too long and now they're not tired.

Try to keep your children on a daily schedule for naps. Your children will go down easier knowing that nap time comes after lunch and a story.

NO NAP!

If your children doesn't seem to want to take a nap, consider these things:

✔ **Did you get them ready for a nap?**

This means calm, quiet activities. Or did you just take them off of the trampoline to put them to bed?

✔ **Did you check for dirty diapers?**

✔ **Is the room conducive to a nap?**

Make the room quiet, no bright lights, no piles of toys in bed, not too hot or too cold, but just right.

✔ **Is it nap time?**

If not, have they displayed signs of needing a nap, such as being cranky, rubbing eyes, and whining? Perhaps they got overexcited and are too wound up for a nap. You'll have to take time to wind them back down so they can rest.

✔ **Are your children getting too old for naps?**

Perhaps your children are getting to the age — which varies from child to child — when they won't go to sleep, but they still need to lie down with a book and rest.

You know you've become an adult when you look forward to naps. — Dan Gookin

Sleeping with Children

There's a lot of talk over family beds. This is when the parents and children sleep together. Every remark has been made from "Oh, what a great idea" to "That's gross." This section covers the pros and cons of a family bed — and the compromise that can come from both sides of this debate.

Yeah for sleeping together

People who like the idea of sleeping with their kids all agree that it's a great time to bond and spend time with their children. They love the idea of cuddling. Mothers agree that it's easier for breast feeding, and they're able to have a quicker response to their babies. Some mothers even think that their babies sleep sounder and longer if they can feel their mother close by. Besides, parents have been sleeping with their babies for thousands of years.

Boo for sleeping together

People who disagree with the idea of sleeping with their kids feel that it's a bad habit to start. It doesn't allow either the children or the parents to sleep well (obviously there are differing opinions here). Kids need to learn independence, and having their own bed is the first step to that independence. It also makes the *private time* that parents need more difficult to achieve (if you know what I mean — wink, wink).

You also have to be careful not to roll over on a baby or small child, or have big pillows and comforters that would smother them.

Then there's always the time when you have to finally end the family bed — or do you have four teenage boys sleeping with you? It's hard to stop something once you've started it. How do you tell your children that now they can no longer sleep with you — and not have them feel rejected?

The compromise

Like most situations in parenting, there's always room for compromise. The family bed situation doesn't necessarily have to have a strict set of rules that you either follow or you don't. Here are some things to think about:

 ✔ Most women who breastfeed won't have to get up several times in the middle of the night to feed a newborn who is already in their bed. Keeping a baby nearby is handier and quicker for everyone.

✔ As your baby starts to sleep more, put him in a bassinet next to the bed so that you can easily grab him without having to go anywhere far. Lay him in bed next to you, nurse, and then put him back in his bed when he's finished. If you doze off and he ends up staying for a few hours, that's fine. He'll eventually spend most of his time in his own bed. You'll sleep more soundly.

✔ You can always welcome your older kids into your bed for those times when they don't feel well and are having a hard time falling asleep. Let them fall asleep next to you, but then take them to their beds. This strategy is especially helpful for kids who share rooms. If they can't sleep, they may wake the others up.

✔ You can also bring children to bed with you in the morning when they happen to wake up a little too early and you're hoping to con them into just a few more minutes of sleep. Sometimes this will work — and sometimes you may all lie in bed and giggle (and get little fingers shoved in your ears and up your noses).

✔ And, of course, everyone is welcome into the bed (including grandmas, grandpas, aunts, and uncles) when it's time to watch *Beauty and the Beast* or *Aladdin* for the 10,000th time.

Your lesson for the day

Getting your kids to bed and keeping them there is a process that involves time — and sometimes a lot of imagination. Don't get frustrated, and definitely don't expect miracles overnight. Changing a habit, or starting a new one, takes patience.

Part III
Dealing with Babies

The 5th Wave   By Rich Tennant

And now, I'd like to share some of my day with you.

In this part...

This section is dedicated to those soft, cuddly, sweet-smelling, precious, puking, drooling, poop machines that have made our lives the true blessings that they are. Call 'em *babies* for short.

Babies have amazing talents. In the middle of the night, they can get up people that even the strongest of earthquakes can't budge. They can get a 300-pound biker named *Tiny* to sit on the floor and play with building blocks. They can amaze, confuse, entertain, and inspire. And, like a movie star who's had too many Academy Awards, babies have their own special needs that must be catered to.

Chapter 13
Holding and Handling Baby

. . . .

. . . .

This chapter is going to talk generally about holding and cuddling your kids. Since kids seem so flexible, parents forget that their little joints are sensitive and things like shoulders and elbows can be easily pulled out of their sockets if you're not careful. There are definite ways to go about hoisting something small, cute, and very wiggly into your arms.

I'm not going to go into all the details of how to pick up a baby. It's not much different than lifting up a bag of sugar. There are a few exceptions. Bags of sugar are a little more compact — and nothing bobbles around or flops over.

Is It Possible to Spoil a Baby by Too Much Holding?

The old school of thought was that you would spoil a baby if you held that baby too much. To set the record straight, that's simply not true. The only way to spoil a child of any age is to give in to whining and temper tantrums. Sometimes it's OK to compromise with your kids. After all, it's no fun never to get what you want. (But there is a definite difference between compromise and letting your children whine, kick their feet, and cry to the point where you give in just to shut them up.)

So what happens when you hold your baby all the time? You develop great arm and back muscles for one thing. Your baby also gets to feel your warmth and love. Babies may get used to being held and want to be held a lot, but as your children get older, they'll want to go out and explore the things around them.

So basically, since you won't be tied to a child forever, never think of an excuse not to hold your baby.

Nothing feels better than cuddling a baby. — Debra Coppernoll

✔ Babies need to be held, touched, and cuddled. This helps in their development and feeling of security.

✔ Actually, it's unfair to limit holding to babies. All kids need to be held. (This doesn't mean you have to pick up your 80-pound children.) Even if your kids get too big to hold, there's nothing that should stop you from cuddling with them on the couch while you read a book together.

✔ Babies who are held more cry less often.

Read your kids *Love You Forever* (Firefly books)by Robert Munsch. It's a great book that demonstrates your kids are never too big or too old to cuddle.

The Joy of Cuddling Newborns and Infants

The special thing you need to remember about newborns and infants is their lack of muscle control. When you hold them or pick them up, always put an arm or hand behind their necks. Never, ever, pick them up by their arms. You can hurt them by pulling their little arms and elbows out of their little arm and elbow sockets.

You should hold newborns either cradled in your arms, or hold them up against you, chest-to-chest. Remember to keep a hand on the back of a baby's head because it'll bobble on over if you're not supporting it.

Don't try the one-handed hold with newborns. It works OK with older babies, but newborns are too floppy, and you can't hold them well with just one hand.

The head slam

Watch for the head slam. As babies start to get control of their head muscles, they'll start looking around and using these muscles. Then, all of a sudden, with no warning, the muscles will get tired — and a cute, bobbly head now becomes a weapon as it rockets toward you, slamming into your head at a painful velocity. This contact hurts both you and your baby. Keep a close eye on this flinging head and be prepared to support this same head when it goes out of control.

Lugging Older Babies (the Easiest Stage To Hold)

As babies get older and their muscles develop more, they'll have better control over their heads and they won't bobble around. But there are still safety precautions you need to remember:

- ✔ Don't throw babies up in the air. It may seem like fun, but there's always that chance you could drop them, or catch them wrong and hurt them.
- ✔ Don't pull babies by their arms. You can dislocate their shoulders and elbows by doing this. Always pick them up from under the arms or by holding one hand behind their necks and the other arm under their backs.

Tugging Toddlers through Tantrums and Tenderness

Toddlers are the hardest to hold, especially when they don't want to be held. They squirm. They push against your chest to be let down. They arch their back obviously not caring that they could fall on their noggins (noggin: very technical term for *head*). When toddlers want down, nothing will stop them.

If holding resistant toddlers seems like a chore, try picking up those toddlers who don't want to be picked up: They throw themselves on the ground as if for some reason being that extra foot away from us makes it impossible to reach them. They also raise their arms up and drop to the ground. This technique is taught in self-defense courses for escaping from an assailant. I have no idea how kids know this stuff. They must sneak off at night and watch Bruce Lee movies.

Even though toddlers like to behave like rag dolls, you must still resist dragging them by their arms. This action can dislocate their delicate shoulders and elbows.

Avoid roughhousing with toddlers because this type of activity can lead to accidents. Typical rough play includes tossing children in the air or hanging them upside down by their ankles. Even the famous "airplane" game can be dangerous. Not only are you stressing their shoulder and hip joints, but you can fall and hurt yourself while sending a kid into a suborbital flight pattern that would anger the FAA.

Your lesson for the day

Just because your kids resemble little bags of sugar doesn't mean that they should be tossed around as such.

Chapter 14
The Diaper Thing

- -

In This Chapter

▶ Let's talk poop

▶ Diaper rash

▶ Dealing with a difficult diaper

▶ Cloth or disposable diaper

- -

*T*his is a messy chapter. It contains words like poop, stink, diarrhea, and other things that may offend the politically correct reader. These are the words you use. Words like bowel movements, feces, and *odoriferously challenged* may seem appropriate in other books, but that's not what your child will yell out when the time comes to let you know what must be done. Your child will say *poop* or *potty* . . . or some other not-so-delicate word to express the mess. And this kid doesn't care if it's in the middle of Aunt Melba's funeral to make the announcement.

Get used to this vocabulary. Get used to talking about bodily functions, examining messy diapers, comparing and contrasting. It's all part of being a parent, and after a while it won't seem so gross — though your zest for guacamole may subside for a few years.

Other words for going to the bathroom

There are many phrases and words that describe the evacuation process. Here are some of them you may be familiar with. Can you guess which ones mean what?

caca	go potty	make a BM	go #1
pee-pee	po-po	poo-poo	go #2
poop	stinky	tinkle	doo-doo

This book uses the common noun-verb *poop,* which is how we describe it at our house.

Talking the Messy Language of Poop

Your family doctor is very interested in your kids' poop. This examination is a way to measure how well your kids' elimination system is working, which is a reflection of their general health. Your doctor will want to know how many times a day kids go poop and pee — and what it looks like (for about the first year).

As parents, you'll become familiar with what's normal for your kids and what's not. You'll learn to recognize what looks like diarrhea and what may be common. The important thing is that you keep track of these things: If there are drastic changes in the number of poops per day, or if your children stop peeing as much, this is an alert that something may be wrong.

Newborn poop starts out looking like black tar. It changes to look like Dijon mustard, and then goes on to look like dark brown putty. Your babies will have anywhere from one to several poops per day. Just like adults, every baby is different, and so is their pee and poop schedule.

Creating a Diaper-Changing Station

Change your baby's diaper in a safe, sturdy place. In fact, I recommend creating a permanent diaper-changing area equipped with everything you need close at hand. Ensure that the table (or whatever) can withstand the force of a 7.7 earthquake. Coincidentally, this is the force exerted by children who don't want their diaper changed.

Diaper changing tables are OK, but a lot of them wobble, and you don't have access to a sink. If you don't want to pay the money to buy a changing table, use your bathroom counter (if it's long enough). Set up the bathroom counter by removing all your makeup, cologne, or whatever may be in the way, and put it somewhere else. You don't want anything close at hand that your little one can grab and pop into an eager mouth.

Put a clean towel down as a cushion, and set aside one of the drawers that's close at hand for all your diaper-changing paraphernalia: diapers, butt-wipes, ointment, and so on. Be sure to include gadgets and toys to keep your baby's mind off the actual diaper-changing process. Mobiles are great to hang over your changing station.

This bathroom sink setup is a great alternative to changing tables. You have at least one wall to keep things secure so that baby doesn't fall off, and you have a sink in which to wash diaper bottoms that are truly messy from those explosive diapers — when those tiny little baby wipes just won't do the job.

✔ If you want to be really careful, you can buy straps and side bars to turn your bathroom counter into a changing table.

✔ Consider your child on a changing table just like you do the ocean or a class of kindergartners: Never turn your back on them. Always leave one hand on a child who's on the changing table.

Changing a Diaper: The Step-By-Steps

Changing a diaper is not like brain surgery, but there are some similarities. Both are delicate procedures in dealing with sensitive body parts — just at opposite ends of the body. Both can be very messy, both take special tools and equipment, and it would be nice if you used a mask for both — although when it comes to diaper changing, we seldom take the time to put one on. The only difference (that I can see) is that brain surgeons get paid a lot of money and parents don't. And once an operation is finished, the brain surgeon doesn't have to go back and do it over and over and over again.

Changing soiled diapers on a wee li'l baby

Brain surgeons have a list very similar to this one. Really. They carry the list with them to surgery. But, of course, their tools and preparation are a little different.

1. Open and unfold the new diaper. Lay baby wearing used diaper on top of new diaper.

2. Unfasten used diaper. If it's a boy baby, open just a little bit at first because air tends to make junior want to go right then and there.

3. Gather baby's feet and lift. Remove the dirty diaper, wad it up, and — if it was his or her turn to do this — toss it at your spouse.

4. Clean baby.

5. Gently lower baby onto the new diaper.

6. Fasten diaper on baby. Say something cute, such as "Oogie booga do boo." Baby will smile and prepare to soil diaper again.

Believe it or not, these steps were taken from a computer book, Dan's *DOS For Dummies*. It shows that even a computer guru can change a diaper. And this was written *before* Dan even had kids. Obviously Dan should have thought more about the baby talk before he composed this. Had he known then what he knows now, he would have realized that saying "Oogie booga do boo" is a definite *no, no!*

Newborns get a very insecure feeling when they get their diapers changed. This is obvious by the crying and the way their arms reach out to the side. To help them feel a little more secure, either keep one of your hands (or a blanket or towel) on their stomachs for as long as possible. This pressure helps to keep them calm.

When you change your little girl's diaper, remember to wipe her bottom from front to back. This approach will help avoid any kind of bladder or urinary tract infection from the bacteria being spread.

"There's no way you're changing my diaper!"

To handle those difficult diaper changes, keep a stash of toys or interesting objects close at hand so that when you lay your little poopy bottom down for a diaper change there will be something to keep those idle hands busy. You can also hang a mobile over the table for your baby to *ooh* and *ahh* at.

Change periodically the stash of toys that you keep hidden for only diaper-changing time. You don't want to find out your child is bored with a toy when you're in the middle of changing a full diaper.

- ✔ Another way to keep babies preoccupied is for you to lean over them, look them in the eye, and sing or talk to them. It's a great time for you two to have a quiet moment and to talk over life's major issues.

- ✔ Doing the occasional *tummy tzerbert* also preoccupies babies. Tzerbert by placing your lips on baby's tummy and blowing out to make a *bpbpbpb* sound. Babies go nuts over this.

When your baby wakes up in the middle of the night, wait to change the diaper until he's half through with the feeding (either half the bottle, or done with one breast if breastfeeding). This way you'll satisfy your baby's hunger right away, and you won't have to wake him up to change a diaper after the little one has dozed back to sleep.

Dealing with Diaper Rash (or the Itchy Bottom)

Diaper rash occurs because of two reasons:

- ✔ dirty diaper left on too long
- ✔ stomach problems

Your baby's dirty diaper needs to be changed immediately. The combination of the moisture from the diaper and the lack of air to dry it out causes rashes and chafing. Just because you have a diaper on your child that is advertised to hold 20 gallons of fluid and can block more liquid than the Hoover Dam doesn't mean you have to test it out for yourself.

Second, a rash can develop because of poop that's very acidic — due to a stomach virus, teething, or something your child ate that was too strong for the system (such as citric foods for babies under one year old). In any case, this kind of poop can cause an instant rash that may resemble little blisters.

The best way to take care of diaper rash is not to use baby wipes, but to wash the little bottom off in a sink with warm, soapy water (baby wipes are soapy cloths that may irritate the rash). Pat the bottom dry and apply a zinc-oxide ointment. If the rash lasts more than three days, contact your doctor who'll prescribe an industrial-strength ointment that will clear it up pronto.

Rashes occur a lot in the groin (top of the legs area). This area tends to be overlooked. Don't forget to pull this skin back to wash and dry it well.

To prevent diaper rash, or help clear up a rash that's already started, expose the rashed area to the air for a while. After changing the diaper and washing off the area, pat dry and then let your baby crawl or walk around without the diaper for some time. Don't put diaper rash ointment on a baby who's walking around bottomless (the ointment will get everywhere!). Allow the *bottomless look* only if it's warm out and there's no chance for baby to get chilled. Keep a close eye out though; your baby may take the opportunity to water the carpet for you . . . if you know what I mean.

Diaper Rash

Situation	*Solution*
allergy to the type of diaper you're using	Change diaper brands.
allergy to the type of baby wipe you're using	Change baby wipe brands or just use soap and water. Try the *unscented* wipes.
detergent used for cloth diapers is too strong	Change detergent.
leaving a wet or dirty diaper on too long	Check your child's diaper often.
hot weather	Your baby sweating, combined with the pee or poop, along with the diaper bottom being warm, dark and wet, begs for diaper rash to occur. This is a good time to go diaperless.

(continued)

Diaper Rash *(continued)*	
consistent diarrhea	Diarrhea can be caused from teething, a stomach virus, tension, drinking too much juice, a food allergy, or eating something that is too strong for a child's system. Look at your child's diet, health, and mouth.
food sensitivity	Change formulas, or take your child off the solid food recently started. Diaper rash can be a sign of your child reacting to a new food.

The Great Diaper Mystery: Cloth or Disposable?

The freckle-faced kid at the checkout counter asks, "Paper or plastic?" The choice is easy: Do you want to use paper and kill a tree to take home your groceries, or do you want to use plastic and have all your groceries roll around the car every time you turn a corner (in addition to the plastic filling up landfills)?

Another major life puzzle you'll face as a new parent is cloth versus disposable diapers. People can get fanatical on the subject, and boxes of literature have been produced arguing the pros and cons either way.

My advice: Use cloth or disposable and don't feel bad about your choice. It's a diaper. It collects poop and pee. Nothing more. The choice of what diaper to use seems to be a hot topic among parents. Some may look at this as wasted energy.

Disposable diapers

Good luck when you start hunting for disposable diapers. The shelves are plum full of different brands, sizes, shapes — those for girls, those for boys. It's amazing. Here are some pros and cons for using disposable diapers:

Pros

- ✔ Disposables are easy; you just throw them away.

- ✔ It's easier to travel with disposables.

- ✔ Disposables are great for kids who have diarrhea because these diapers don't leak.

Cons

- ✔ Disposables don't disintegrate — so they fill up landfills more.

- ✔ Disposables can be expensive.

- ✔ It may take longer to potty train your child because the little one can't feel it when wet.

Cloth diapers

Moms have been telling stories of how they used to hang diapers out to dry when there was snow piled up to their knees. Can you imagine how cold those diapers were when they took them down? Do you wonder if they let them warm up before they used them? Oh well, cloth diapers have some advantages as well as some disadvantages.

Pros

- ✔ Cloth is more natural.

- ✔ Cloth diapers now come with Velcro straps, so you don't have to worry about safety pins.

- ✔ If you don't like to wash diapers, you can use a diaper service that will pick up, wash, and deliver diapers to you on a weekly or biweekly basis (provided you don't live too far out in the hills).

- ✔ Washing your own diapers is less expensive than using a service. Cloth diapers, whether you use a service or wash them yourself, are less expensive than disposables.

- ✔ Cloth diapers make great burp rags (placed on your shoulder so the *liquid* burps don't get on you). When your kids grow out of them, they make great dusting rags.

Cons

- ✔ Cloth diapers use water and electricity to wash.

- ✔ Cloth diapers have to be rinsed out in the toilet, and you have to deal with the mess and the smell.

- ✔ Cloth diapers leak more than disposables (even with the plastic outer pants).

- ✔ Cloth diapers are not good for travel because you have to carry the used diapers with you.

Disadvantages of both

- ✔ They can cause diaper rash equally.

- ✔ They both smell really bad after they've been used.

A Suggestion (if You Just Can't Make up Your Mind)

One possible solution to the diaper dilemma is to use a combination of both. Use cloth at home and then use disposable for trips, outings to the store, when your child has diarrhea, and possibly even for nap and bedtime.

If you decide to go with the cloth diapers, use a diaper service for the first couple of months after you have your new baby. You're going to be too tired and busy with your newborn to take the time to be washing out diapers. You'll be surprised at how much poop and pee a little newborn can produce.

Your lesson for the day

The debate about what kind of diaper to use can go on and on. Don't worry about your choice and feel that you're going to be an outcast if you don't use the socially correct diaper. Just make sure you change diapers often and keep your little diaper-bottom clean.

Chapter 15

Breastfeeding vs. Bottlefeeding

● ●

In This Chapter

▶ The lowdown on breastfeeding

▶ Breastfeeding guidelines

▶ The truth behind breastfeeding

▶ The decision to wean

▶ Using bottles for babies

▶ Author's thoughts

● ●

As a parent, you're going to make a lot of decisions about your child. One of those decisions is whether or not you're going to feed your baby. That's a good decision. Now the hard part comes. *How* are you going to feed your baby? This topic is a big deal. There are a lot of misconceptions about breastfeeding and bottlefeeding (at the beginning, those are your only choices), and they are covered in this chapter.

Breastfeeding Pros, Cons, Myths, and Truths

Once you let people know that you're going to have a baby, they start shooting the questions at you. "So, do you want a boy or a girl?" (like you can put in a request and get what you want). "What are you going to name it?" (If it's a girl, Mary, if it's a boy, Mary, if it's a Vulcan, Mary.) "Are you going to breastfeed?"

If you're planning on breastfeeding, the only honest answer is, "I plan to try." If the thought of breastfeeding turns you off, that's OK. Your answer is simply "No, I think not."

When you're pregnant, your doctor will happily supply you with a forest full of information on breastfeeding and bottlefeeding. Then somehow you magically get on a mailing list and you start receiving this information from people you don't know, along with samples of different types of formula. *Then*, while you're in the hospital delivering, some candy striper comes by with even more information. At this point you'll probably forget your earlier stated convictions, break down, and admit that being a mother is too technologically unbearable and, by golly, how did grandma ever manage?

Should I breastfeed?

"Should I breastfeed?" is a question all new mothers have to ask themselves. It's not always an easy decision, especially when you have every person you ever met giving you advice on the subject (like you really want it). The changing times — and those people from those times — give different perspectives on breastfeeding. There was a time when the only way to feed a baby was to breastfeed. Then doctors came along and decided that mothers couldn't handle such an important job: Even though breastfeeding is quite natural, mothers should use formula to feed their infants. Breastfeeding was banned, and only the outcasts would do such a dastardly deed. Now there's a mismash of opinions. Some people have gone off the far end of the spectrum and feel that everyone should breastfeed; these same people see no reason why anyone shouldn't or couldn't. The most important opinion is yours. To help you along with your decision, I've listed the pros and cons of breastfeeding.

Pros

- Breast milk is the best food for your baby. The vitamins and minerals in breast milk can't be duplicated.

- Babies that are breastfed are less likely to get ear infections and upper respiratory infections.

- Breastfeeding can be a great, quiet, bonding time for you and your baby.

- Breast milk doesn't take any preparation time. Quick and easy access.

- You don't have to wash and sterilize bottles or nipples (and wouldn't *that* be painful?)

- Night time feedings are a breeze. Bring your baby to bed with you, lie down, and nurse. This is especially nice during those cold winter nights.

- Breastfeeding forces you to sit down and rest. You can't breastfeed and work at the same time. It's a nice break.

- If you have to be away from your baby during feeding times, you can use a breast pump and *express* milk for later use so you're not always tied down to a nursing baby. You can get away for short periods of time.

✔ Breastfeeding helps your body return to normal quicker. It also helps to shrink the uterus back to normal size.

✔ Breastfed babies are more likely to accept a wider variety of foods when they get older. Breast milk has different flavors (not like chocolate, vanilla, or strawberry — but *subtle* differences based on what you eat). Experiencing different tastes at an early age leads babies to be more open to other tastes.

✔ It's cheap! Breastfeeding saves money. No extra food to buy.

Cons

✔ Breastfeeding can be uncomfortable. For some, it hurts like heck, and they would scoff at the word *uncomfortable*. When you first start to breastfeed, your nipples get sore and, for some mothers, they crack and bleed.

✔ Your breasts get engorged (filled with too much milk) if you don't nurse on schedule. This is painful.

✔ Using a breast pump may make you feel like a dairy cow.

✔ For a lot of mothers, their breasts leak and cause embarrassing wet spots on their blouses. They look like they leaned up against a wet window.

✔ You can get a breast infection, which is painful.

✔ Using a breast pump takes some time (anywhere from 10 to 30 minutes). Unless you have some breast milk already frozen, you have to plan ahead to leave your nursing baby.

Breastfeeding myths and truths

Like most activities that have been around for a gazillion years, breastfeeding is filled with myths and old wives' tales. Allow me to shed some light on a few of the more popular ones:

Myth: Everyone is capable of breastfeeding.

Truth: This is the number one myth that has left mothers feeling frustrated and inadequate. Not everyone can breastfeed. This situation happens for a variety of reasons, ranging from not having enough breast milk to a baby simply being unable to nurse. Breastfeeding advocates have a hard time admitting this fact.

Myth: Breastfeeding is a natural event, and you and your baby will fall into the breastfeeding ritual like you've been doing it for years.

Truth: It takes a while for you and your baby to get a pattern down and both be comfortable with breastfeeding. For many mothers, it takes anywhere from a few days to a few months to get the process down.

Myth: Doing nipple exercises helps to make your nipples not so tender, and breastfeeding will be less uncomfortable.

Truth: No matter what you do to prepare, nothing is going to prepare your nipples enough for the colossal sucking force from babies.

Myth: As long as you breastfeed, you can't get pregnant.

Truth: Allow me to introduce my third son, Jonah, to you. He's only 11 months younger than my second son, Simon. *Ahem.*

Those parents who have children 11 months apart laugh hysterically at this myth. Although you delay your menstrual cycle (for about six months) while you breastfeed, you still ovulate and can get pregnant unless you use a contraceptive. Abstinence is the best kind of contraceptive, but not as much fun.

Myth: The only way to bond with your baby is by breastfeeding.

Truth: There are several ways to bond with your baby and breastfeeding is only one way. Bottlefed babies are just as capable of cuddling up with their parents and bonding. The breastfed babies don't have this bonding thing cornered.

Breastfeeding Guidelines

Don't assume that just because you naturally produce breast milk that you will without a doubt know how to nurse your newborn. It doesn't work that way. For many mothers, breastfeeding takes time and practice before everything goes along smoothly. Then there are those mothers who grab their babies while on the birthing table, hold their newborns to their breast, and never have to think twice about nursing their children.

Keep these thoughts in mind when you're nursing your child:

 ✔ **Don't get nervous or upset if your baby doesn't latch onto your breast the first, second, or even third time.**

 You both are new at this, and it may take coordination, time, and practice between you two. The older your child gets, and the more practice you have, the easier breastfeeding will be. Sometimes newborns are just too darn small and floppy to try to hold and feed at the same time. Just keep trying.

✔ **Don't assume that just because you've successfully nursed one child, the second or third child may be just as easy.**

Remember, these babies are different people, and they have to start out new at nursing. They weren't able to get any good advice from their siblings.

✔ **Don't feel pressured to succeed the first time you try to breastfeed.**

You will probably have a nurse, husband, or a roomful of spectators anxiously awaiting to see your performance. Don't get nervous or flustered.

✔ **Don't be surprised if you tend to sweat a lot during your first tries at breastfeeding.**

This state is a combination of your body going back to normal (all that hormonal stuff), any nervousness you have breastfeeding, and the letdown process your body goes through when it's time to nurse.

✔ **Get comfortable when it's time to nurse.**

You'll be nursing quite a bit, so find a comfortable chair, couch, or bed, use pillows to prop yourself up, put pillows underneath your arm that is supporting your baby's head, lean back, and relax.

✔ **Have your supplies ready.**

New mothers are busy, busy, busy. So take the time while you're nursing to have a large glass of water and a snack. Look at it as sharing lunch with your baby.

✔ **Don't forget the football hold.**

If you're having problems nursing your baby with the cradle hold (baby's belly against your belly), try the football hold. You hold your baby like you would a football, tucked under your arm: your baby's belly is against your side.

✔ **Take care of yourself.**

Nursing is not the time to go on a diet to shed those extra pounds. You have the rest of your life to diet. Now is the time to think about your baby, and your baby needs you to be eating and drinking. Simple food is the best, so have plenty of fruit around for you to grab, keep bowls of nuts and raisins out, and keep a sports water bottle filled with water for you. (Don't fill it up with soda pop. Your body needs pure, healthy water.)

✔ **Watch what you put in your mouth.**

Many things can be transferred to your breast milk: alcohol, medications, illegal drugs, and even some spicy foods. Always consult with your doctor before you take any medications.

✔ **Drink lots of water.**

You are producing milk — a liquid. The more water you drink, the more liquid you'll produce. You should drink at least eight 8 oz. glasses of water per day.

✔ **Follow the basic rules of breastfeeding.**

Hold your breast with your thumb and forefinger behind the aureole (the brown area behind your nipple), make sure your baby's mouth is wide open like a little bird's, and quickly put the nipple in his mouth before he shuts it. Holding your baby tummy-to-tummy will make sure he doesn't pull your breast or break away from it.

If you want to breastfeed, but are having troubles getting started, consider using a breast pump. This pump will keep your flow of breast milk going, and you'll be able to feed your baby. But it also buys you some time so that you can continue working with your baby to get him to breastfeed without the fear of him going hungry.

Some hospitals have breastfeeding classes or lactation consultants to educate mothers about breastfeeding. They cover basic breastfeeding techniques, suggestions on how to reduce sore nipples, and a lot of other helpful information. You can also contact childbirth educators (like Lamaze instructors), midwives, or the La Leche League.

Lick by lick, the cow ate the grindstone. — Texas saying

Working through the soreness

You can do some things to help get over sore nipples from breastfeeding. Most women will breastfeed longer if there's a way to *endure* the pain of sore nipples.

✔ Don't pull your baby away from your breast without *unlatching* your baby first. Do this by sticking your finger in the corner of your baby's mouth to break the suction.

✔ *Air dry* your nipples when possible.

✔ Don't use soap on your nipples (soap can dry your skin). Water is all you need to clean your nipples.

✔ Break open a vitamin E tablet and rub the oil on your nipples. Remember to wash your nipples before breastfeeding. You don't want your baby eating the vitamin E.

✔ Limit the feeding time on the sore nipples. Many babies like to nurse and doze off to sleep with the nipple still in their mouths. Once your baby has stopped eating, take him off the breast.

✔ Express a little milk before breastfeeding to stimulate the let-down process of the milk.

✔ Put warm washcloths on your breast and nipples before breastfeeding. This action also helps with the let-down process of the milk.

✔ Use a breast-pump on occasion to give your nipples a rest.

Breastfeeding away from home

You're in luck if you breastfeed and you and your baby are going on an outing. When your baby gets hungry, just plop down where you are and start feeding.

Don't be embarrassed about breastfeeding in public. Be as discreet as you need to be, but remember that this is your baby's food — and your baby deserves to eat now. Look at it like this. If you were hungry and had a candy bar in your bag, you wouldn't feel like you needed to go hide to eat it. Well, if you breastfeed, you're carrying your baby's lunch in a very unique way.

If you're on the modest side and prefer to breastfeed in private, most restrooms have couches or chairs so you can breastfeed your baby.

If your feelings about publicly nursing your child are somewhere in between the plopping-down-anywhere or sitting-in-a-restroom scenarios, you can always use a blanket to cover yourself and the baby so that you can nurse in public. Use a lightweight blanket, or just wear a shirt that can be unbuttoned or lifted up easily. Between your body heat and the heat your baby will generate simply from the eating process, you'll need something light so you both won't get overheated. Of course, if you're really shy, duck into a dressing room or restroom.

Breastfeeding away from baby

Taking a trip without your breastfeeding baby is possible. It just takes advanced planning and some extra pumping on your part.

Figure out how many feedings you'll miss; then give yourself plenty of time to pump extra breast milk and freeze it for later use. When you're away from your baby, your babysitter can defrost and use the frozen breast milk. The milk should be thawed in the refrigerator and used within 24 hours.

While you're gone, continue to use a breast pump during your regular feeding times. If you don't, your breasts will become engorged (filled to capacity), and you'll stop producing more milk.

Warm thawed breast milk by placing the bottle in a pan of warm water, or hold it under the hot running water for a few minutes. Test the milk on your inner arm. It should be just a tad warmer than lukewarm.

To give Mom a treat, have her express extra breast milk and let her sleep in while you take the 2 a.m. feeding.

The Truth of All Truths about Breastfeeding

Some women have it in their heads that if they don't breastfeed, they won't get to bond with their babies and somehow will be a failure if they don't, won't, or can't breastfeed. I don't know when this happened, but we've been brainwashed into thinking this way.

Some women have gotten to the point where they have unintentionally starved their newborns because everyone insisted that they should be able to breastfeed — but they couldn't. So many things can happen to prevent breastfeeding: You may not have enough breast milk, the baby's mouth may not be able to suck properly, or the baby may just not want to breastfeed for some unknown reason. There's a long list of possibilities, but the breastfeeding experts will usually insist on trying every known contraption or strategy for getting that newborn to breastfeed.

My advice is to listen to your gut and do the best thing for your baby. There's no question that breast milk is the best food for your baby, but the most important issue here is that your baby be fed. If you've breastfed your baby and he still cries like he's hungry, he may still be hungry. You may be told that babies will continue to nurse for as long as the breast is being offered. If you've finished nursing, give him a pacifier. If he's still not satisfied, he may still be hungry. Be your own best judge of when your baby is full. Some babies eat and eat and eat. Don't stop feeding your baby because some *average chart* claims he's full.

If you can't breastfeed, try using a breast pump so that your baby still has the benefit of getting that breast milk. This practice will also keep your breast milk going so that you can continue to try to breastfeed your baby.

If you don't think that your baby is getting enough food, get a breast pump (Medela is a great electric one) and express some milk. You'll be able to see if you have any milk, for one thing. Second, if the baby takes the milk, you know he's still hungry. If he doesn't then go on to see if he has gas. (Read Chapter 16, "Cranky Babies.")

Breast pumps that you buy at the store don't work as well as those that you can rent from a drugstore or pharmacy. Ask your doctor or pediatrician for a recommendation for a breast pump. The nursery in the hospital where you deliver may also be able to give you information on breast pumps. You may find that you have to experiment with a few breast pumps. There are both electric and manual pumps. Some women love the electric pumps because they don't take any effort and are quicker. Other women find them quite painful — and of course they make you feel like a dairy cow hooked up to one of its automatic milking machines.

You're not a failure if you can't breastfeed. You can still be just as close to your baby by bottlefeeding. Curl up in bed in a nice quiet room and take your time giving your baby a bottle. If you can breastfeed, that's great. Enjoy it. Don't get too frustrated over the sore nipples and leaky breasts. It'll pass, and breastfeeding will go smoothly.

Cigarettes cause breastfeeding problems. Studies have found that female smokers produce about 40 percent less breast milk, and that milk has less fat in it. Babies wean themselves early and miss out on the vitamins and nutrients necessary to ward off respiratory illnesses and ear infections.

To Wean or Not to Wean (That Is the Question!)

You won't want to breastfeed your five-year-old, so at some time you're going to have to wean your child from breastfeeding. Some kids wean themselves.

The decision to wean is very difficult for a lot of mothers. After all, breastfeeding is a special time that just you and your baby have together. No one else can share in the act, and for most mothers, there's nothing more relaxing or fulfilling.

Because of busy schedules, going back to work, or simply being tired of having leaky breasts, wearing big blouses, and not having the freedom to skip a meal or two, the decision to wean your baby from breastfeeding may not be difficult at all.

The easiest and least painful way to wean your baby is slowly, over a period of time. Mothers have actually been told that the best way to wean a baby is to go cold turkey. Just stop breastfeeding. An honest reaction would be, "Well, won't that hurt? I mean, my breasts will get engorged." The response: "You'll experience some tenderness. Take Tylenol and put cold packs on your breasts; after three or four days, you should be fine."

Going cold turkey has to be the worst advice ever given in the history of advice giving. Mothers usually try this for one day. By the end of the day their blouse is soaked with breast milk and their breasts feel like they're going to explode. The smart moms are the ones who grab their babies and say, "Eat, *please!*"

There is a better way. Start weaning your baby by taking one feeding at a time and replacing it with formula (or baby food if your baby is old enough to start eating solids). Give yourself plenty of time for your milk supply to start reducing. After anywhere from a few days to a week of replacing one feeding, replace another. Do this again and again until finally there's no more feedings to be replaced. This process is longer, but it's not painful. Anything without pain is the best.

For some mothers, their babies will start weaning themselves once they start on solids. Don't feel rejected. Once your baby gets to taste the wonderful world of real food, milk may simply not be enough.

- ✔ Statistically, half of all women stop breastfeeding during the first four months. Why? Lots of reasons — from the pain from tender breasts that some women never get over to having to go back to work. The saddest reason is that some mothers feel they're looked down upon for breastfeeding an older child.

- ✔ Many women wean their babies when they start the teething process. When those little teeth start coming in, babies may take the opportunity to use your breast as a teething ring. Unfortunately, there's not much you can do to ease the discomfort. You can unlatch your child every time you feel biting, and eventually your baby may get the idea. (But repeatedly latching and unlatching your baby can make your nipples sore.)

- ✔ Don't let anyone's opinion about breastfeeding influence you. If you want to breastfeed your kids until they go off to college, so be it.

- ✔ You may want to wean your older baby onto a cup rather than a bottle. This transition may be easier in the long run. You won't have to go through the weaning process again to get your child off the bottle.

- ✔ If your child weans quickly, you may have some *discomfort* (another word for *excruciating pain*). Use a breast pump and express just enough milk to ease the pain. Eventually, you'll stop producing as much milk as you did.

- ✔ Other ways to help with the pain of engorgement is to wear a good, supportive bra to hold those puppies up (don't even think about going braless), put ice packs on, or put chilled cabbage leaves inside your bra (Kathy Lee Gifford claims to do this).

Keep a close eye on your kids as they make the transition from breast milk to formula (or cow's milk if they're over one year old). Bad reactions to the change include getting diarrhea, developing a rash, spitting up or vomiting, getting a stuffy or runny nose, or wheezing or coughing.

Bottles for Babies

Bottles are another confusing area for parents. The truth? There's not a whole lot of difference between any of them. The only real difference is the type of bottle in which you put plastic liners and squeeze out the excess air. Other bottles come in different shapes and sizes; some are plain, and some have cute little pictures on them. Some are angled for babies to get their milk without getting a lot of air. Honestly, they're all about the same.

Some babies are particular about the type of nipple you use, however. You may have to try a few different kinds if your baby turns a pug nose up at a particular nipple. Most babies won't give it much thought. They'll get used to whatever you stick in their mouths.

Bottlefeeding Guidelines

You have just as much of an opportunity to have a strong, healthy, loving baby who is bottlefed, just like those babies who are breastfed. Don't feel guilty if you choose to bottlefeed your baby. Or, if you're in that group of people who don't have a choice about it, accept the fact that bottlefeeding your baby is the only way to go. Just be happy that you have a baby to feed.

Here are some guidelines to help make your bottlefeeding experience as wonderful as it can be:

- **Expect to feed your newborn anywhere between $1/2$ to 4 ounces of formula at each feeding.**

  As your baby gets bigger, finishes all the milk, and seems hungry at shorter intervals, increase the formula. You'll eventually increase the formula and be feeding your baby less often.

- **Hold your baby during feedings.**

  Take the opportunity to hold, cuddle, and sneak in those kisses while your baby is eating. Never prop the bottle up to feed your baby. This is extremely unsafe. Your baby could choke and would be unable to push the bottle away. Holding your baby during feeding also helps to prevent ear infections. Babies who lie down with bottles are more likely to have the milk or juice drip from their mouths, run across their cheeks, and drain into their ears. When your baby is old enough to hold the bottle, allow him to do so. This is the first step to independent feeding.

✔ **Heat the formula by placing the bottle in a pan of hot water or holding it under hot running water.**

The formula should feel a little warm when you dribble the milk on your inner wrist. If it feels hot on your wrist, it's too hot for your baby. (You also heat bottled breast milk this way.)

✔ **Don't change formulas.**

Babies have a very delicate system. Changing formulas can cause gas pains. If you find a formula your baby likes, stick to it. If you want to change formulas for some reason, ask your doctor for a recommendation. Not all formulas are the same.

✔ **Sterilize bottles and nipples.**

The recommended way to sterilize your bottles and nipples is to wash them with soap and water, place them in a pan of water, and boil for five minutes. This process will get rid of any germs that simple washing will miss.

✔ **Burp your baby halfway through feeding.**

Feed your baby half the bottle and then burp him before you continue with the rest. This practice not only helps your baby feel better (because there is no buildup of gas), but it also reduces the chance of your baby burping up the food.

✔ **Don't *handle* your baby right after feeding.**

Allow your baby some time to lie in your arms after feeding before you hoist the little one up to burp (this advice also applies to babies who are breast-fed). Giving your baby those few extra minutes allows the food to settle — and thus avoids the possibility that the food will come spewing out.

Heating formula in the microwave is not a good idea. Microwaves heat food unevenly, which causes hot spots in the milk. These hot spots could burn your baby. Microwaves also cause the plastic sack-type bottles to burst. Not a good idea.

Avoid the guilt and do what's best

It was necessary to include a whole chapter on breastfeeding and bottlefeeding for a very important reason. If you mess around with your baby's food, you can severely hurt your baby. You must feed babies when they're hungry. Don't feel guilty with whatever choice you make. As parents, we go through our children's entire lifetimes feeling guilty about one thing or another. Try not to make this area one of those guilt-ridden decisions. Just feed your baby.

For more information on nutrition, read Chapter 10, "Understanding Food and Nutrition."

Bottlefeeding away from home

It's inevitable. At some point in time, you are going to have to travel with your baby. This may mean only to the grocery store. But you'll look like one of those parents who totes around a 50-pound bag full of goodies for the little tyke.

That's okay. At least you'll be prepared. Remember these things when you get ready to go on your outing:

✔ **Prepared formula (the liquid kind, not the powder) must always be refrigerated.**

If you can't — or don't want — to keep a cooler with you, use the powdered formula.

✔ **Put the powdered formula into the bottle and take a bottle of water with you.**

When your baby is hungry, just add water and shake the bottle.

You can take along the ready-to-feed formula in the cans, but I don't recommend it. Not only do you need a way to open the can, but you'll also have to throw away the unused milk if you're not able to use it immediately (or store it in a refrigerator or cooler). I just wouldn't mess with it.

Your lesson for the day

Breastfeeding your baby is the best thing you can do for your little one. Actually, it's not the breastfeeding, but the breast milk, that's most important. But don't feel guilty if you can't breastfeed. No one in the medical field seems comfortable admitting that sometimes — for mysterious reasons — it just can't be done. Feed and love your baby. That's what is important.

"SCREAMING OR NON-SCREAMING?"

Chapter 16
Cranky Babies

Crying babies make you feel so helpless. That's one of the reasons why you get upset when your baby cries. That — and it's an annoying sound that interrupts the television.

Crying *usually* means something is wrong. New parents all tend to do the same thing when their babies cry. They stand there, rocking back and forth and say, "Our baby's crying. What's wrong?" As if their spouse knows what's wrong but would rather stand there and let the other person figure it out. No, that's not it. The problem with new parents is that, in the midst of all the crying (by both you and the baby), you forget, or perhaps don't know, all your options for calming the little dear.

Working with the Crying Baby Flowchart

Babies cry. It's a fact of life, and no matter how good a parent you are, your baby will cry. It's the only way your baby can let you know about a problem or a need that you haven't noticed.

You don't need to get upset, mad, or anxious when your baby cries. If you start to get upset, just stop and remind yourself that the only reason you're feeling this way is because you feel helpless and frustrated that you don't know what's going on. For your baby's sake, get control of yourself and relax. You can't be of much help if you're crying, too.

When your baby cries, just follow the Crying Baby flowchart and take each step one by one.

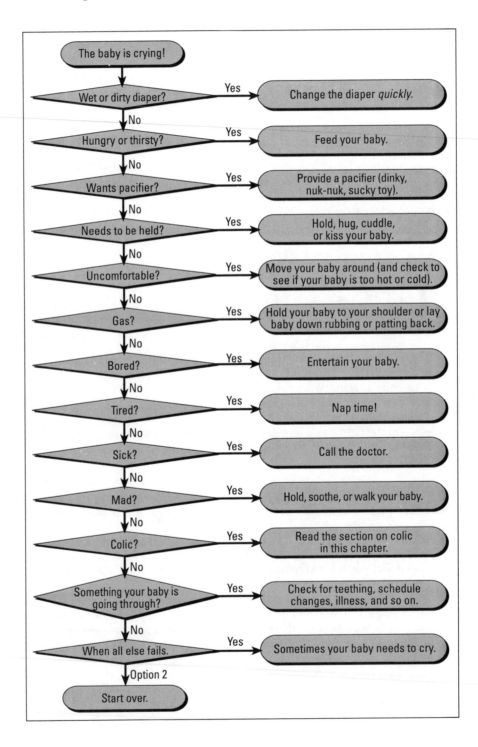

Why Babies Cry

When baby starts crying, there are a number of things you can do to *fix* the problem. Please take a look at the Crying Baby flowchart illustrated in this chapter. Each of the following sections goes into an explanation of the steps on the flowchart, expanding on what you can do to assist your cuddly li'l megaphone — and get the volume turned way down, hopefully off.

You'll learn the different type of cries your baby has. They're not all the same. As you and your child get to know each other better, you'll be able to distinguish one cry from the other. Also, don't be quick to pick up your baby when he lets out a little peep. He may just be letting off a bit of gas (oops), or just starting to fall asleep.

Wet or dirty diaper?

It may be a shock to learn that babies don't like to sit in their dirty diapers. I thought they were sort of apathetic one way or another, but they *do* care. They do, they do, they do! That's why they cry when they're wet or dirty. If your baby is teething or has an upset stomach, the poop gets acidy and can cause little blisters. As you may guess, this stuff hurts. So your baby appreciates it if you get those diapers off in a hurry.

The best way to clean your baby's bottom is to rinse it off with a wet washcloth. Remember to use lukewarm water. Your baby won't appreciate the invigorating feeling of cold water.

For poopy diapers, wipe most of the poop off with the edge of the diaper (which can be done with either cloth or disposable diapers). Then wash the bottom first with a wet washcloth (warm water), and next the genital area. Remember to wash front to back for girls so as not to cause infection. Pull back the foreskin on a boy's penis to clean that area thoroughly. (Remember to be very careful, not to pull hard, and only if the penis has been circumcised.)

For the knee-deep info on diapers, read Chapter 14, "The Diaper Thing."

All some people need to make them happy is a warm bath, warm food, and a dry bottom. — sign in a truck stop

Hungry or thirsty?

If changing your baby's diaper doesn't seem to help the crying situation, think about the last time you fed your baby. Your kids will always be on a feeding schedule, even though that schedule changes as they go through growing stages. They may not seem hungry for a while (like a day or two), but then they'll act like they're starving and will eat anything that sits still (watch out for small pets, household insects, and bark chips).

Try giving your baby something to eat or drink. Remember, he has a mind of his own. If he doesn't want milk, try juice, water, or (if you live in Scarsdale) a little chilled Perrier with a twist of lime.

If you're trying to give your baby solid food and he won't stop crying long enough to eat, give him a bottle for just a moment (or offer a breast if you're breastfeeding). He's gotten too hungry and is too angry to stop to see that you're trying to feed him. Once he realizes what you're doing, he'll stop crying so you can feed him.

Don't always assume that crying babies need food. If you feed your baby too often, he'll never expand the time between feedings. Thus, you'll always be feeding your baby every couple of hours. And never try to force feed children. They know when they're hungry and when they're not. If your child pushes the bottle, spoon, cup, or plate away, get the hint. This kid's not hungry!

For more details on your child and the world of food, see Chapter 10, "Understanding Food and Nutrition."

Wants a pacifier (dinky, nuk-nuk, sucky toy)?

Not all babies love a pacifier. If yours is one who likes the pacifier, don't keep it too far away. When babies feel the need to suck, they want to do it now. No waiting. Pronto. Hurry, hurry, hurry!

Most babies have the strongest need to suck during their first six months of life. But don't force your child to take the pacifier. If you give it to a baby who continually spits it out, take the clue. Your child doesn't want it.

You can buy clips that attach the pacifier to your baby's clothes so if the little one drops it, it doesn't get lost or fall on the ground. However, never attach a pacifier to your baby by putting a band around the baby's head to hold the pacifier in. This practice is dangerous and very unnecessary. Also, never use these clips while your baby is sleeping. Your baby could roll around, and the string to the pacifier clip could get wrapped around his neck.

Read Chapter 17, "Tools of The Trade," for more information on pacifiers.

Needs to be held?

Your baby needs a lot of physical contact — which means that your baby needs to be cuddled, hugged, kissed, loved, and held. Sometimes the only thing that will stop your baby from crying is if you pick him up and walk around with him. It's a simple solution, and it works.

It's been proven that babies who are frequently held cry less. And you can't spoil a baby by too much holding. That's an old wives' tale, and only old wives still believe it. The only way to spoil any child is by giving in to temper tantrums and by letting a child bully you into getting his own way.

 Invest in a baby sling for your baby. (Read Chapter 17.) The baby sling lets you carry your baby with you, but leaves your hands free so you can go about your day. We've stolen this idea from women in Africa and Asia who have been carrying their babies like this for centuries.

Uncomfortable?

Like you, babies get uncomfortable. But unlike you, they can't get up and put on another sweater, take their shoes off, or move to another chair. They have to sit there and be miserable until you figure it out.

Check to see if there's anything poking or jabbing your baby. Sometimes toys can get lodged in rather uncomfortable places. Also, check your baby's clothing. Zippers, hard threads, or tags can be uncomfortable for delicate skin.

Maybe you've left your baby in the swing for awhile, and he needs to change positions. You know what you feel like after you've sat in a two-hour movie. Your baby can feel the same butt-numbness if left in one place for too long.

Feel your baby's hands, feet, and face. Are they too hot or too cold? If they're cold, put additional clothing on. If they're too hot, start taking off the clothes. You can also give a lukewarm bath to help cool a baby off. Let baby play for a while to get into a better mood (but never leave baby alone in the bath).

 Avoid using baby lotions in hot weather. Lotion only blocks a baby's pores and makes the poor thing feel hotter. Also, offer lots of liquids — but avoid giving too much juice. Give water. Babies get diarrhea if they drink too much juice.

Has gas?

Babies tend to get gas rather easily. And I don't mean gas as in leaded or unleaded. Gas, as in pockets of air in the intestines, has to be relieved by coming out one end or another. These are some signs that your child has gas:

- ✔ Pulling legs up
- ✔ Stiffening or stretching body
- ✔ Making a high-pitched, honking noise

To relieve this uncomfortable state, you can:

- ✔ Hold your baby to your shoulder and gently pat him on the back.
- ✔ Hold your baby to your shoulder and gently rub his back in a circular motion.
- ✔ Lay your baby on your lap, stomach down, and gently pat his back.

You know you've been successful in helping to relieve gas when strange noises come from either end of your baby.

Bored?

The thought of a bored baby may sound goofy to you, but it happens. Your baby needs stimulus. If you've ignored him for too long, he may need some entertaining. So, get out those tap shoes and top hat and get to work. Make that baby happy.

Bored babies don't really take a lot of creative thinking to make them happy. Move them to a different place, give them different toys, or take them for a walk. A walk will do you both good.

Or talk to your bored baby. Even if you bore your friends, you'll find the baby enthralled with your babble.

Tired?

Sometimes it's hard to keep track of the time when you have kids. The day seems to fly by and you forget that you haven't laid the baby down for an afternoon nap until he starts rubbing his eyes and doing that yahhh, yahhh, yahhh, kind of cry/whine.

The hardest situation to deal with is when your baby gives you all the signs of fatigue but doesn't want to go to bed. That's when your baby has become over-tired. You'll have to work extra hard at your go-to-sleep baby rituals, but don't give up. Putting babies to bed and letting them whine it out is sometimes the only thing you can do. If your baby is rubbing his eyes and is obviously tired, make him take a nap. Don't fall into the trap of thinking that just because your baby is crying in bed means he's not tired. You know better than your baby does.

Read Chapter 12, "The Joys and Perils of Bedtime."

Sick?

When kids are sick, they don't really tell you they're sick, they just start acting differently. It's not that they necessarily get cranky or whiny (although that can be an indication), it's just that their behavior changes.

Signs of illness are numerous:

✔ **fevers**

Slight increases in temperature are usual signs of the beginning of an illness. If your child's temperature abruptly rises, call your doctor.

✔ **difficulty breathing**

One indication is to watch your baby's chest to see if he seems to be breathing deeply.

✔ **screaming loud with knees drawn up**

When babies draw their knees up it may mean gas or colic. Read on for ideas on how to handle colic.

✔ **pulling at their ears**

If babies pull at their ears, it may mean an ear infection. Ear infections are common in kids but should never be taken lightly. Take care of it immediately.

✔ **swollen glands**

These glands are located just below your child's ears and down the neck.

✔ **sleeping past feeding times or not eating as much as normal**

Don't take one day as an indication, but if it continues, you may have a need to be concerned.

✔ **changes in their sleeping schedules**

This means *drastic* sleeping changes as opposed to sleeping an additional 20 minutes.

✔ **difficulty in waking up from sleep**

This situation includes waking up from naps during the day, or in the morning.

✔ **looking pale or a little gray, perhaps with dark circles under their eyes, or blue lips**

The truest sign of kids' health is the way they look. A child with any of the symptoms above will *look* sick.

✔ **acting limp and without any energy**

Since kids are generally on the go every waking moment, this quietness may be a real shocker.

✔ **bad breath (other than the fact that your baby just ate all the fried onions off your liver)**

Kids normally have very sweet-smelling breath.

✔ **smelly private parts even after a bath**

Babies' genitals will smell somewhat because of dirty diapers. But this odor should go away after giving baths.

These are all signs of a problem. Get your baby to the doctor. Don't ever take chances on your child's health and hope these things will go away. You should also check out Chapter 23, "Health and Hygiene."

If your child has a cold that lasts for more than ten days, call your doctor.

Mad?

Babies not liking dirty diapers surprised me, as did the fact that babies get mad. It would be fun for us to throw as big a fit as babies do when they're mad, but as adults we're supposed to suppress that kind of behavior. You can't help but admire the amount of energy kids put into being mad.

You'll learn to recognize what your kids look like when they're mad. Typical signs are stiffening of their legs, screaming, and their cute little faces turning red. Sort of how your mother-in-law looks when you let her know you aren't coming home for Christmas.

There's really nothing you can do when your kids get mad at you. If they're older, you can try talking to them, but you can't reason with babies and toddlers. Just hold them close and try to soothe them — if they'll let you. Don't be surprised if they push away or fall to the floor. Just walk away when they do this. They'll have to learn that this behavior is not going to get your attention.

Your children get mad for a variety of reasons. It may be because they don't get what they want, or it may be out of frustration — it's very frustrating to young toddlers who aren't able to communicate their needs well. They may be mad because they're trying to tell you about a toy dropped behind the couch or a favorite toy stuck in the toy box. Or perhaps they're just hungry, tired, or sleepy.

Colic?

We can send people to the moon and we can teach cats to pee in the toilet, but no one really knows what causes colic. The old tale that colic is caused by a nervous mother is stupid and untrue. Mothers are not responsible for a colicky baby. You just have to do your best to try to comfort your little babe. Understand, though, that there's not a lot you can do.

Colic is a term that describes unexplained crying. A colicky baby will usually cry between one to two hours at a time. Colicky babies will draw up their legs and act like they're in a lot of pain, but they usually aren't. If your child under the age of three months cries but is not hungry, tired, or ill — and then acts fine for a while — your child probably has colic. But go to your doctor and let an expert decide if it's colic. Your doctor will tell you to try a variety of things, such as changing the baby's formula. Or if you're breastfeeding, you'll be asked to cut out dairy products from your diet. It'll take a while to see if any of these steps helps. Sometimes they may, sometimes they may not. Every baby is different.

A colicky baby is a nightmare. There's very little you can do to comfort a baby with colic. Picking a fussy baby up usually stops the fussiness. Picking up a colicky baby doesn't do anything.

Try these ideas for relieving colic. They may or may not work, but at least it'll give you something to do.

- ✔ You can try laying your baby on his stomach on your lap. Place one hand on his back and the other on his bottom, and then bounce your legs lightly. Sometimes you'll get a big burp out of him, or maybe he'll just puke down your leg. If you're really lucky, your baby will fall asleep.

- ✔ Try putting a warm water bottle on your baby's stomach. This may or may not work to comfort your baby, but at least it's worth trying.

- ✔ Give your baby weak mint or diluted chamomile tea. This may help with colic.

- ✔ Give your baby diluted 7-Up (half water/half 7-Up).

- ✔ Leave your baby with a family member or friend for the evening. You need your rest and some quiet time to help rekindle your nerves.

Colic will probably be pretty hard on your nerves — brutal for most parents — but just remember that it will pass and will not have any lasting effect on your baby. You just have to remember to keep calm and have some quiet time of your own: When you feel rested, you have more energy to deal with a colicky baby. Colic is usually over by three months of age. If your baby continues to have symptoms of colic past this age, consult a doctor.

Something they are going through?

When your children cry and you haven't been able to figure out the cause, sometimes you have to stop and think about what's going on with them at the time. Maybe they're teething, starting to get a cold, or have had their schedules interrupted and had a nap cut too short.

When all else fails. . .

If you've gone through this list and you haven't found the reason for your upset baby, maybe it's nothing at all.

Newborn babies cry about two hours out of 24 for no reason other than to exercise their lungs. Six-week-olds cry about three hours out of 24. This crying for no reason usually ends around the age of three months.

After your baby starts to calm down, start the list over, go through it slowly, and try again. Maybe this time when you offer the bottle of juice, your baby will take it.

Crying Babies in Public

New parents look terrified when their baby starts to cry in public places. It's like they're afraid the *Baby Police* are going to come by and arrest them for neglect. They have that look on their faces because every other parent who walks by has apparently forgotten that sometimes babies cry, and these observers give them a look like, "My Lord, can't you take care of your child?" Ignore everyone who's walking around and just take care of your baby the best you can.

When you go out in public, you should have your bag of goodies to take with you to ward off any crisis that may happen. Nothing in your little bag will help you with a toddler who's too tired from shopping and refuses to nap in the stroller. You have to do your best there.

Don't misunderstand me when I tell you to ignore others who are giving you dirty looks because your kids are upset. You also have to take into consideration where you are and what the situation is. If you're in a movie theater and your kids cry, leave. There's no need to disturb the other people because your kids are cranky. If you're in a restaurant and your kids cry, try to comfort them — but if it doesn't work, excuse yourself and your cranky child, go to a restroom or lobby, and try to fix whatever the problem is. Don't let others upset or intimidate you, but respect those around you, too.

Read Chapter 20, "Social Skills to Be Proud Of," for information on creating a bag of goodies for social outings.

Your lesson for the day

When your baby cries for no apparent reason, try comforting him the best you can. Rubbing a baby's back while you hold him to your shoulder, or simply walking around with a baby, is the best you can do. Just don't stary crying yourself.

Chapter 17

Tools of the Trade

- -

In This Chapter

▶ Satisfying the immediate needs of your children

▶ Getting ready for the later needs of your children

▶ Just-for-fun stuff that you may or may not want

▶ What you don't necessarily need — but people will try to sell you

▶ Safety equipment that's a must

- -

> If you truly love your child, you'll buy this super-duper, highly improved, extra special, guaranteed to make your kid laugh, six-pack of Green Goop — so it can be ground into your carpet!

Companies like Fisher Price, Graco, Carter, Playskool, and all the other hordes of similar companies out there must be enormously rich off all the junk they sell to parents. Yet, you really need only the very basics to operate with your children. Most kids turn out pretty well and are able to live fulfilling lives without having had special Disney knee pads to protect their precious little knees when they crawled around as infants.

This chapter will take all that junk that's out there for sale and break it down into stuff you need now, stuff you need later, fun stuff, and stuff you don't really need. Happy shopping!

Names you'll soon be way too familiar with

It's said that by the time kids reach the fourth grade, they can identify most major beer brands. In fact, ten percent of them actually have a brand loyalty without ever having tasted the stuff (I hope). Well, on or before your child's fourth month of life, you'll find yourself becoming familiar with a whole new grab bag of product names. Just for fun, expect to see more from the following:

Barney	Carter	Fisher Price
Kolcraft	Little Tikes	Playskool
Sesame Street	Johnson & Johnson	Beech-Nut
Dr. Seuss	Carnation	Gerber
Pampers and Huggies	Playtex	Tonka
Toys "Я" Us	Evenflo	Graco
Disney	L'Oreal (this is for when your hair starts to turn gray)	Similac

Stuff You'll Need for a Baby

Having a baby is no cheap endeavor. The first good news is that you don't need everything all at once, so save taking a second mortgage for a later time (like when your kids go to college or maybe start T-ball). The second bit o' good news is that you really don't need everything that you see advertised on TV or in those parent-type magazines.

Food supplies (or "bottles and nipples")

If you plan to breastfeed, you'll still need bottles for giving your baby water during those times after breastfeeding, or when just a swig is needed to wet your baby's whistle. It's also needed for those times when you decide to go out and leave the baby with grandma for the night (you'll need to do that at some time just for your own sanity).

There is a moderate selection of different types of bottles and nipples. Honestly, your baby won't care if one has a bunny on it and another has Elmer Fudd. There are, however, two types of bottles you should watch out for:

- Avoid bottles (or anything) made of glass. They break easily, and your child will throw his bottle at some point in time!

✔ You may also want to avoid the bottles with the plastic liners. These bottles are supposed to reduce the amount of air your baby gets, thus reducing the amount of spit up. There hasn't been any research that proves this belief to be true. Also, sometimes those plastic liners leak. And if you're an environmentalist, need I say anything about the waste of plastic liners? Waste! Waste! Waste!

For more information on food, you can turn to Chapter 10, "Understanding Food and Nutrition," or Chapter 15, "Breastfeeding vs. Bottlefeeding," if your baby is still wee, helpless, and cute.

Clothing supplies

Your baby's primary item of clothing is the diaper, though it's actually more of a tool than an article of clothing. Yes, like a clean-up tool. (Imagine life without them!)

Your only choices for diapers are cloth and disposable. Read Chapter 14, "The Diaper Thing." It contains information that will help with your diaper dilemma, and take care of your baby's number one task and product.

Other clothes for baby can get more creative. Even so, don't trust anyone who tells you that you need *this* many shirts, *this* many nighties, and so on. The rule is that however much you have is however much you'll need. (Yet the more you have, the less often you have to do laundry.) If your baby is growing at a fast rate, you may have too many clothes and end up not using them. Only *you* can decide how much of everything you need.

Try to buy clothing that is flame retardant (which is usually found only for pajamas.) The label on the clothing — or packaging — will mention whether or not the clothes are flame retardant.

Avoid clothes with drawstrings in them. The drawstrings have been known to get caught in a variety of things — like slides, elevators, escalators — and can cause your children to get hurt.

An easy way to shop for children's clothing is through catalogs. You don't even have to leave the house! Right in the comfort of your own home you can sit and order clothes without having to drag your kids all over the place. One of my favorites is Hanna Andersson (800-220-0544). The clothes seem a little pricey, but they won't fall apart, and you'll end up using them longer than a lot of other clothes simply because of the way they're made.

Bathroom equipment

No, don't go buying pint-sized porcelain toilets for your precious little poopmaker. At least, not at first.

Actually, baby's first bathroom equipment will probably be a bathtub, specifically one of those small plastic bathtubs that have a sponge lining. These tubs are great for newborns. They're sturdy, they keep the baby at your level so you're not leaning over, and they make bathing in the sink safe and easy. Granted, this special tub is not a must-have item. It's still possible to bathe baby in a sink. However, the plastic tublet is inexpensive, washable, and portable. For bathtub safety, read Chapter 11, "The Joys and Perils of Bathtime."

Another bathroom item you'll eventually get for babies is a potty. That's their own, wee toilet, upon which they'll hopefully one day — and with much glee — take their first real poop. See Chapter 18 for more information on potty time.

A place to sit. It sounds silly. Babies aren't yearning for that 18-foot-long, L-shaped sofa/recliner with built-in popcorn tray. Still, babies need a few core items, maybe not tiny furniture, but some special things just their size.

Infant seats are those little chairs that you plop your baby in while you're trying to get things done around the house. They're light enough that you can take them to any room you're going, along with baby. Some seats are adjustable so your baby can be sitting up, or lying back. Some bounce with your baby, some even have little covers so the mean, bright sun can't get into baby's eyes.

Changing tables

Changing tables are tables for changing — not anything a magician may demonstrate. They're like backless bookcases with a small holding pen for baby on top. Below you store the diapers and other changing paraphernalia.

Fortunately, changing tables are getting bigger and better than ever. Where they used to be these wobbly, flimsy stands that swayed back and forth when you put your baby on top, they're now sturdy and truly handy. So if you stumble upon one of the old-time wobbly ones, keep looking.

Obviously, changing tables should be large enough to hold your baby. They also need a strap to hold down a baby who gets to that squirmy stage. If you are using a changing table that doesn't have a safety strap, you can buy these straps and put them on yourself. Voilà! Other nice amenities are drawers or shelves for storing diapers, wipes, and the other goodies you need.

A fun replacement for a normal changing table is a piece of furniture called a *dry sink*. It has a large flat surface for your baby, and lots of drawers or cabinets to put your supplies in.

If you have a house that has more than one level and you don't feel like walking up and down stairs to change diapers (or have the energy), use one of your bathrooms as a changing station. Use a bathroom counter that is long and wide enough to lay your baby on. Clear away everything from the counter, put a towel down for your baby to lie on, and place all your supplies in the drawer under the counter. This way you have access to a sink for washing away *really* poopy diapers.

Bedding (and the stuff associated with it)

Baby's biggest piece of furniture will probably be a crib. But before a crib, you may consider a bassinet, which can be much more handy than a crib, especially for a newborn.

Bassinets are small, compact, and easy to move around — just like your baby. You can easily take this bed anywhere baby goes. But if you don't like the idea of spending from $50 to $200 on something that you'll probably use for a short period of time, forget it. Use a crib.

Anymore, cribs are fairly easy to pick. Crib manufacturers have to abide by federal regulations with cribs so that these products are safe for your baby. Your only decision is to find one that will *match* your nursery theme.

For baby's crib you'll need both receiving blankets and heavier weight blankets. Receiving blankets are light weight and used for keeping your baby wrapped in as you both just hang out. Warmer blankets wrap around a sleeping baby. Never use heavy comforters. Your baby could get caught up in them and suffocate.

Bumper pads are *side blankets* that should fit all the way around the crib and either tie or snap together. These fasteners should be attached on the *outside* of the crib so that your baby can't play with them. If the ties are excessively long, tie them where you want them, and then cut off the extra string. This way baby won't be tempted to pull on the ties and, of course, eventually want to stick them in his mouth.

If you forgo a bassinet, you can bring the crib into your room with you. Keep baby there until you feel he's old enough to sleep on his own (usually in six or eight weeks). Parents usually like to keep their newborn in their room so they can respond quicker. They also don't have to tromp all through the house

---

A night light

Night lights are for more than scaring away the Closet Monster. It's nice to have a night light stationed wherever you could possibly walk in the middle of the night. Turning on a bright bathroom light at 2:00 a.m. is an awful experience for both you and your baby. I suggest you buy the light-sensitive night lights. These turn on automatically as it gets darker, and then shut off as it gets light. The last thing you want to do is stumble around in the dark trying to find the night light to turn on because you forgot to do it before you went to bed.

---

every two hours (or however often baby is eating). But there's not a law or anything that says baby must sleep in your room with you. It's just a matter of convenience.

Never use antiques for your crib: They may be cute, but they could also be dangerous. Old furniture wasn't made with newer safety precautions in mind — rules that manufacturers now have to follow. For example, crib slats should be no more than 2 ³/₈ inches apart, and the mattress should fit so snugly that you can't wedge more than two fingers between it and the crib.

With the mattress fitting so tightly, changing the sheets is difficult. The easiest way to change sheets (without hiring a maid) is to lift the mattress up, stand it on one end, and then change the sheets. This maneuver puts the mattress up to eye level, and the corners are easier to reach.

When the little one goes a-travelin'

As a baby of the late 20th century, your tot will soon enjoy the rigors of traveling. Maybe not to the south of France or Aspen, but soon your child will be going with you to the grocery store, to grandma's, to the park, and maybe elsewhere — providing you're bold enough to take a little one supplied with all the right equipment.

The all-important-wouldn't-leave-home-without-it diaper bag

Mary Poppins had quite a bag. It was a good size, held everything, and it didn't make one of her arms longer than the other. If only they made such a bag. (Who could forget Julie Andrews pulling all that wonderful stuff out of her bag in Disney's *Mary Poppins*? Little Michael Banks even looked under the table to make sure it wasn't trick photography. Amazing.)

Important baby bag contents

The good news is that as your baby gets older, you'll find that there will be less that you have to carry with you. Also, if your trips are short (like a run to Baskin-Robbins to feed that *post-baby-craving,* if there is such a thing), you don't have to necessarily load up with everything. (Use the checkbox list in Appendix B to make sure you're well-stocked.)

- diapers
- burp-up towel
- change of clothing
- water
- bib

- baby wipes
- changing cushion
- pacifier
- bottles
- doctor's phone number

- diaper-rash ointment
- food/spoon
- blanket
- nipples
- insurance and allergy information

Today, you'll see a lot of parents using oversized travel bags or large purses for diaper bags in place of the hard-to-get-but-buy-em-when-you-find-em Mary Poppins bags.

Big travel bags are a great idea. They're bigger so they can be used as a purse in addition to having the diapers, wipes, clothes, blankets, and the kitchen sink — which you now have to carry with you whenever you go anywhere.

The only thing that regular diaper bags have that these oversized bags don't are those special slots to put bottles in so that the bottles don't tip and leak all over the bottom of the bag. (Of course, there *are* bottle lids and caps so that stuff doesn't happen.)

Medications

No matter how close you watch over your baby, he will catch a cold on occasion, get diaper rash, and fall down at least 100 times before it's all over. Read Chapter 23 for some suggestions on keeping a well-stocked medicine chest.

A baby-sized chair for the car

It used to be that the only thing you needed for a car seat was a solid box and rope. I'm serious. We once rented a car with a car seat for our baby, and it was essentially a fiberglass melon box with a nylon rope. At $40 for the week, it was a gyp — and probably unsafe. Times are tougher now.

You *need* a car seat. It's the law. It doesn't matter if you never plan on taking your baby anywhere. Hospitals won't let you leave with your new baby unless you have a car seat.

Many brands of car seat are out there — with subtle differences between them in design and fashion. The type of car seat most popular is the one where the seat detaches from the base and you can carry your baby and the seat all in one. Or there are those where you carry the seat and attach it to a stroller. You don't have to wake up a baby to get him out of the car, or unwrap a baby in cold weather. Just unlatch the seat and go.

Detachable car seats (where you carry the baby and the seat) are not good for older, heavier babies. For them, you'll have to invest in a larger seat — or just buy the detachable kind that goes with a stroller.

✔ Don't use a car seat that has been involved in a car accident.

✔ Don't use an infant seat (like those from swings) as a car seat.

✔ Strap the car seat down with the car's seat belts.

There is a special doohickey you'll need to use to lash the over-the-neck seat belt with the lap belt. Attach this to the side of the car seat opposite from where you buckle the belt. This keeps the seat from tipping over when you round a corner (and with the way you drive . . .).

✔ Strap your child down with the car seat's restraining belt.

If the idea of buying more than one kind of car seat doesn't appeal to you, look for a car seat that you can use until your child reaches 40 pounds or 40 inches in height. It's required by law that your child remain in a car seat until that time. Or until they're four years old. In fact, most states' written driver's test have the 40 lbs/four-year-old limit as a question. Don't miss that one!

If you have a big baby or towering toddler, consider getting one of those lap-restraint type of car seats. Commonly called toddler seats, these abbreviated car seats are ideal for kids who are too big for traditionally-sized car seats.

For more child-safety information on car seats, read Chapter 9, "Making a Safer Lifestyle."

"If you loved me, you'd wear our baby around your neck"

Baby slings. They make you look like you're recovering from surgery that attached your baby to your hip, chest, or back. Still, people who've had such surgery tend to compensate for their wobbliness by using both free arms — and are otherwise unencumbered. For this reason, baby slings can be extremely handy.

Personally, I love baby slings and feel babies love them, too. It's a nice idea having your baby physically close to you. Your baby will love the closeness and, in return, will fuss less often while riding in it.

Keep the following stuff about baby slings in mind:

- Baby slings are harder to get the hang of, but they're good for newborns up until toddler age. It takes some time and practice to learn how to arrange your baby in it. But once you get used to a sling, it's great.

- Babies like being all scrunched up, which is how they usually get in a sling. However, don't let them stay that way too long or they will get uncomfortable.

- Front packs are great for newborns, but bad for older babies and toddlers. There's no support for your back, so the heavier your baby gets, the harder your baby is to carry.

- Back packs offer fairly good back support so you can carry your kids in them as they get heavier. However, back packs are *not* good for newborns. They don't have the body weight to hold themselves up, and there is not the support needed for a baby's head and neck. A newborn in a back pack would just crumple down into a little ball. You don't want that to happen.

- Back packs offer open invitations for hair pulling.

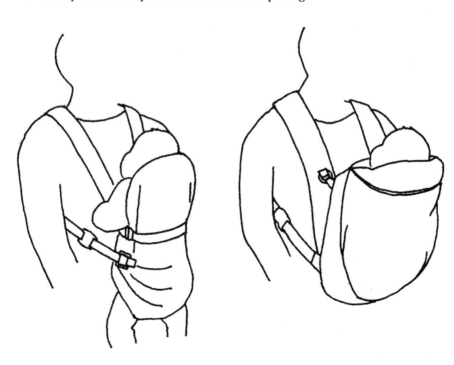

Goodies Your Child Will Eventually Need

As babies gets bigger, their needs change. Along with those changes come some new equipment you'll consider buying. Again, most of these are common, baby-associated items. The following sections offer some pointers on what to get and what to avoid for the slightly bigger baby.

New tools for chow time

Soon will be the day when your beautiful little baby will be sitting in a high chair throwing spaghetti all over your kitchen. So, of course, you want to have a chair that gives your child the optimal amount of throwing power.

High marks for high chairs

The things that are important in high chairs are:

- **crotch strap**

    It's not enough to have a belt for the waist. If the belt is too loose, your child can slide under this belt just enough to get caught and possibly get hurt. The crotch strap is attached to the waist belt but doesn't allow your baby to slip much.

- **one-handed tray latching**

    These latches are usually in the front, underneath the tray. There will be many a day where you'll hold your baby with one hand and try to get the tyke in the high chair with the other. It's much easier if you only have to use one hand to unlatch the tray. (Two-handed latches are common in restaurants.)

- **adjustable seat**

    This chair should be adjusted up or down, so if you want to include your baby in a family dinner, or if your toddler is getting to the point where he can eat with the family but the dining chair is too big, you can adjust the seat up or down to fit at the table.

Like all baby products, don't buy an antique high chair. If you like the antique look, there are new products that are made to look like antiques. These are fine. They have the safety requirements that you want for your baby equipment.

Don't forget to use a plastic mat or old, ugly sheet under your high chair if it's sitting on carpeting. Nothing will stain your carpet quicker than baby food. (Strained carrots. They're the worst.)

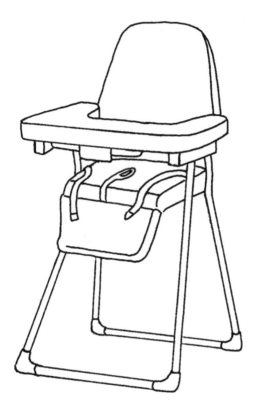

Finding proper baby flatware

Eventually baby will grow to the point where he can manage a spoon or fork. You may notice this new talent when he sees you eating that way and refuses to be hand-fed. "I want my own fork, darn it, and I want it NOW!"

Baby flatware comes in the predictable baby sizes and styles. If baby wants to feed himself, start with a spoon. Don't use an adult spoon, not even a teaspoon. Go out and buy a spoon just the right size for baby's mouth.

Forks are little riskier to use, since they are pointy and baby can jab himself. Small, dull forks are available in baby sizes. Start baby off with them if he demands a fork (which he'll probably call a *spoon,* by the way).

Never, ever, under any circumstance give a baby any type of knife. Steak knives, definitely not. Butter knives, no way. Babies do not needs knives. You use the knife, cut up baby's food, and then put the knife out of reach. Babies and knives go together like electricity and bath water. No way.

A simple dining set for baby

By the time your kids turn one, they'll want to start holding their own cups and feeding themselves. Break out the camera — and consider the following:

- **cups with a weighted bottom (a spill-proof cup), two handles, a lid, and a spout**

- **plates with separate compartments**

  Such plates are good for toddlers who can be really picky about their food. Sometimes they don't like their food to touch. (Heck, I know some adults who refuse to eat a sandwich if it has been sliced in two by the same knife used to previously slice a sandwich made with mayonnaise.)

- **bowls with suction bottoms**

  This item helps little ones to learn to eat from a bowl without the bowl ending up on the floor.

- **toddler-size fork and spoon**

  These small devices are easier for little hands to operate and to aim for little mouths.

Avoid glass. It breaks. Soon you'll discover that babies likes to throw their plates, bowls, and glasses when they're done with them. It's part of a child's joy at discovering gravity. If Newton would have had kids, he wouldn't have needed an apple to fall on his head.

The ever-unpopular bib

The function of a bib should be obvious. Not to an adult. Even the fastest eaters take time to carefully guide food into their mouths. That caution just isn't possible when you're 14-months-old and eat spaghetti by the fistful.

You have quite a selection of bibs to chose from. Some are plastic, some look like towels with a hole for the head, some are even worn like smocks. Buy whatever suits you. If your baby likes the bibs with yellow ducks on them, buy those. (What is that connection between *bibs* and *ducks*?)

To save a lot of extra washings, *invest* in bibs. Once children turn around one year old, they'll be determined to feed themselves. May I suggest you also wear clothing that you don't mind having spaghetti flung upon?

Cloth bibs are also good for teething babies. All that drool has to go somewhere, and cloth bibs will absorb all the liquid, whereas plastic bibs just let the water keep rolling off. Actually, plastic bibs aren't really good for anything. They don't absorb the food or liquid (which is what you want), and if you wash and dry them, they begin to turn hard and crack. Then they start to smell bad. YUCK! Just avoid the plastic bibs.

Never tie the bib too tight around baby's neck. Dan still has memories from childhood of fearing grandma would strangle him with his bib. (Seriously.)

Out and about

Nothing hurts me more than seeing some parents dragging their toddler along, pulling a chubby little arm out of its socket. Baby legs are very short, and it takes babies many more steps to keep up with your slowest walking pace. And sometimes babies just don't want or know how to walk. In either case, it's time for a stroller.

You remember strollers from your single days. Remember going to Disneyland and loathing the Stroller Armada that would block every tight passage? Remember stubbing your toe on a stroller pushed by some surly mother with a snarly brat? *Déjà vu!*

There are basically two types of strollers: the umbrella stroller and the super-deluxe limousine type of stroller. The difference (aside from price) is that the umbrella stroller is light weight and doesn't take up much room, whereas the super strollers are bigger and do take up some trunk space.

The choice of which stroller you use is up to you — and baby. Keep in mind that umbrella strollers aren't good for newborns: Babies can't lie down in them, and there's no support for their little bodies. A baby in an umbrella stroller just sits there and sinks down to look eventually like a little ball of clay. Then the baby will ever so slowly tip over frontward — and splat onto the ground.

Super strollers can be used from the day your baby is born way up into toddler age. They're designed for storage of diaper bags and all the goodies that always have to go with your kids. These strollers are also great for shopping; you just pile your bags beneath the stroller and take off.

Look for these items in a stroller:

- ✔ **seat belt with crotch strap**

  Seat belts aren't always enough. The crotch straps keeps your kid from using the seat belt as a chin strap.

- ✔ **big basket underneath the seat for storage**

  These baskets are great for storing diaper bags, along with any extra paraphernalia you manage to need — or pick up — while out shopping.

> ✔ **wheel locks**
>
> Strollers will roll away if parked on hills, so the wheel locks are absolutely a necessity.
>
> ✔ **a wide wheel base**
>
> The distance between the front and back wheels, and from side-to-side, should be wide enough so that if your toddler leans forward, there's no risk of tipping both himself and the stroller over.

Strollers are also great when you're trying to get through crowds. All you have to do is ram the people in front of you with the stroller, and they get out of your way. (Remember Disneyland? *Revenge!*)

The only time when umbrella strollers are better than the super strollers is when you're traveling. On most airplanes, you can wheel your baby on in an umbrella stroller where the larger ones aren't allowed. (There's no place to store super strollers on the plane.)

A bionic ear for Mommy and Daddy

Those baby monitor listening devices are great to keep in your baby's room while he sleeps. You keep your end with you so that when baby wakes up or makes some unusual noise, you know immediately. This way the poor little tyke doesn't have to sit and scream for 15 minutes before you hear the commotion.

Use the baby monitor only as a signal for when your baby is sleeping. Don't rush to your baby at the first signs of stirring because he may go back to sleep on his own. Be sure that your baby's really awake and ready to be taken from the crib.

Don't use the baby monitor to justify leaving your children alone while they play. You should always supervise young children, especially babies and toddlers.

Just-for-Fun Stuff

There are so many gizmos designed to make your baby happy you'll get dizzy looking at all of them. Meanwhile, your baby will get happily dizzy from playing on some of these wonderful and often useful toys and contraptions.

Jump for joy in your jolly jumper

A jolly jumper is a great babysitter for your kids (those that aren't any heavier than 25 pounds, anyway). This device hangs in a doorway with a seat attached to it. You place your baby in the seat, and the little one is able to jump up and down — and basically be jolly.

If you need a justification for buying this, it's great for developing your children's leg muscles. It's a lot of fun for your kids. But on the whole, it's rather unnecessary. (Then again, so is a permanent.)

Swinging babies

Swings are a great babysitter, and your baby will love them. Back-and-forth. Over and over. The swings are good for a short time. But when your baby feels the need to sit up or move around, these things will be history.

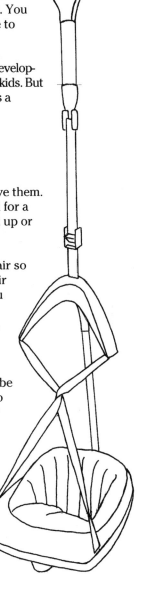

Look for the kind of swing that has a detachable chair so you can take it with you around the house. The chair comes in handy when setting baby down. And if you get this type of swing, remember to stop the swing and remove the chair *before* you remove baby from the swing.

Most swings have a weight limit, which is usually around 25 pounds. For some babies, that limit may be a long way down the road, but for those people who have Miracle Grow babies, it can come along pretty quickly.

"Grind me up some green beans, Mommy"

Food grinders are nice to have when your baby is making the transition from baby food to regular food. They're kind of unnecessary because you can just as easily smash the food yourself with a fork, but sometimes food like green beans just doesn't *smash* real well.

What You Don't Necessarily Need

Here are few choice items you'll be pressured into buying — often while being threatened with guilt if you neglect them. Here's the short list:

- ✓ **knee pads**

    These pads are for your toddlers to protect their knees from the cold, hard ground. It's a miracle that generations of kids were able to grow up to be well-rounded people without these things.

- ✓ **bath seats**

    These little plastic doohickeys are supposed to keep your baby from falling over in the bathtub . . . as if our arms are much too weak and the thought of having to hold that baby up for ten more minutes is going to do us in.

- ✓ **plunger infant feeder**

    This plunger-type bottle is supposed to help you feed cereal to your baby. Bah! The only thing you need to feed your baby cereal is a spoon and bowl. Babies need to learn to eat *normally* at some point in time. This type of feeder only delays the inevitable. Don't buy it.

- ✓ **playpens**

    I don't like playpens. They're like little prisons — which is, of course, the point. They'd be great during the day when you're cooking and you don't want the baby crawling around your feet while you juggle hot pans. But parents tend to abuse the idea of a playpen and keep their babies in them for hours. You also have to keep in mind that playpens take up space. Don't make your company crawl over the back of the couch to get to the bathroom just to get past the playpen.

    Playpens are only good until your child gets to the crawling age. A baby who learns this new mode of transportation won't be happy to sit in a playpen.

> ✔ **walkers**
>
> Walkers have been found to cause way too many accidents — more than what having a walker is worth. Falling down stairs, or wheels getting caught on doorjambs or thick carpeting, make these seemingly fun devices too dangerous.

Babies are the ones who always get all the cool toys. I never get anything. — Blake, age 5

Safety Equipment

Invest in some safety equipment. You can't have too much of it. The trick here is to know your child. If your children seem fascinated with the toilet and can't seem to keep their hands out of it, you need a toilet lock. Toilets are extremely dangerous for little ones who are too curious. They like to lean into the toilet for a better look, lose their balance, and *plop*! They're in the toilet. If you're not there, unfortunately they drown. (Luckily, toilet locks are made with quick-and-easy access for those times when you need to open the lid in a hurry.)

All of these safety devices can be obtained wherever baby supplies are found. You can also find some of the locks in hardware stores.

Some basic safety stuff

Generally, the safety equipment you need, no matter what kind of child you have, consists of the following:

> ✔ electrical outlet covers
>
> ✔ locks for drawers and cabinets
>
> ✔ gates for stairways and other forbidden places
>
> ✔ doorknob covers to keep little ones out of rooms they shouldn't be in
>
> ✔ Syrup of Ipecac for those babies who think Lysol is apple juice

Read Chapter 9, "Making a Safer Lifestyle," for more information about keeping your child safe.

More and more and more stuff

There are lots of things you can buy to protect your kids:

- ✔ You can get knob covers for your bath so your kids don't accidentally turn on extra hot water.

- ✔ There are safety knobs for your stove, and stove shields so that your kids can't reach over the stove and touch a hot pot.

- ✔ There are plastic covers for the edges of your coffee tables to protect little ones from sharp corners.

- ✔ A newfangled gizmo will adjust the water temperature in the bath and shut it off when it gets too hot.

- ✔ You can even buy air filters to protect your kids from allergies.

The list goes on and on. There is so much stuff you can buy that I'd have to add another chapter just to list it. Instead, get the catalog *One Step Ahead* and have a heyday spending all your money. *One Step Ahead* (800-274-8440) offers a lot of safety equipment along with general merchandise for your kids.

The more you know your children, the more you'll know what you should buy to keep them as safe as possible. But avoid the urge to overprotect your children. Safety is important. Paranoia is not. Please refer back to Chapter 5, "The Art of Keeping Your Cool," for more information on being a relaxed type of parent.

Your lesson for the day

Always inspect your children's *equipment* for cracks, tears, or broken pieces. If you find anything damaged, get rid of it. This stuff isn't foolproof, and your kids will give it much more of a workout than any testing facility could possibly reproduce.

Chapter 18

Watching Baby Grow

*T*here are people who get the dry heaves if they see a baby drool. Who knows what would happen if they actually got this *drool stuff* on them?

As for the drooling, there will come a day when your kids won't always have drool hanging from their lips. Of course, some people never lose the drooling habit. And old folks drool, too. Actually, come to think of it, drooling is a part of the human experience. Alas, this chapter has to go into more depth on the baby side of drooling. (Maybe you can hold out for *Drooling For Dummies*?)

Drooling is a part of watching your baby grow, as is teething, learning to walk, and (everyone's favorite) potty training. This chapter covers these areas so that when they happen, you'll be prepared to handle them — hopefully without heaving.

The Fine Art of Sucking and Slobbering

Sucking and slobbering are never found together. If your baby is deeply involved in the sucking process, you know this kid's not slobbering (otherwise known as drooling). And drooling just can't happen when you're sucking. It just doesn't work that way.

Some things just suck

Babies are sucking before they're born. In the womb, some babies manage to find their thumb and suck away. So it's fairly easy to conclude that sucking is a natural process that babies find comfort in doing.

Because sucking is one of your baby's high priorities, two things should be on your list of immediate needs: *pacifiers* and *pacifier clips*.

There are only a few different types of pacifiers on the market, so don't spaz about which one to buy. The difference between the two is in the shape of the sucky part. One is rather round and traditionally nipple-shaped. The other is flat on one side, supposedly designed to fit better into baby's mouth. Whatever.

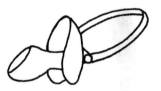

Don't be surprised if your baby never seems to have the need to be in the constant companionship of a pacifier. Some kids never get attached to them.

A pacifier clip attaches the pacifier on to your baby's clothing. Its purpose is to keep hold of the pacifier so that when your baby spits it out, it won't fall on to the germ-infested ground. Don't ever use anything that holds the pacifier *in* your baby's mouth. A baby needs to be able to spit a pacifier out when finished with it.

Babies do have a preference as to what's stuck in their mouths. But since you can't really ask them what they like, you'll just have to guess. I suggest you buy both types of pacifiers. If your baby doesn't seem to like one, you'll have the other to fall back on. Some pacifiers are designed for newborns and are smaller than the other types.

If you give your baby a pacifier and he doesn't seem to like it, you can try a different kind. But don't keep trying to shove a pacifier in a baby's mouth thinking he wants it. One of the hard parts of parenting is knowing when your baby wants to suck (*suckle* for the grandparents out there) or eat. Try the pacifier first. If your baby seems irritated at you for sticking the pacifier in, or more obviously spits it out or even gags on it, take the hint and quit forcing the pacifier.

Does the pacifier keep getting spit out? Then try feeding your baby . If that doesn't seem to help, you need to read Chapter 16, "Cranky Babies."

See Chapter 17, for more information on pacifiers and other interesting toys.

Thumb sucking

A habit that has many parents concerned is thumb sucking. The general rule is that you should *not* let your kids suck their thumbs. Not that it's gross or bad. It's just not fair to your kids to let them start something that someday they'll have to end. Kids form habits easily, and thumb sucking sometimes turns into a habit more than a means of satisfying that sucking urge.

Babies who suck their thumbs during the time their teeth develop will alter the way these teeth should naturally grow — and may end up with crooked teeth. These kids can also develop a tongue thrust, which may affect the way they talk.

You can't always rely on the idea that your kids will outgrow thumb sucking. Parents have tried everything from putting tape to hot sauce on thumbs for their elementary school children to try to get them to stop sucking their thumbs. (By the way, the kids eventually grow up to like the taste of hot sauce. You see these people in Denny's all the time, ordering Tabasco with their poached eggs.)

- ✔ Elementary school children who still suck their thumbs are perceived to be less attractive, less fun, not as happy as other children, and not as likable. This perception is by other elementary school children. You don't want your child going to school sucking his thumb and having school mates think less of him because of a habit you could have prevented.

- ✔ Dan's grandmother put a sock on his sister's hand to dissuade her from thumb sucking. So she sucked the sock.

If your kids are determined to suck something, take their thumb out of their mouths and give them a pacifier. This way they'll learn that they can suck, but that they need to keep their hands out of their mouths.

Ninety-eight percent of all illnesses are transferred by hands. The last thing you want is for your kids to have a habit that requires them to stick their fingers in their mouths.

Slobbering

Slobbering in babies is usually caused by only one thing: teething. Slobbering in men is usually caused by scantily dressed females, but that's the subject of another book.

The only thing you need to know about slobbering is that it's wet and it gets everywhere. So don't get grossed out when you pick your baby up and you get a string of drool draped across your face. It's really not as bad as it sounds. (My favorite situation is lying on the ground, picking my baby up over my head, and having him drool either in my eye — or if I'm not careful, having it land right in my mouth.)

✔ When your kids drool and slobber, things get wet, especially their clothes. You can either keep a bib on them to catch the drool or change their shirts several times a day.

✔ Don't get lazy and leave wet shirts on a baby. Cold air on a wet shirt can lead to sickness (even pneumonia) if a baby has it on all day.

✔ By the way, women don't slobber — at least they never admit to it.

The Happy Days of Teething

Nothing makes the drool flow like teething.

Teething means that your otherwise good-natured, happy-go-lucky baby is going to get in a really bad mood. For about a year. Not all the time, just every now and then. You'll also notice that your baby will drool excessively. You can expect swollen and sore gums; some babies develop a fever, their poops will be acidy at times (which can give instant diaper rash), stomachs will be upset, and some babies have bouts of diarrhea. It makes you wonder if teeth are really worth it.

There are a few things you can do to ease the discomfort of teething:

✔ **Acetaminophen** (for example: Baby Tylenol, or Infants' Tylenol) helps reduce the fever and ease the pain. (Always ask your doctor for dosage recommendations before giving your baby any medications.)

✔ **Freezer popsicles** to gnaw on will temporarily make your child's gums feel better. The cold on the gums feels good. Freezer popsicles are extremely messy. This mess generally goes way beyond what a bib can control. Look for the sugar-free kind or those made of 100 percent real juice (no sugar added).

✔ **Teething rings** can sometimes help. Some teething rings are filled with water and can be frozen. Again, this cold feels good on sore baby gums.

✔ **Baby Orajel** is something you may want to try. This is a gel you put on your baby's gums to ease teething pain. You can buy it at your local pharmacy. Just read the instructions. Oh, good luck trying to put the gel on your baby's gums. Your baby may not want to cooperate when you start sticking your finger in an already sore mouth.

✔ **Infant toothbrushes** have soft bristles that your baby will like chewing on. Don't let your baby walk or run around with a toothbrush in his mouth, however. If he fell with one in his mouth, he could severely hurt himself. Give him the toothbrush when he's sitting in his high chair.

Your child's gums will be sore during the whole teething process. Remember that nothing you do is really going to help that much or for very long. Even Orajel doesn't last very long.

Some kids don't suffer much from teething and you may not see very many of the symptoms. Consider yourself very lucky!

Toddling (or the Walk on the Wild Side)

Nothing causes parents to brag and compare like a child's first steps. Parents always try to outdo each other on whose kids start walking at the earliest age. Just tell them that your child was so big at birth that this *wunderkind* jumped off the delivery table and walked over to the scales to be weighed.

The truth about those first steps

Here's the truth: It doesn't really matter when your kids first walk. No future employer is going to ask for that age on their résumé. This date has nothing to do with their growing up to be successful, well-rounded people.

Doctors like to know when baby first steps to make sure your baby is developing properly. Even so, the walking age varies from child to child. Some kids start walking as early as five months, while others don't feel the need to walk until they're 17 or 18 months. (These are extreme rarities. Normal walking time is anywhere between 9 and 13 months.)

The important part of your baby walking is that this kid is now considered a toddler: a person who toddles around the house and pulls the dirt out of your house plants and tries to stick toys into electrical outlets.

If you haven't babyproofed your house yet, this is the time to do it. Read Chapter 17, "Tools of the Trade," and go buy all the safety equipment that applies to your household.

Preparing the home for your little stunt person

You should also be reminded that once your toddler is mobile, the bumps and bruises increase tenfold. To reduce the chances of these bumps and bruises, consider doing the following:

- ✔ **Watch the feet.**

  Don't let toddlers walk on wood floors or tile with socks on (unless these socks have grippers on the bottom). Toddlers will slip and slide, and it'll be harder for them to keep their balance. Either let them go barefoot, or put shoes on them.

- ✔ **Keep junk picked up off the floor.**

  Junk means newspapers, magazines, shoes, vacuum or extension cords, blankets, couch pillows, and toys. These obstacles are easy for you to walk over, but to your toddler they can be the difference between standing and falling to the ground.

- ✔ **Keep toddlers off wet floors.**

  Restrain your toddler in the high chair when mopping the floor. Toddlers are lighter than you; they slip and slide (and of course fall) on wet floors.

- ✔ **Watch for sharp corners.**

  If possible, keep toddlers away from sharp corners when they're practicing their walking skills. Glass tabletops are the worst. These corners are extremely sharp and can cause some nasty cuts and bruises.

- ✔ **Teach the siblings how to play.**

  Educate older children on how to play around toddlers. Older children need to be extra careful because toddlers fall over so easily. Even a strong wind from another child running by can knock over a toddler.

Don't be surprised if your baby walks at first on tippy-toes. Lots of new toddlers walk on their toes but eventually outgrow this practice. If you're concerned about your child taking up this new walking style, ask your doctor about it. She can put your mind at ease.

Potty Training Perfected

Most parents don't look forward to potty training. You'd think that kids would *want* to learn how to use the potty. After all, peeing or pooping in their pants can't be comfortable. And having a cold butt-wipe slathering their nice warm bottoms must be miserable. But when you think about how awful it is to get up in the middle of the night to go to the bathroom (the cold draft when you lift up the covers, sitting on the hard, cold toilet seat), maybe doing it in your pants isn't such a bad idea in certain circumstances.

The truth is that your child *will* want to use the potty. Some day. Maybe not as soon as you'd like, but it will happen. But not at nine months old, nor at 12 or 16 months old. Also, potty training is not all that hard. The trick is not to start too early, or have the attitude: "As of today — as God is my witness — my child is going to learn to use the potty." Your child has to be both physically and emotionally ready to use the potty. No matter how much you want it to happen, it's really up to your child.

Time is the greatest innovator. — Francis Bacon

Like everything else your child learns, going pee and poop in the potty takes time. Toddlers learn to use the potty between two and four years old. If that span seems old to you, keep in mind that it's not until the ages of eighteen to twenty-four months that toddlers begin to recognize what it feels like when they have to go pee or poop. Before this time, these bodily functions just sort of magically happen. You know, sort of how *Lucky Charms* are *magically delicious!*

The myth of potty training at an early age

If you have friends who say they have potty trained their babies at nine months old, feel free to snicker behind their backs. What has actually happened is that the parents themselves have been trained. They've learned their babies' habits well enough to know when their children have to go potty. When that time comes, the parents whisk the unwitting babies off to the bathroom, plop the victims on the potty — and the children then sit and do the doody.

If you talk to these parents in more depth, you'll find that their babies have *accidents* all the time. (But these babies don't really have *accidents* because the poor kids have never really been potty trained.) What has happened is that their babies get older and their bodies change. So just because their kids used to go poop right after lunch doesn't mean they will for the rest of their lives.

When to start the potty train

Most toddlers will give signs that they're ready to use the potty. I'm not talking about written notices placed strategically around the house saying, "Hey, I'm ready for that potty thing you gave me," but nonverbal signs like the following:

- Running to the corner, squatting, making grunting sounds, and maybe even turning red.
- A dry diaper for several hours.
- A dry diaper after naps. Although for some children, this one may not happen until long after they've been potty trained during the day.
- Regular bowel movements.
- Tugging at a diaper when it's dirty, or other indications that your kid knows there is a mess in the diaper. Your child may even tell you that he's dirtied his diaper: "Poop!"
- Letting you know that he *has to go* poop or pee.
- Bringing you a clean diaper.

Don't panic or get frustrated if your child never does any of these things. Every child is different and, because of their particular situation, they may never have regular bowel movements, may never let you know when they go poop, or may always seem to be wet.

The education stage

After you start noticing signs that your toddler may be ready to use the potty, start educating him about his body and the potty. You also get your child used to the idea of going potty. It would be too frustrating for both you and your toddler if you all of a sudden say, "OK, today you are going to learn to use the potty. Here it is. Go for it!"

Imitation is a wonderful way to learn, so if you're not too modest or shy, let your toddler in the bathroom with you to see what a potty is used for. Tell your child what it is you're doing. If your toddler has an older sibling, encourage this sibling to help with the teaching process and to demonstrate the potty.

After your toddler is potty trained, you'll also have to teach how to wipe after using the potty — and don't forget the washing-of-the-hands ritual.

There are a lot of wonderful books and videos about using the potty that will help with your potty training. A big time favorite is the video, *Once Upon A Potty* by Alona Frankel and produced by Frappe, Inc. *Once Upon A Potty* is also a book, but the video has this great song that you'll hear over and over and over again (even in your sleep).

Sitting on that potty

Sitting on the potty — and using it — is a critical moment that will be different for everyone. Pay close attention to your children to see how they react to the whole potty thing. Potties can be cold and hard . . . and can make you feel like you don't have any support down there. So don't be surprised if your kids don't like the feeling. Keep trying every now and then and they'll get used to it, just like you did.

There are three different approaches to the actual process of setting your toddler on the potty (hoping for positive results):

- Set your child on the potty at regularly scheduled times when you know the kid tends to go poop and pee.

- Don't go by any schedule, but watch for signs that your little one may need to go to poop (like when your kid squats, grunts, and turns red).

- Do a combination of both. You may want to set your child on the potty first thing in the morning, or after naps. During the rest of the day, watch for signs that your toddler may have to go poop. You can also ask if your child has to go poop or wants to use the potty.

After you've accomplished the *sitting-on-the-potty* process, it's just a matter of consistently placing your child on the potty and encouraging its use. It takes time before you can stop asking your child to use the potty and he automatically does it on his own.

Fun you can expect from the potty experience

Training to go potty takes time. Even after the first successful "Mommy, I have to go poop," there will be interesting episodes. Here are some things you may expect:

- Accidents up to age four or five. For some kids, even up to the age of ten.

- Accidents or setbacks if schedules or events change in your toddler's life. Over-excitement or being upset over something can cause accidents (sort of like Cocker Spaniels).

- Your toddler may not be able to go through the nights dry even though the day is without accidents. Keep diapers on your toddler at night, and every couple of months or so try to go through a night with underpants. Let your child know that he needs to try going through the night without a diaper.

✔ Don't be upset or angry if your little one doesn't make it through the night. Don't make a big production of changing pajamas or bedding. And definitely don't shame your child for having this accident. Be sympathetic to the accident and let your child know that sometimes these things happen. Believe it or not, your child won't wet the bed on purpose. And it has nothing to do with laziness or stubbornness. It's bladder control, pure and simple.

If your toddler is having a hard time going all night staying dry, you can try limiting the amount of liquid intake right before bed. Give small sips of water, but don't allow 7-11 Big Gulp glasses of juice before bedtime. Also, ask your child to try to go potty before going to bed.

Some helpful potty things to keep in mind

Learning to use the potty is a major event in a toddler's life. It takes maturity, body control, and body awareness. Don't get upset and yell at a child, or worse yet, don't call names like *baby* when your child has accidents. You didn't scold your child when he fell learning to walk. You didn't yell when the same child got messy starting to feed himself. And you shouldn't get upset, yell, or shame a child who's learning to use the potty.

✔ Bedwetting can continue until age five. A small percentage of kids continue to wet the bed until age ten.

✔ The golden rule in getting your children to bed is that they must be sleepy. The golden rule in potty training is that children must be willing and ready to be trained. They have to want to use the potty. If they fight you on the idea, wait and talk to them about it later.

✔ Let your kids pick out their own training pants. You can let them know that you're going out to pick up *big kids'* underwear. They may be more aware of their body functions if they know they'll soil *Beauty and the Beast* when they have an accident.

Step by step one ascends the staircase. — Turkish proverb

Warning: potty problems

If your child seems to be having problems using the potty, maybe you're trying too hard with your training. Your child won't be in diapers forever. Give this potty thing lots of time and don't pressure your child to do something he may not be ready for. And don't allow yourself to feel pressure from other parents or family members who feel they know what's best for your child. I hate it when that happens!

The harder parents try to potty train, the longer it takes and the more upsetting it is for the child. — Chris Boyatzis

---

Your lesson for the day

Potty training can seem to last forever for some parents. Don't get frustrated or angry at your child during this time. And don't make the mistake that a lot of other parents make: They try to start too early and they push their kids too hard. Have patience and read Chapter 5, "The Art of Keeping Your Cool."

Part IV

Help for Desperate Parents

By Rich Tennant

In this part...

*I*t's OK to admit you're desperate about something. In the film *The Ten Commandments,* Rameses was desperate for Nefretiri's love. Moses was desperate to find the daughters of Jethro (because he got mighty thirsty out there in that desert), and the Israelites were desperate to cross the Red Sea before the bad guys caught up to them. As parents, we can get pretty desperate looking for the right answers to those parenting questions we all face, such as finding good child care (without going broke), finding (and going to) a doctor, dealing with discipline and punishment, and parting the bath water — should it ever become necessary.

Chapter 19

Guidelines for Co-Parenting (The Two-Party System)

1 f you want to find a chapter that you can skip over, you came to the wrong place. You've just gotta read this chapter. Not only that, but you have to make sure that your mate reads it, too. Even if that means catching your partner on the toilet or reading bits and pieces over the answering machine until the whole thing has been heard. Do it.

This chapter covers the teamwork part of being a parent. It's about taking care of you so that you can, as the Army says, "Be all that you can be." It's about coming up with a plan so that both you and your partner can act as full time parents *together*.

Parenting is more than dealing with your children effectively. It's also about being a family. Both parents should work as a team, with everything involved in keeping your family going. That teamwork makes parenting easier, and you'll grow stronger as a family, spending more time together doing fun family stuff.

One unfortunate fact that we must bring up is that many families consist of single parents. This chapter is still for you. Your co-parent can be a roommate, a grandmother or grandfather, uncle, aunt, rent-a-spouse. It can be anyone in your life who can be there to help you raise your kids. It doesn't have to necessarily mean a Mom and Dad, although that is the ideal situation.

If you're a single parent with no one to help you raise your kids or support your efforts, this chapter has a section called Single-Parenting Guidelines.

Parent + Co-Parent = Teamwork

Being a parenting team is like tag team wrestling. When one parent gets too tired, she tags the other parent who then struggles on with the fight. When that doesn't happen — when one parent sits back and the other one does all the wrestling — the child is the loser. The child suffers because you start to let things slip. You'll turn your head rather than take the time and effort to stop what's going on when you see your child crawling on the table (for the 100th time) or playing in the toilet.

Parenting is not an on/off thing. It's a job that never ends. It doesn't matter if both parents work outside the home, or if one parent stays home and the other one works outside. You both have to be full-time parents whenever you're with your kids — regardless of when that is.

Being a parent who stays home all day with a child is no easy task. It doesn't mean that you have all day to clean the house and keep the laundry going. Your major task during the day is taking care of your kid. You'll still be doing it at night, and you'll need the help of the parent who has the outside job.

The business of being fun together

There's a line from the movie *Honey, I Blew Up The Kids* that goes, "Daddies are for fun; Mommies mean business." Who came up with this? I don't know any Mom who would say, "Oh yes, I guess playing with the children would be nice, but I would much rather discipline the children, put cranky babies to bed when they don't think they're sleepy, or (my favorite) change those really explosive diapers." Do you know what happens if Daddies never partake in the really tough stuff? Resentment by the Mommies.

I've heard both Moms and Dads say how they feel like a single parent because their partner won't help with any of the *difficult* parts of raising a child. You both have to be involved in every aspect of raising your kids. Both Mommies and Daddies are for fun. Both Mommies and Daddies can mean business. Make it so.

How to be of one common mind without brain surgery

Fairyland is the place where Wishful Thinking is the capitol. Before parents in Fairyland have children, they sit down and discuss the philosophy of how they're going to raise their children. Reality sets in when you actually have *your* child and nothing happens like you thought it would. That's because no one lives in Fairyland.

There will be times when you and your mate disagree on how to handle certain situations with your child. But you have to treat such situations delicately. You don't want to turn a coloring-on-the-walls incident into a raging debate over how things should be handled, especially as your little one is standing there absorbing everything you're saying.

Here are some suggestions for handling mutual decision making:

✔ **Don't argue about discipline.**

   Especially in front of your kids. They'll interpret this as one parent taking their side and the other one not. They'll store this information away and eventually use it against you — not in an evil kind of way, but they'll remember it and bring it up later.

✔ **Respect each other's ideas.**

   Your child-raising ideas most likely will come from your background — either how you were disciplined, or how you've seen others handle their children. Be open to what your partner has to suggest. Don't always assume your way is the right way.

✔ **Talk out disagreements.**

   You both should feel comfortable with the outcome. You need to be in agreement about household rules and how to handle it when those rules are broken. If you're inconsistent with these rules, your child will be confused, decide not to listen to either one of you, or — worse yet — play you both off of each other. You know the scene, "But Dad, Grandma always lets me jump on the bed."

✔ **Don't jump into an ongoing situation.**

   If you walk into a room where your partner is already handling a situation, try to keep quiet. Things aren't always as they appear, and you probably don't know what's going on.

✔ **Don't gang up on your child.**

   If you both see something going on that shouldn't, let one parent deal with it. You both don't want to seem like you're ganging up on your child. If you see that your partner is having trouble, offer to step in and help.

Thou shalt share thy housework

Housework or *chores* may be a sore subject in some families. Maybe this is a good time to catch your mate on the toilet so that running away is impossible.

Sharing housework doesn't necessarily mean that you have to divide the chores up equally so that everyone has five each. It means that you divide the chores up equitably (which means fairly or reasonably). Sit down and make a list of things that you all are willing and able to do. If you hate vacuuming, let your partner do it. If your partner detests the laundry, you do it. If you both hate doing the dishes, wait a few years and force your *children* to do them for you. If your regular chores get boring, make changes to your chore schedule every week or so, just to keep things interesting.

The Co-Parenting Chore Chart							
	Mon	**Tue**	**Wed**	**Thur**	**Fri**	**Sat**	**Sun**
Parent #1							
Make the bed							
Vacuum							
Load the dishwasher							
Fold the laundry							
Parent #2							
Sweep/mop the kitchen							
Take out the trash							
Feed the dog							
Wash a load of clothes							

Children and chores (kind of like involuntary servitude)

There's a reason they say children are *emancipated* when they reach 18 years old. Honestly, before that time, some people consider kids as property. Nine months of cooking; then birth; then for 18 years a helping hand around the house. Our ancestors knew this. They had children more as a way of building a small labor force (though I'm certain some *love* was involved as well).

Forget their political status for a moment; there's no reason why your kids can't help around the house. Try not to turn them into little Cinderellas and have them do everything while you sit around and watch *Wheel of Fortune.* Anything done together is more fun, and your kids will be more willing to help if they see that everyone is helping.

Start your kids off with little chores they can handle, like putting the forks, spoons, and napkins on the dining table. Remember not to criticize their efforts; praise them and let them know they're doing a good job. Also remember that they may not set the table exactly how you would have done it. That's OK. They may have their own ideas on how things should be done. That's a part of growing up and experimenting. As long as they've got the right idea, give them some room to experiment.

Chore time is family time. Teach your children at an early age to take on new responsibilities that will not only help with the family chores but will also build your children's self confidence, teach them that work is fun, and promote the family unity.

The best way to teach is by example. If your children see that everyone in the family is working, they have no room to complain about their chores. (Not that it will stop them; they just won't be justified.)

Sharing child care (or: It took both Adam and Eve to raise Cain)

If you're busy with the kids, it may seem that there's little that your partner can do to help. Wrong! There are a number of things that may seem very small, but they'll be a ton of help:

> ✔ **Pick up the clutter.**
>
> Pick up toys, blankets, bottles, or towels that you see lying around the house. It always baffles me that whole families can walk over a napkin on the floor, as if someone had placed it there as a sacrificial piece of garbage and only certain holy hands are allowed to touch it.

> ✔ **Share the child care duties.**
>
> Take turns changing diapers, putting the kids to bed, giving baths, feeding (obviously with the exception of breastfeeding, which could get painful for Dad), burping baby, helping with homework — and whatever needs to be done to take care of your kids.

✔ **Give Mom some special time.**

If you really want to make Mom happy, give her some special time in the morning to have to herself so she can shower, put on makeup, get dressed — or whatever her morning ritual is. This luxury is overlooked, especially when there's a newborn that only Mom can feed. New mothers can go through most of the day before they have a chance to get cleaned up. They will feel better if they can have a few minutes to themselves to wash off the baby puke and leaked breast milk.

✔ **Give your partner some free time alone every now and then.**

As much as we love our children, sometimes it's good to get away for an hour or so just to spend time alone. This goes for both parents.

Sharing the ties that bind

It's unfortunate that some Dads feel left out of bonding because they aren't able to breastfeed. Some fathers feel that newborns are a time for Mom and baby. Dads need to get involved with their newborns with as much interest and vigor as Moms do. They can spend just as much time with their baby if they take some time and a little imagination.

✔ Dad can lie down with Mom and baby while she nurses. It's a nice, cozy time with baby in the middle and Mom and Dad on either side.

✔ Dad can bottlefeed the baby (with the help of a breast pump from Mom).

✔ Mom and Dad can play with baby together.

✔ Mom and Dad can give baby a bath together.

I asked my students what they preferred to get from their parents, money or time — they all chose time. — Jonnie Johnson, 7th Grade Teacher

As your children get older, you'll still want to spend that bonding time with them. Make dates with your children where just Mom and child or Dad and child can go out alone and do things together. This is a great time not only to get close to your child, but also to spend uninterrupted time talking. These outings don't always have to be costly. Go out and run errands, go grocery shopping, or just go out for a walk or bicycle ride.

Single-Parenting Guidelines

Being a single parent has its good points and bad points. The good points are that you don't have to argue with a partner over parenting issues — you just do what you want. And you may have wonderful children who will love you until the end of time — provided you don't embarrass them when their prom dates come to the door.

The bad point of single parenting is that you don't have anyone to help you. Doing it on your own means you don't have that back-up person to help you parent when you're ill or tired from a long day at work. You have to do all the disciplining, punishing, cleaning, cooking, washing . . . and the list goes on.

The key to single parenting is finding the thing that makes parenting the hardest for you and dealing with it. The lack of help and support may be that one thing, so work to solve that problem:

- ✔ Enroll your children in Big Brothers/Big Sisters.

- ✔ Ask your family (if available) to spend time with your kids.

- ✔ Find a play group for your children. They'll get to interact with other children, and you'll get to interact with other parents.

- ✔ Join organizations that encourage family togetherness. Examples are family sports (gymboree for toddlers, snow skiing for older kids), religious groups, volunteer programs (feed the homeless), and so on.

If you've got lots of support, but you don't seem to have the *time* you want to spend with your children, try some of the following:

- ✔ Hire someone to help with housework once a week, once a month, or whatever you can afford.

- ✔ Teach your children to help with housework and cooking. Kids are great at ripping lettuce apart.

- ✔ Do an exchange program with your friends. Everyone takes a turn cooking dinner (or cleaning for the others) one day a week.

- ✔ Go home from work when it's time. The pressure to do well at work is even stronger when you know that you don't have another income to fall back on. But you still have a responsibility to your kids to go home and be with them.

Being a single parent is a *choice* for many people. For others, it's not a choice, but something they have to deal with. Whatever your situation, remember your first priority is your children. Good luck.

Look! Driving the Minivan! Over at the Mall! It's Super Mom!

The 1980s bore the term *Super Mom*. It was a syndrome of mothers who tried to be the best at everything there was to do, and did everything to be best at. She tried to be a super mom, a super employee, a super wife, and a super house-keeper. Super cool!

Unfortunately, Mom found that she wasn't effective at doing any of these — not because of lurking kids with Kryptonite, but because she was trying to do too much. The solution for the Super Mom was to let something go. (Some let their bedrooms be a mess, some left work at 5:00 so they could be at home with their family instead of putting in the overtime.)

The Super Mom syndrome is not limited to the 80s. It's still happening today. The only change is that it's not limited to mothers. Fathers have joined the ranks of being *overdone*.

The cure to this disease is to have priorities. Number one should be your family. Everything else should be secondary. Since you can't ignore everything else (although ignoring laundry would be nice), it's time to look at things differently.

✔ **Get help from your family.**

There's no reason why one person in a family should be responsible for doing everything. Yeah, even though Batman has lots of cool toys, he still needs Robin. Get everyone involved in cooking, cleaning, yard work, and grocery shopping. The possibilities are endless.

✔ **Leave work when it's time to go.**

It's a job. If your job is like most, the work will still be there when you go back tomorrow.

✔ **Get organized.**

Have your daily house and work chores arranged so that you don't waste time on anything. Make up chore lists for everyone in the family so everyone knows what it is they're supposed to do.

> ✔ **Limit yourself to three things.**
>
> Most people can juggle three things at once. When you add a fourth thing — being team leader, volunteering to drive the church van, tutoring at school — that's when you'll trip up, wear down, and fizzle out.

Be Gooood to Yourself

To be the best parent you can be, you need to be the best person you can be. When you feel your best, others around you also get that good feeling from you. When you're tired and haven't been taking proper care of yourself, others, including your kids, can tell. You'll have less patience, your energy level will be low, your enthusiasm will be less. You'll also have a tendency to have a shorter attention span, and you may even be — even though you'll probably deny it — a little cranky.

So that you have enough energy to be the terrific kind of parent you always wanted to be, make these three areas an important part of your life: exercise, diet (meaning eating right, not *not* eating), and rest. Try to think of an original excuse for each of the following:

Why you can't exercise.

Why you snack on junk food too much.

Why you never get enough rest.

Ha! It can't be done. There's no excuse you can offer that hasn't already been said. Even the Aliens-came-down-and-forced-me-to-eat-this-doughnut excuse has been used — but no one believed me.

Exorcise the demons of laziness!

Exercise doesn't mean you have to join a Health Club, put on spandex, and sweat to the Golden Oldies to get in shape. It means loading the kids in the stroller, pulling them in a wagon, or have them ride along on their Big Wheel, bicycle, go-cart whatever — and walking for 20-30 minutes, 3-4 times a week. That's what the *health experts* say that you really need.

There are plenty of floor exercises you can do that involve your kids, too. Do sit-ups while holding your baby on your stomach. Do leg lifts while your toddler lies beside you with a favorite toy. Race to see how many sit-ups you and your kids can do in ten minutes This isn't brain surgery here. I'm sure you can also think of a few things to do.

The best way to have time for exercising is:

- ✔ Turn the TV off. TV can be evil. It robs you of your life.
- ✔ Have everyone help with dinner and housecleaning so that *everyone* can take a walk after dinner.
- ✔ Schedule your exercise time. You're more likely to exercise if it's a part of your schedule.

Realize one very important thing. Once you have a baby, your body may not be the same size as it was before you had the baby (Dads, there's no excuse for you). Your weight may go down to the same weight, but your body may be shaped differently. Women tend to spread out more in the hip area, their breasts may become larger or smaller, or their feet may grow (this happens if you wear tennis shoes or go barefoot more than you used to). It's a necessary price to pay for a great baby.

There are some women who go down to exactly their same tiny selves, but we don't like these women.

Jogging is a great way to hear heavy breathing again. — quote from someone really funny

Eat right (put that doughnut down!)

It's easy to gain weight after having a baby. Not necessarily because you're overeating, but because you tend to stop eating well and snack on foods that are high in sugars and carbohydrates.

Remember how well you ate while you were pregnant? (Yes, you were supposed to be eating right.) Don't let the busy schedule you have with kids make you fall into that bad habit of eating only fast foods, or snacking all day on crackers.

Alternative Snack Chart

What you want to eat	What you can eat instead
graham crackers	steamed soybeans
potato chips	baby carrots with spinach dip
Honey Nut Cheerios	raisins and unsalted nuts
bagel with cream cheese	fresh fruit
Wheat Thins with Cheez Whiz	celery with peanut butter
Reese's Peanut Butter Cup	Reese's Peanut Butter Cup

You don't have to be Julia Child to fix well-balanced meals. Grab some frozen bags of vegetables, stick a chicken in the oven, *et voilà!* Dinner! Don't forget to let your family help with dinner; you don't have to do it all by yourself. Ask for help and delegate those chores.

Hurry up and get some rest!

When you're young, you don't want to take a nap because if you close your eyes, you know you'll miss out on something great. As adults, most of us would pay cash for the opportunity to take naps.

As a parent, you owe it to your kids to be well rested. If you can, lie down and rest when your kids do. But don't try to get them to nap when *you're* sleepy. It just doesn't work. Don't stay up and watch David Letterman if you know you're going to have to get up in four hours to feed the baby.

Some parents say, "Oh, I just can't miss the late news." What they're really saying is that the late news is more important to them than their rest. They don't care that they're tired and unproductive the next day. They also don't care that they don't have the energy to have a tea party or color with their kids for a while. As a parent, you have to do what's *right* and that's not always what's the most fun.

Some parents don't feel that they have enough time during the day to get everything done, so taking a nap would be a waste of time. This is why you need everyone's help in cleaning, cooking, and taking care of your kids. The work will never get done. Someone will always dirty a dish or want to be fed. So don't worry that you don't get to everything during the day. There's always tomorrow. Yes, the sun will come out, tomorrow. Betchya bottom dollar that tomorrow there'll be sun.

Don't Neglect Your Mate

Pick up any magazine in the grocery store and you'll find at least one heading that says *How to keep the romance alive* **or** *Take our survey, are you a good kisser?* **or** *Is beer more important to him than you are?* This whole chapter is about being good to yourself so that you feel good about who you are — and in return teach your children to feel good about themselves. Remember, your kids learn by example. If you're happy and laughing and having a grand old time with your partner, they also have a better chance of becoming happy people.

Make an effort to spend time with your partner. Don't get so caught up with your kids, work, housekeeping, or whatever that you forget to go out with each other for time alone. Your kids need to know that you have a life outside of them and that you are more than just Mom and Dad.

The most important thing a father can do for his children is to love their mother. — Theodore M. Hesburgh

This is what you need to do:

✔ **Go on dates.**

Just you two. You don't have to spend money on dinner and a movie. Walk around the mall, go to a free concert in the park, go play tennis, cruise to Tahiti (no wait, that would cost a few bucks). Do something together without the kids. If your lives are so busy that three weeks have gone by and you haven't done anything yet, get a calendar and write it down so that it's scheduled. Make a rule that if it's on the calendar, neither one of you can back out.

✔ **Keep the romance alive.**

Yes, there probably was a time when you both used to have sex together — and at the same time. This may be another area that you'll have to write down on the calendar. I know that sounds really unromantic, but make it that way. Flirt with each other all day. Don't forget to hug and give kisses and all the other lovey-dovey stuff you used to do when you were trying to win the other one over during your dating days.

✔ **Do something special for each other.**

Bring her home a flower. Send a love note in his lunch. Make an effort to show each other that you care for each other.

✔ **Remember the important words.**

It's imperative that you let your spouse know that you think he or she is special. One way you do this is by the words that you use. Don't ever, and I mean ever, say, "Well I don't need to tell him/her that I love him/her. He/She knows." This is such bull. If anything, your children need to hear that you love each other. Besides, if you don't profess your love to your mate, are you remembering to tell your children that you love them?

The day we become parents, our *guilt gene* is born, and we are forever feeling guilty about what we do. (Unless, of course, you were raised Catholic; then guilt comes naturally.) Don't feel guilty about wanting to spend time alone. Your children will learn that you both love each other, you want your relationship to grow, and you both don't take each other for granted.

Important words you need to tell your mate

- I love you.
- You're special to me.
- You're doing a great job.
- Thank you.
- My, you have a nice butt.

- Please.
- Your eyes are like crystal blue pools.
- Want to get lucky tonight?
- I appreciate all that you do.
- Want a date?

Don't be surprised if your sex life is not what it used to be after you have kids. This doesn't necessarily mean you have a sexual problem. It takes some parents several months after having a baby before they remember that they used to have sex. Pure exhaustion from a new baby tends to block that part of your life out. Keep in mind the other ways the two of you can be intimate.

Let's Behave, Shall We?

Everything that you and your partner do together is sending a message to your children. If you are loving, kind, and fair to each other, that's how they learn to act with their siblings and friends. They will also learn how to deal with conflict and fighting based on how you handle it.

Fun things to do with your mate

- Take bubble baths together with lit candles and share a bottle of Diet Coke. (OK, wine may be a little more romantic — but don't get drunk in the tub.)
- Write each other love notes and hide them in places the other is sure to find later.
- Go out with another couple. It's fun to have other adult company. Of course all you'll end up doing is talk about your kids.
- Don't forget how fun staying at home can be. Order take-out food, light candles, listen to music, and cuddle on the couch (maybe even a little smooching would be nice).
- Send the kids to the neighbors and give each other massages.
- Go to bed early and try to remember what you did to make those kids in the first place.

Keep your communication open and honest with your partner. It's OK to say that you're tired, unhappy, upset, sleepy, happy, grumpy, dopey, or whatever. Don't feel like you need to try to hide disappointment or anger. Learn how to handle these feelings and resolve them. Your kids need to learn that these feelings are natural. More important, they need to know how to behave when they have these feelings and how to make themselves feel better.

Alexander and the Terrible, Horrible, No Good, Very Bad Day by Judith Viorst (Macmillan Publishing) is a good book to read to your kids about having bad days — which we all have.

It's all right to argue in front of your kids as long as you keep it to a clean, honest fight. No throwing things, no cursing, no yelling, no sarcasm, and no low punches (bringing up situations or events that don't belong in this argument, but maybe in some other one). Your kids will learn that you may not agree with someone, but that doesn't mean you don't love that person. It would be awful to go through life thinking that every time you had an argument with someone, the relationship was over. The key to arguing is having your children see that you've both come to a happy conclusion and that you've kissed and made up.

What counts in making a happy marriage is not so much how compatible you are, but how you deal with incompatibility. — George Levinger

Keep arguments or disagreements about your children private. Even though it's OK for them to know that you have disagreements, they don't need to hear the back-and-forth arguments you have about them. They'll use this information against you both later on (that is, if they're old enough to understand what you're saying).

And on the other hand, don't be afraid to be affectionate with each other in front of your children. It's healthy for your kids to see you kiss and hug. But please leave the heavy petting for the privacy of your bedroom or car.

Your lesson for the day

We rely so much on our mates that if the relationship isn't going so well, any breakdown falls over into our relationship with our kids.

Chapter 20
Social Skills to Be Proud Of

. . . .

In This Chapter

▶ Keeping realistic expectations

▶ Taking children out to eat

▶ Traveling with children

▶ Taking your children to the movies

. . . .

Someone well-versed in social skills knows that you don't pick your nose in front of others. It's the knowledge that you don't comb your hair at the dinner table, belch out loud, or scratch yourself in front of guests. This stuff should (hopefully) be pretty obvious. Then there are the more subtle social skills: if there's more than one fork on the table, start with the one on the outside and work your way in; send a thank-you note to someone who gave you a gift; after she's colored her hair, never tell your Aunt Debra that her hair looks orange.

Social skills aren't easy to learn, but they're a necessary part of life that we need to teach our children. The hardest part of it all is that you have to take your kids out in public to practice it.

Great Social-Skill Expectations

Social skills (such as dining out, going to parties, traveling, or even playing with others) are a learned behavior that takes a lot of practice and, in some cases, advance planning. You need to keep some things in mind as you train your children to be proper little ladies and gentlemen.

Don't expect too much from your little ones. They're just learning and, quite honestly, this is hard stuff to learn. Many adults haven't learned any social skills — like your Grandma Shirley who puts her false teeth on the table after dinner. Some things just shouldn't be done.

Many social activities require long periods of sitting, which can be very boring to children. As adults, we usually amuse ourselves when we're bored. It's our job as parents to amuse our children when they're in boring social activities. If we don't, they'll find their own amusement: kicking the back of the pew in church, throwing spit balls at the waitress, screaming just because it sounds cool, making fart sounds with their armpit during your best friend's wedding, and more.

Any type of social activity turns out better if you remember to go to these activities when your child is not tired, sick, or hungry. In addition, let your child know what is to be expected at the event and what is to be expected from his behavior. Read the section, "Explain what's to be expected," in Chapter 2.

Children prefer to play with other children who are well-behaved and well-mannered. You'd be doing your children an injustice by not taking the time to teach them the proper way to act and play.

Dining Out with Children (other than McDonald's)

Yes, it's possible to eat out other than at McDonald's. Your children don't have to be going through puberty before they realize that not all restaurants have a golden arch out front — and that some places actually put your food on real plates.

Eating with the little ones

Eating out with infants is a breeze. They're *easy*. They're happy to sit quietly, be cute, and look around. Occasionally they'll spit up just to impress those dining around them. Just follow these guidelines:

✔ **Try to arrange your restaurant meal during their nap time.**

Ideally, if you can feed your baby when you first get to the restaurant, the little one can sleep while you and your dinner date enjoy your food.

✔ **Ask to be put in a booth.**

Booths are usually wide enough for a baby seat so that your child can nap next to you. In addition, booths are a little bit more secluded, darker, and better for napping kids. If you're breastfeeding, a booth will give you a little more privacy so your baby can nurse. The perfect booths are those in a corner.

✔ **If you can't arrange the outing around nap time, bring plenty of supplies to keep your baby happy.**

There is nothing more annoying for both you and those dining around you than to have dinner with a screaming baby. Your supplies should include: plenty of diapers and diaper wipes (otherwise known as butt wipes); milk, juice, and water bottles; spit-up towel; a blanket (since restaurants can be drafty); soft cushy toys that are good for biting.

✔ **Avoid giving hard toys, like the hard plastic rattles, to your infant.**

Babies won't have enough arm control and will eventually hit themselves on the head. This act is funny in a Three Stooges movie, but it's not so funny when your baby does it.

Dining with older babies, toddlers, and up

The toddler age group takes more planning and imagination than what you need to summon with infants. Older babies, toddlers, and your older children aren't so happy just to be cute; they want to be entertained. They want to get up, cruise around the restaurant, and check to see what others are eating (maybe even taking a bite or two).

✔ **Have enough supplies with you.**

These supplies include diapers, diaper wipes, milk, juice, water, food (if your child is not going to eat off the menu or from your plate), blanket, and toys. Again, no hard toys: Hard plastic toys are great for banging on the high chair or table. That's a no-no. Good toys to bring are soft picture books, crayons, and a coloring book. Many restaurants supply some of these things already. Give toys and finger food only when needed and only one at a time. (In other words, don't dump the whole bag of goodies on the table.)

✔ **Go out to eat when it's your children's mealtime — not when it's past this time.**

The best way to keep children or anyone else quiet is to have them eat (nice to know for when your in-laws come to visit). Chances are good that if you go out to eat when your children aren't hungry, they'll get antsy quickly. Nothing is more boring than sitting around waiting for someone else to eat.

✔ **Ask the server to get your children's food as soon as possible.**

But only if your children are acting cranky because they're really hungry. Otherwise, just have them wait for their food like everyone else.

✔ **Don't fill your children up on pre-food stuff (like crackers, juice, or milk).**

Keep children happy by quietly playing games with them. That's why you need to have a book or crayons with you. For little ones, spoons or napkins can be a source of great amusement.

If your children seem to be getting cranky and the food hasn't arrived yet, you and your dinner date may want to take turns taking them for a walk. Go visit the enticing restaurant lobby, but avoid meandering around other eating guests. And never let your children walk around by themselves unless it's in the lobby — away from the other guests.

Restaurant rules and regulations

The sooner you and your children learn the basic lessons about going out to eat at a restaurant, the easier it'll be for you both.

No loud screaming or talking

Remove screaming children from the restaurant until they've calmed down. Most people can tolerate a whimper or crying because you're not getting food to your kids fast enough. But you need to handle the *getting mad* type of crying elsewhere.

Obviously you can't teach a baby not to cry, but you can try to find out why a baby's crying. Go through your list of reasons why babies cry (read Chapter 16, "Cranky Babies"). Is your baby hungry or thirsty? Does your baby need a pacifier? Does your baby have wet or dirty diapers, or need to change positions, or is simply tired? Of course there's the I'm-mad-because-I-can't-play-in-your-mashed-potatoes cry and the I hit-my-head-with-this-stupid-rattle-you-gave-me . . . and it h-h-hurts!" You can handle this type of crying with hugs or by leaving the restaurant for a moment. The change of environment sometimes makes kids forget why they're crying.

If you practice these guidelines, your children will grow up to understand what's acceptable and what's not while they're eating out. You may still have to give reminders to your kids as they get older to hold their voices down while they talk. Kids' voices tend to get louder the more excited they get.

No wandering

When your children are at the age where they can walk, that's what they're going to want to do. Don't let them. They have to learn that it's not acceptable to walk around a restaurant and pick food off other people's plates.

No unnecessary lingering

When you eat out with your youngsters, realize that the long, casual dinners are a thing of the past. If you want to linger over dessert while sipping coffee and talking about the pros and cons of Rush Limbaugh, get a babysitter and leave the kids at home. If you want a good meal with the kids, go someplace where children are welcome and the restaurant is equipped for them. Such restaurants will have a child's menu, maybe some crayons, high chairs, and booster seats. Order your food, eat, and then leave. This strategy doesn't mean eating out can't be fun. It just means it may be quicker than if you were alone. If you keep your outings short and sweet, your children will be less likely to lose their patience with the situation. As they get older, you can try expanding the time. Just be very sensitive to how they are acting. If your kids seem happy to sit there and play with the napkins, sit back and enjoy. If they're getting antsy and are beginning to squirm, take their hint and leave.

It's possible to have a long, relaxing dinner with five-year-olds and up. All you need is a pen and pad of paper for them to draw on. That will keep them happy while you complain about your job, neighbors, the government, and so on.

Practice politeness

You are in a public place. Practice your good manners while you're out. No food throwing — by anyone. That includes you too, parents. Don't leave a huge mess for your server to clean up. Be respectful of the fact that tidiness is greatly appreciated. Say "please" and "thank you" to your server. Their job is not exactly easy.

Children on the Go

Traveling with your children can be fun. No, really. Say this out loud:

Traveling with my kids can be fun.

All you have to do is prepare for the trip. This advice applies whether you're traveling by car or by plane. Remember, a lot of this is your attitude. You're taking your kids with you, so you must act as a *family*. Gone are the days when you took off for Europe with a duffel bag and your dad's credit card. Things are different now.

Hither and thither with the kids (general travel information)

Traveling with your kids can be fun, providing you keep in mind a few basics. Make sure you tell your kids what's going on and give them an idea of your schedule. Traveling often involves a lot of waiting, so let them know that, too. Like everything else, if you inform your kids what's to be expected of them, they'll be better able to comply.

If you have a young one, try to leave before nap time. If your baby or toddler is able to sleep through most of the trip, it'll make everyone a lot happier.

Finally, take plenty of snacks, drinks, and entertainment. Sometimes the entertainment may mean you, so be prepared to sit with your child and play some games (only if someone else is driving). If that doesn't appeal to you, you can buy all sorts of travel toys to keep your little one happy.

Here are a few tips that will help make traveling with your kids less like an episode of *The Simpsons*. (Be sure to check off these items on the form found in Appendix B.)

> ✔ **Allow yourself plenty of time to get to wherever it is you're going.**
>
> You'll have to stop for potty breaks, rest stops, and to stretch your legs.
>
> ✔ **Ask your travel agent about vacation sites that are equipped for children.**
>
> A travel agent should be able to give you a list of hotels that accommodate children, along with resorts that have special children's packages. For example, the Hyatt Regency in Scottsdale, Arizona has a water playground and a special all-day camp designed for kids.
>
> ✔ **Have snacks and toys close at hand.**
>
> You don't want to be contorting all over the place, or digging in the bottom of bags trying to reach the things you need.
>
> ✔ **Take the phone number of your doctor with you.**
>
> Kids get sick, even when traveling. Don't forget your insurance card, too. You never know when you'll have to pick up medicine on the road.

Some children don't sleep well in an unfamiliar place. Take along a favorite blanket or stuffed animal to make them feel more comfortable. You may also find that you'll have to stay with them until they fall asleep.

See the USA in your Chevy minivan (automobile travel)

No one likes to try to do marathon trips where you drive and don't stop until you've reached where you want to go. Keep these things in mind when traveling by car (and use the checkbox list in Appendix B):

> ✔ **Make regular stops.**
>
> Even when no one needs to pee. Stop for stretching and letting off energy. Your kids will get tired of sitting and want to stop on occasion.

✔ **Clean up.**

Stopping at a roadside park not only means playing tag and going on short walks. This is also a good time to change diapers, wash hands and faces that may have gotten sticky, and clean out your car. Your trip will be much more enjoyable if everyone feels clean and isn't having to fight the trash that's piled up on the floor.

✔ **Exercise caution.**

Play tag or chase only if you're in an area that is away from cars. Don't play in driveways or parking lots, and never let your kids play unsupervised.

No matter what, don't let your young ones out of their car seat while you're driving. It only takes a second to have a car wreck and have your little ones thrown from the car. If your kids get tired of sitting, pull the car over to a McDonald's and let them play on the McPlayground, on the McSlide, and in the McBall cage.

Up, up, and away (airplane travel)

Basically the same rules for car travel apply to airplane travel. The only difference is you can't pull the plane over to a roadside park and let the kids run around. (Use the checkbox list in Appendix B to make sure you're prepared.)

✔ **Pack extra diapers and clothing.**

You never know when you're going to have extended layovers on connecting flights. Don't forget to pack a plastic bag for dirty diapers or dirty clothes. You'll also want to pack an extra set of clothes in case diapers spill over, or the eating process doesn't go so well.

✔ **Be prepared for ear un-plugging.**

Bring something to suck on such as a bottle, pacifier, sucker, or piece of candy (hard candy and gum works well for older children who know how to suck on a piece of hard candy without choking on it). Breastfeeding also works. The hardest part of flying with a child is the takeoff and landing. The air pressure changes hurt those delicate little ears, and they'll not hesitate to let you know.

✔ **Take a car seat when you travel with your toddler.**

Yes, you'll have to pay for the seat your kid occupies, but flight-safety experts will tell you a child is better off in that seat than in your lap. Besides, your toddler will be used to the seat. And since he knows that if he's in the seat he's not allowed to get up and stroll, he'll be less likely to want to get up and walk around the plane.

✔ **Take snacks and beverages with you.**

Your kids may not be happy with the given snack of stale peanuts and a thimble of soda. So it's best if you bring along snacks and beverages that your kids would enjoy.

✔ **Limit your carry-ons.**

Airplanes have a limited amount of space, and just because you have children doesn't mean you are allowed more than your two carry-ons. A purse, diaper bag, overnight case, and stroller are not two carry-ons. The less you have to carry with you, the better off you'll be.

Combine your purse and the diaper bag, check the overnight case at the ticket agent's desk, and check the stroller at the boarding gate. If you let the ticket agent know that you want to check the stroller, the agent will ticket the stroller. Then you can drop it off at the gate as you're about to board the plane. Airport personnel will have it ready for you as you leave the plane (just let them know that you'll need it to get off the plane).

✔ **Don't let your kids walk the aisles.**

The flight attendants have a hard enough job getting all those drinks to everyone. The last thing they need is to try to work around kids bouncing up and down the aisle.

✔ **Reserve a bulkhead seat when flying.**

This area has extra room in front of you, which you may need to juggle kids, bags, food, toys. You get the idea.

Kids up to two years old fly free, but you have to hold them in your lap (and that rule may change soon). Those older than two can sometimes get lower fares, but it depends on where you're flying. Whenever you travel by plane with your child, always call a travel agent and let the agent know that you'll be flying with your child. Every airline is different, and sometimes children's fares are more than the lowest excursion fares. It's too confusing. Just call 'em.

Kids can be great on a plane. The rocking and the low hum of the plane usually put them to sleep.

Warnings: Please observe these flying-safety guidelines

Do not put your children through the X-ray machine.

Do not check your children as luggage.

Do not store your children in the overhead baggage area. They may shift during the flight and fall out when the door is open.

Do not use your children as a flotation device.

Do not tamper with, disable, or destroy the smoke detector in the lavatory.

In case of an emergency, the oxygen mask will fall from the overhead bin. Do not fight with your children as to who gets the oxygen mask first.

Remember that your children must have their own passport when traveling to a foreign country. And call the Center for Disease Control Travelers Hotline (404-332-4559) for information on immunization requirements. You may need immunizations if traveling outside the country.

To make traveling a little more fun for your kids, pack them a new toy or surprise. The newness of the toy will keep them busy through most of the trip (all of the trip if you're lucky). Don't bring any toys that have a lot of small pieces. You'll be spending the rest of your trip trying to find all the parts.

The following *supply list* can also be found in Appendix B. Feel free to make copies of the form: Every time you need to take a trip, go down the list and check off your supplies.

- ✔ diapers
- ✔ baby wipes (or hand wipes if your child is past diapers — get the travel size)
- ✔ spit-up towel
- ✔ bottles and nipples
- ✔ light blanket
- ✔ eating utensils (cups, spoons)
- ✔ plastic bag for dirty diapers or dirty clothes
- ✔ change of clothing
- ✔ beverages (juice, formula, water)

✔ food

✔ entertainment for the kids (books, stuffed animals, crayons, small portable TV with attached Nintendo)

✔ current passport (if traveling outside the United States)

✔ name and phone number of your pediatrician and medical insurance

✔ medications (Baby Tylenol — or similar acetaminophen product — diaper-rash ointment, any other medications your children are taking)

Lovin' those family vacations

When you're traveling with your family and little kids are involved, keep these things in mind (and use the list found in Appendix B):

✔ **Don't over-schedule.**

Vacations are for rest and spending time together. The goal here is not to shove everything possible into one day. You'll all get too tired and cranky if you feel that you're rushing from one place to another. In fact, when we travel as a family, we schedule in periods of *down time* where nothing goes on. It's better that way, and it makes things more relaxed.

✔ **Keep your kids on their schedules.**

Eating and sleeping schedules have to be kept as much as possible. If your kids get over-tired or too hungry, they'll become unpleasant. Very unpleasant.

✔ **Have plenty of free time for goofing off.**

Playing in the pool, going on hikes, building sand castles, or frolicking in the lake is the ultimate in fun for kids. Don't overbook your vacation so that you leave out time to relax, read, and let the kids run around and explore.

✔ **Don't eat too much junk food.**

Snack on some healthy stuff every now and then. You don't want your vacation cut short because someone is puking all the time after having ingested too much of the cotton candy/grape soda combo. Worse yet, you don't want your little ones to get stomach cramps because they haven't eaten vegetables for four days — and now they're constipated.

Do I need to remind you to never let your kids play around water alone? And don't leave an older child in charge of younger ones when it comes to water. Older kids can also get distracted and forget that they have the job of watching their younger siblings.

Food on the road

Consider this nightmare: You're driving down the road on your family vacation and you see a sign that says, "Last stop for the next 50 miles." The last thing you want is to be 20 miles past this stop and have your children announce that they're hungry. For kids, that means they're hungry NOW!

Remember these feeding tips the next time you take a trip (and use the checkbox list in Appendix B):

> ✔ **Have enough supplies.**
>
> Take a bib, baby spoon, juice cup (the kind that has a *closable* spout so juice or milk doesn't leak everywhere).
>
> ✔ **Keep enough food on hand.**
>
> Put dry cereal in plastic bags to add milk to later. Bring small jars of baby food (although you'll have to throw away the extra if you aren't able to refrigerate the leftovers). Have dry finger foods like Cheerios, crackers, and chewy granola bars.
>
> ✔ **Keep plenty of liquids with you.**
>
> For bottle-fed babies, put dry formula in bottles and add water when needed. Avoid using canned formula. You'll end up throwing away the extra formula that you aren't able to immediately use. Try to avoid having a bunch of sweet sodas for your only liquid. Water works the best for quenching thirst, and it's better for you.
>
> ✔ **Keep a bottle of water from home with you.**
>
> It's great for a quick swig, or for adding to formula bottles. Your home water is less likely to upset your child's stomach.
>
> ✔ **Keep a supply of juice.**
>
> You can refill your child's juice cup by keeping a large jug of juice with you, or buy the boxes of juice. Remember, buy the fruit *juice* and not the fruit *drink*. (Fruit drink has added sugar that your child doesn't need).
>
> ✔ **Limit fresh fruit.**
>
> Unless your trip is short and you can store the fruit in a refrigerator or a cooler, avoid taking it with you. It gets hot and mushy (with the exception of apples — but don't drop or step on them).
>
> ✔ **Yum, Restaurants.**
>
> Don't forget the joys of eating out while on vacation.

Read Chapter 15, "Breastfeeding vs. Bottlefeeding," for more information about feeding babies while traveling.

Ask your child what he wants for dinner only if he's buying. — Fran Lebowitz

Children and the Movies

Keep an open mind and realize that you may be going to a movie — but you may not be watching it. Every child is different and doesn't respond to the movies the same way. Some kids, no matter what age, will sit quietly and watch the movie. Some kids won't be able to sit still until they're five or six years old. (And even then they'll have a hard time not announcing, "Oh, this is the part where he dies!")

Now is the time to rediscover those comfy aisle seats in the back. If you have a child who will not be quiet, take him out to the lobby until he quiets down. If he doesn't ever quiet down, leave. Don't sit in the theater with your crying or fussy child. Other people have paid to watch the movie, too. But they didn't pay to sit in a dark room and listen to your little one — even if your kid is adorable.

Your lesson for the day

Always have some sort of entertainment for your kids when you go to eat — no matter what their ages. Even a pad of paper and a few crayons can make your kids happy long enough until the food comes.

Chapter 21

Finding Good Child Care

• •

In This Chapter

▶ Your options for child care

▶ The good and bad news about day care centers

▶ Using private sitters, either in or out of your home

▶ Co-op programs — a new idea in child care

▶ Considering after-school programs

▶ Questions to ask during your child care hunting

▶ Child care referral services

▶ How to start your new day care situation

• •

As a parent, there are two times in your life when you will be scared to death (actually, there'll be tons more times, but for right now just say two). One is when your child starts to drive. But before you even have to deal with the "Dad, can I borrow the car keys" situation, you'll have to decide what kind of child care you'll provide for your children — which can also be a very scary situation.

If you plan to stay home with your child, you have the best possible solution. You can't buy care as good as what you can give. But what if you have to work outside your home? Or even if you want to go out for a romantic evening with your partner? You're back to the child care issue.

(Be sure to look at Appendix C: The important lists given in this chapter are also found in Appendix C — but in easy-to-use forms.)

What Are My Options?

You must promise yourself something: You'll be optimistic about finding someone to take care of your children. A lot of wonderful people and schools have great programs where your children can play, have fun, and become little geniuses. Your job is to avoid all the undesirable and rat-infested schools to find what you *really* need and want. Your first decision concerns what kind of care is best for you and for your particular situation.

Whatever you choose as a means of child care, always consider the location. It's like real estate; everything is *Location! Location! Location!* You want something that is not only close to home, but preferably close to work, or close to whoever will be picking up your child. You don't want to spend a good chunk of your mornings and afternoons driving to and from the child care center. And you want to be close in case your child gets sick or has an accident.

Trust your gut! Even though the person or center you pick out for your child care may have all the qualifications, if you don't *feel* right about this person or place, keep looking. You have to feel good about the person and place where you're going to leave your child.

The Ever-Popular Day Care Center

Your first option for child care is a day care center. These centers are easy to find; they are staffed with teachers; and the day is usually organized with arts, crafts, and music. If you look, you can find one that actually tries to teach the basics like the alphabet, counting, and printing.

The good news

The teachers usually have teaching credits, the environment is bright and clean, your child will have other kids to play with, you have a backup in case your child's teacher is sick, they provide a nice play area, and these centers are usually required to have licenses and are reviewed by the licensing agency to make sure they are following day care standards.

Notice I've said *usually required to have licenses*. Sometimes you may walk into a place and not find this at all. That's why you should get nosy, poke around, and ask a lot of questions. If you find a place that doesn't have a license, turn around and run: These places without a license are not held accountable by anyone to operate safe and sanitary centers.

The bad news

The bad part about day care centers is that parents who feel too obligated to work to think sensibly (and thus keep their sick children home) will send their sick children to school. Yes, this means if you put your children in a day care, they will get sick, harboring the latest strain of flu from their playmates.

You also may have problems finding a day care center that will accept children who haven't yet been potty trained. Or the center may just charge you an extra fee to change diapers.

A third concern with day care centers is that your children may not get a lot of individualized attention if the classes are at full capacity. What is full capacity? It depends on the ages of the children and the square feet available to the center. Call your local Child Welfare Department to find out what your local requirements are.

To keep illnesses and germs spreading from your children to you, give your children a bath as soon as you pick them up from day care. This strategy helps prevent the spread of germs.

Watch to see if day care workers wash their hands — which they should do every time they change a diaper, wipe a nose, or help someone on the potty. Toys should be washed daily, and the staff should be wearing plastic gloves when diapering little bottoms or handling food — which hopefully isn't happening at the same time.

Your friendly corporate day care center

The new movement in day care is the sponsored center, supported by individual companies. If a day care center is the route you're going to take, check to see if your company has one available. These centers are in the same location as the company, so your child simply goes to work with you each day.

Company-sponsored day care is a great idea. Your child can go to work with you, you can visit your little one during the day and even have lunch together, and you're close enough to breastfeed your baby (if they take babies). You may even find, with some research, a center that has more than one corporate sponsor. These centers sometimes accept children from people who aren't employed there.

Private Sitters (is not some Army guy)

The babysitter of old still exists. Maybe you remember getting hired by the neighbors for 25 cents an hour to watch their kids. Heck, maybe you even remember them not paying Social Security taxes on your wages — and that omission keeping them out of politics. It takes all types.

There are two options for private sitters:

- at their home
- at your home

Generally, you have to be very careful with private sitters since they aren't governed by any regulations (unless the sitters apply to be certified child care workers). With no certification they don't have to comply with any cleanliness, health, or safety standards. Most of the questions at the end of this chapter should also apply to private sitters, so be sure to ask before you hire anyone.

Sitting on your children at their home

Keep your eyes open when interviewing a private sitter. Go to the house and look to see if it's clean and tidy. Are there safety locks on cabinets or on electrical plugs? Is there a place for kids to play? In addition to the questions at the end of this chapter, you should ask about the number of kids the private sitter takes care of at one time. Does the sitter ever leave the house with the kids? Does the sitter get a lot of company during the day? Is the sitter certified in CPR and first aid? You may also be concerned if the private sitter doesn't schedule activities for the day. You don't want your little one getting bored.

Private home sitters are usually less expensive than day care centers or having a sitter come to your home. They typically have a small group of children, so your child will get more attention than at day care; and if your child is ill, you can usually still use the sitter (although some sitters will not allow sick children). Some home sitters will allow your schedule to be a little more flexible, as opposed to day cares that require you to pick up your child at a certain time or else pay a humongous fine.

The bad news is that private home sitters may not have a back-up person when they become sick. They also may not be required to be licensed (this varies from state to state), and so there's no way to monitor their work. You also have to be careful that they don't decide to take every December off to take hula lessons in Hawaii. Having a sitter gone for a whole month can really leave you in the lurch.

You want someone whose main concern is taking care of your child. It would be nice if the sitter offered arts and crafts and games similar to that of a day care center. You don't want someone who looks at this work as going about the day as usual with someone's kid hanging around.

Babysitting is one step better than parenthood; you get paid for it and you can quit when you want. — Debra Coppernoll

Sitting on your children in your own home

If you have a private sitter who comes to your home, you can determine what it is you want your children to do all day. If you want them involved in art projects or park outings, you're the one who makes the decisions.

You also don't have to worry about other children making yours sick, or you having to stay home from work with a sick child. If you're really lucky, your sitter may also do some housework. Heck, if you lived in Ancient Greece, you could have just *bought* a sitter — and that would have been that.

The only problem with private sitters is that they're hard to find, they tend to be expensive, and you need a back-up person if they get sick. You also aren't able see how a sitter does during the day since no one is around but the sitter and your kids; a sitter is not required to be licensed; and you also have to keep in mind that this person coming into your home every day will be alone with your children. It would be nice if you could find someone you already knew and trusted. Remember to thoroughly check references, and if the sitters are willing, have them fingerprinted by your local law enforcement agency. It's good to have them on file and also to check that your new nanny isn't Charles Manson's evil sister.

A babysitter is a teenager who comes in to act like an adult while the adults go out and act like teenagers. — Harry Marsh

Prepare your sitter for your children

When you start using a private sitter, you want this sitter to be as much informed about your children's schedule and likes and dislikes as possible. Before your sitter starts, have this person come over and spend time going over the following:

- ✔ the schedule for eating and naps
- ✔ favorite toys and any nicknames for them (example: your child may call her favorite doll "Bud")

✔ food favorites or allergies

✔ fears your children might have (like the vacuum, thunderstorms, big purple dinosaurs that sing to you)

✔ things to do to help calm your children if upset

✔ a list of phone numbers for emergencies

✔ a release form (like the following example) in case of an accident

You can also find this form in Appendix C where you can copy it or cut it out.

_____ has my permission to authorize
fill in the complete name of your sitter

medical treatment to my child(ren) _____ in case
list the names of your child(ren)

of a medical emergency.

Signed,

_____
sign your complete name

The joy of night-out sitters

Your concern for daytime sitters should also carry through for nighttime sitters (for those special dates between you and your loved one, who is hopefully your husband or wife). These sitters should also know CPR and first aid.

If this is the first time a particular sitter is watching your child, have this person come over one hour early. If the sitter is able to spend time with you before you leave, your kid adjusts to having a new person around. Take time going over the following with the sitter:

✔ the evening schedule

✔ the bedtime

✔ household rules (like no jumping on the bed or eating in the living room)

✔ a list of emergency phone numbers and the phone number where you are going to be for the evening

> ✔ any allergies
>
> ✔ a list of *Do's* and *Don'ts*
>
> For example, *do* keep the doors locked, *don't* stay on the telephone all night.

Take any sitters on a tour of the house so they'll know their way around. Clue them in on any quirks your house has (like a door that automatically locks, or what switches will blow the fuse box). Leaving a flashlight on the kitchen counter isn't a bad idea. If the electricity goes out, you don't want both your sitter and your children sitting in the dark screaming. Are you worried yet?

Write out your children's evening schedule for your sitter and make it as detailed as possible. Include favorite foods, what snacks are allowed, what your children like to wear to bed, if your children prefer certain blankets, and if your children like to sleep with certain stuffed animals. (You can find a combination checkbox list of the preceding information for daytime and nighttime sitters in Appendix C.)

Having a sitter can be more fun if you let your kids do extra special things only when you're going out for the evening. Let them build a fort (made out of chairs, blankets, and pillows), eat popcorn, and watch a favorite movie. They might even start to look forward to your evenings out.

Co-op Programs

A co-op program is organized by a group of mothers who all share baby-sitting time. If you have a full-time, 9-to-5 job, this program wouldn't work. But if you work part time, or don't work outside your home, a co-op program is a great way to get a babysitter for lunch dates or just time away to do shopping. Payment is made by your babysitting when other members of your group need a sitter. Hours are logged so that one parent isn't doing all the sitting and another is doing all the shopping. It works out so that everyone gets equal time.

The good idea behind this program is that you have a group of people to go to for sitting needs. Your child will also have the opportunity to play with other children while you're out. But there may be times when you may not be able to find one member of your group who is able to sit for you. A co-op group can be an unreliable source at times.

When you first meet with your co-op group, go over all the rules, and especially cover situations such as sick children.

After-School Programs

Many day care centers, private sitters, and even some public schools offer after-school programs. These programs are for school-age children who need some place to go after school until their parents can pick them up.

You need to ask the same questions for after-school programs as you do for your children who will need a caregiver all day. In addition to these questions, you need to find out the following:

✔ if their afternoon is organized

✔ if there is a scheduled time for kids to do their homework

✔ if kids get an afternoon snack or are expected to bring their own

✔ what the arrangements are for transporting the children from their school to the after-school program (if it's at a different location)

✔ how the kids are released to their parents

Child Care Hunting Guidelines

You must be aggressive when hunting for child care. Don't be shy or timid; don't hesitate to ask questions and poke your nose around where it probably doesn't belong. Be bold and brave. You're making a very important decision and you have every right to act like an overprotective parent — maybe even on the paranoid side.

Keep your eyes open

There are two main things to look for when you tour a child care facility with the intention of placing a child: the physical environment and the nature of the child/adult interaction.

The physical environment

The room your child will be spending most of his time in should be clean and safe, but not necessarily too neat and tidy. After all, it is a room filled with kids. Look at the toys and equipment (such as tables and chairs). Are they appropriate to your child's age? And are they in good condition? Does the artwork on the walls look like the teacher did it with some help from the kids, or is the art the product of a child who was allowed to be creative on his own?

Try to see this room from your child's point of view. Are the toys, pictures, and working material at your child's level? Now look at the room for safety. Are the room dividers (if there are any) low enough so that a teacher can see what's going on in all areas? You may find that new buildings are designed with lots of windows, low walls, and open spaces; some may even have video monitors to protect children from abuse (not that a video monitor can jump out and protect a child, but you know what is meant here).

The child/adult interaction

Now you need to look at what's *happening* in the room. Do the children seem happy, healthy, and involved in activities? Remember, this is a room full of kids. Sooner or later an argument or accident is likely to occur. That's to be expected. You need to watch to see how the caregiver handles the situation. Ideally, the caregiver will stay calm and step in to help the kids solve their own problem.

Hopefully you'll find a staff that looks happy and is enjoying their work with the kids. You don't want to see caregivers who look like they're on the point of a nervous breakdown, or someone who doesn't seem in control of his or her class. You also want a teacher who practices the same communication skills found in Chapter 2 — someone who physically gets down on your child's level, gives direct commands . . . you know, because you've already read Chapter 2, right?

Questions? Questions? Questions?

Go hunting for child care equipped with questions to ask. Write these questions down and document the answers. When you've researched all the places and people who are possible candidates, sit down and go over the answers. With a written record, you won't have to try to remember which person said what and who promised this or that. After all, you're not as young as you used to be, and memory is the first to go. In the back of the book, in Appendix C, you'll find these questions in a form that you can copy to take with you during your child care hunting.

Ask these questions

These are questions that you should ask any person you are considering for child care:

May I have some names and phone numbers of parents who currently have their children attending here (or of parents whose children you have cared for in the past)?

Ask for a list of parents you can call as a referral. If you can't get this list (because some people may not want their phone numbers given out to strangers), stop parents and ask them how they like the facility or the teachers. The best time to do this is during afternoon pick-up time when parents are a tad less hurried.

Do you allow visitation during the day?

Avoid places that are hesitant for parents to pay surprise visits or do not allow visitation during the day. It's your right to stop in and inspect their work and to see your child if you want. After all, it is *your* child.

What kind of snack or lunch program do you offer?

Avoid places that only serve sugary or nonnutritious foods. You don't want your child eating junk all day, and you don't want to take home a child who is on a sugar high. (It wouldn't be so bad if they made tiny straightjackets, but they don't.)

May I see the play areas?

Play areas should be well-lighted and well-supervised. The area underneath climbing structures (like slides, jungle gyms) should be covered with a cushion-type material such as bark chips, sand, or rubber. This covering minimizes injuries should your child fall off one of these *toys*. Outside areas should have a fence so little ones can't walk off — and big mean bad boogie-persons (the politically correct term) can't walk in and snatch someone.

What is the procedure for releasing the children at the end of the day?

You want a system where there is a sign in/sign out ritual. No place should be so relaxed that anyone is able to walk in and take a child without someone seeing what's happening. It would also be nice to have a place with a prerelease form on your child's application (a form listing the people allowed to pick up your child, such as grandma, aunt, neighbor, and so on). That way if someone's name is not on the list, this person won't be allowed to pick up your child.

What are the rules regarding sick children?

You want to hear something about the school or caregiver separating the sick child from the other kids once they realize that someone is sick. They should also have a policy on sending home a sick child whose temperature reaches a certain point. This may be anywhere from 99 degrees to 101 degrees.

Do you give out medications? What is your policy?

Schools and private caregivers, like most places, are afraid of legal problems, so some facilities will not give out medications. Others will with written release forms and well-written directions. You can count on your child getting sick and needing to take medication, so these answers should mean a lot to you. If the facility or caregiver will not give out medications, do you work close enough so that you can leave work to give your child medicine during the day (and is this something you want to do)?

What will you do if my child gets injured?

Injuries can mean anything from a bump on the head to a broken arm. Most places will handle minor injuries because kids have them a lot, especially if they're playing with other kids. If it's important for you to learn of every bump and bruise, you may want it put in your file that you are to be called *anytime* your child gets hurt.

If your caregiver calls only for an emergency, what constitutes an emergency?

Is anything involving blood an emergency, or just accidents involving broken bones? For your own comfort, you need to have defined for you what this center considers an emergency situation.

What are your fees?

Be prepared for heart failure here. Child care, in general, is expensive. The younger your child, the higher the cost. This is because more staff is needed to care for younger children (their child/teacher ratio has to be lower than that with older children). Ask if the fee includes any meals or snacks. And ask if there are additional costs such as diapering fees.

Do you have a late pick-up charge?

Some of the day care chains have a late pick-up charge that can be anything from a flat fee to $1.00 per minute that you're late. These people want to go home when it's time. They also have these charges so parents won't get the idea that being 10 to 15 minutes late every day is acceptable.

What is your teacher-to-child ratio?

You're basically asking how many kids each teacher is responsible for handling. Every state has a different requirement. You can call your local Health and Welfare Department or Child Welfare Department to find out what your state and city requirements are. You want to know this because if the state says that a child care facility can't have more than 10 two-year-olds to one teacher, you don't want your two-year-old with a teacher who has 20 to look after. These laws also apply to registered private sitters.

What are your teacher qualifications?

You want a child care facility that requires its teachers to have credits in child care classes. These classes include CPR, first aid, and child-development. Private sitters should also be certified in CPR and first aid.

What is the turnover rate of your teachers?

Finding a center that has a low turnover rate of teachers is good for your child: You don't want your kid never to be able to develop a relationship with a teacher because the teachers are always leaving. A high turnover rate also reveals a problem at a center where it can't seem to keep teachers employed.

Do you do background checks on your employees?

It is unfortunate that you have to ask this, but do you want a convicted child molester caring for your children? If that thought doesn't worry you, don't bother asking this question.

How do you discipline children?

If the response is "We beat first, ask questions later," you may want to look elsewhere. It's good for you to know how your caregiver handles discipline problems — if anything so that you can use the same language and discipline style at home. Day cares are usually pretty good about discipline. They rarely fall into the bad habit of saying, "I'm going to give you until the count of three before I act like I may start to do something." They give one warning, and then they act.

On the other hand, you don't want to keep your child someplace that doesn't discipline at all. You'll have a lot of work on your hands if your child is with someone most of the day who lets him get away with anything he sees fit to do.

You also want to find out how teachers reward good behavior. They may give out stickers or candy; or the teachers may simply allow special privileges. This reward system may be important to you if your child is diabetic and can't have candy, or if you hate stickers because your younger child always finds them and eats them.

What kind of communication will I have with my child's caregiver?

You should receive some type of information about what your child is doing during the day and any behavioral problems that occur.

How well does my child have to be potty trained?

This question is for the facility or private sitter who will only take potty-trained children. Your child may have accidents up until the age of four or five. You need to know if they will handle accidents and how well they will clean them up afterward. You don't want to bring your child home and find pants full of poop. You also don't want your child with someone who believes the old school of thought that a child should be potty trained by one year old — and will shame your child every time there is an accident.

What kind of payment schedule do you have? Do you allow time off for vacations?

Some facilities make you pay whether you're there or not. Others will allow you time off during the year for vacation. Each facility handles this situation differently, but you need to know if you're going to have to pay for time even if you're not going to be there. Facilities reason that you're paying to reserve the space for your child, because they're only allowed so many students per teacher.

What is your daily curriculum for the children?

You want to know if the school has the day scheduled with organized activities or if it's a free-for-all during the day. Your child doesn't necessarily need to be put in a preschool environment and forced to learn the *ABC*s at six months old. In fact, forced learning in itself can be very detrimental to very young children. But children do need organization during their day. Take the time to discuss the center's educational goals and philosophies with the teachers and the director. You want someone whose goals are the same as yours.

Do you have a nap time during the day? What is your policy on children who no longer take naps?

Your child may not be a napper, but the facility you choose may require all children to at least lie down to rest. You want to find out so that when or if your child comes home to complain about having to lie down, you can talk about just *resting*. You can explain that there are nap times so the other kids can rest. Actually, it's so the teachers can rest so they can finish the rest of the day without choking anyone.

Can I see your last licensing report?

This document gives you an idea of how well the center measures up to state requirements. You can also call the licensing agency and ask if a particular center has been cited for any violations.

Do you have NAEYC accreditation?

NAEYC stands for National Association for the Education of Young Children. It's is a private association whose accreditation goes beyond the state level. Its inspectors look at a variety of criteria ranging from child/teacher ratios, to developmentally appropriate teaching practices and multicultural curriculum. Basically, if a facility has this accreditation, it's looking mighty good.

Ask your day care provider if it offers alternate activities for children who are not nappers, such as a quiet reading time, painting, puzzles, and so on.

Child Care Referral Services

If you can't seem to find a private sitter who is close to you, call your local Health and Welfare Department for the number of your area child care referral service.

This service provides names and phone numbers of sitters who have been accepted into its program as certified sitters. In order to qualify to be a sitter for the Health and Welfare Department, candidates must complete an application showing current certification of CPR and first aid; they also must list their procedures of discipline, food for snacks and lunches, daily schedules, and any activities.

This service can recommend people close to either your work or home but can't guarantee the type of care that your child will receive. This is where you would want to do your research by talking to other parents, viewing for yourself what the home or facility looks like, and making a few surprise visits to see what happens during the day.

Starting Your New Child Care

You never know how your child is going to act on the first day of day care. Your child may see all those toys and other kids his age and forget you ever existed. Or, what will most likely happen is that your little one will want to go exploring — but with you close by.

If this is the first time you're leaving your child with a sitter or at a day care, make the transition gradually. You don't ever want to just go in, drop your child off, and then leave. This would be hard not only for your child, but also for the people who are responsible for taking care of your child.

Try this process of easing into a new day care situation:

Day 1: Go with your child for the morning and have lunch with him. This will give you both an opportunity to see how lunch is handled. After lunch, you both can go home for the day.

Day 2: Go with your child for a few hours. Sit back and watch, and encourage him to go and play without you. Having you there within eyesight will make your child more comfortable with the whole situation. After a couple of hours, leave for a while. Come back and get your child later. Make sure you let your child know that you're leaving and that you'll be back soon. Never sneak out. That's mean!

Day 3: Go with your child for a few hours, kiss him good-bye, let him know you'll be back later, and then leave. Come back at the end of the day.

Day 4: Go with your child for a few minutes. Make sure he is settled in. Then kiss him good-bye, let him know that you'll be back later for him, and leave.

The idea behind this strategy is that you gradually make your exit. To drop your child off to a new place without him warming up to the idea will be harder on him (and perhaps you too) than if you both wean yourselves from each other.

You don't have to follow this schedule exactly. You can make up your own schedule of how you take the time to gradually wean yourself from your child.

Give your child a few pictures of your family to take to the facility. Being able to look at these throughout the day will be comforting for your child.

Here are a few other guidelines to make leaving your child at a sitter or day care a little easier on you both. (Use the checkbox list in Appendix C to be sure you follow these guidelines.)

✔ **Don't rush in the mornings.**

Kids hate to be rushed and don't handle it well at all. Give yourself plenty of time to get ready at home — even if it means getting your child up a few minutes early so that he can lollygag around. And spend a few minutes getting your child settled in at the day care. Never rush in, drop your child off, and rush out.

✔ **Spend some time together in the morning.**

When our oldest son was in day care, I would take our breakfast to his room at his day care and we would share it together. This gave him a chance to be comfortable with the situation, and we had our own time together. This doesn't have to be a major chunk of time. Allow yourself an additional 15 to 20 minutes. By the time your breakfast is over, your child will be happy to see you leave.

✔ **Never sneak out while your child is doing something else.**

Let your child know that you're leaving and that you'll be back at 5:00 (or whenever). You'll turn any kid into a clingy child who will be afraid to let you out of sight if you're always disappearing.

✔ **Make your good-byes quick and to the point.**

Some children never seem to get over the separation, no matter how much time you devote to making them feel comfortable. When you do decide to leave, kiss your child good-bye and *leave*. Don't hang around and go into long explanations as to why you have to leave — just leave. You can't reason with a mad or upset child, so simply go. It's rare that any child will cry all day; they usually get over it pretty quickly. Once you finally do go, your day care worker or sitter can help your child to get involved in something else that will take his mind off your departure.

✔ **Don't scold a child who cries because you're leaving.**

Being upset is a natural response when a parent is leaving. It's unrealistic to ask your child not to be sad and to instantly stop crying. Just let him know that you love him, you're sorry that he's upset, you'll be back, and then leave.

✔ **Don't be too hard on yourself.**

Children aren't the only ones who shed tears on the first day of a new child care situation. Parents shed a few themselves. Try to hold back these tears until you can hide in the safety of your car. Your child doesn't need to get the impression that the place where he is staying is a bad or sad place.

✔ **Don't be upset if your child isn't as *tidy* as when you left.**

Go ahead and be upset if you pick up your child and there's snot smeared all over that once clean face. In fact, you should talk to the director or teacher about this. But if your child's clothes are on backwards, he may have been practicing his independent self-help skills. If your child has red paint in his hair, clay in his pockets, and playdough under his fingernails, chances are good your little one had a great day.

Read the book *The Berenstain Bears and The Sitter* by Stan and Jan Berenstain (Random House) to your kids. It's a great book to get them accustomed to the idea of a sitter.

Your lesson for the day

Communication between you and your child care provider is very important. Just as you want to be told about school events, your child care provider needs to know about the things going on in your home. For example, if your child was up all night and unable to sleep, your child care provider needs to know. This way he or she can adjust for your child's moods or tiredness during the day.

Chapter 22
Going to the Doctor

. . . .

In This Chapter

▶ Looking for a doctor

▶ What to look for in a pharmacy

▶ Homeopathy

▶ The relationship between your child and your doctor

▶ When you should take your kids to the doctor

▶ Hearing and vision checkups

▶ Going to the dentist

. . . .

1 hate going to the doctor. I hate waiting in the lobby just so that I can go into a very small room that's either too hot or too cold. There I will be greeted with magazines that are older than I am, and I wait some more. Then, just when I've almost forgotten why I even came, the doctor arrives asking, "So, how are you today?" Is this the time when the doctor really wants to know, or is this the time when I politely say, "Fine" all the while thinking, "Of course I'm fine. I just like to come see you so that you can stick that piece of wood down my throat and make me gag."

This is a really *bad attitude,* and it shouldn't be passed on to kids. It's up to us as parents to let our children know that doctors (or any medical person) are for help — and that no matter how much they poke, prod, and stick, they're going to *try* to make you feel better.

(Use the convenient forms in Appendix D for many of the lists found in this chapter.)

Finding the Right Doctor

Before you even have your baby, you should be out interviewing and researching doctors (and their staff) for your child. You can choose either a family practitioner or a pediatrician, who is medical professional specializing in children's medicine.

A doctor is going to examine your baby the day you deliver. It's best if you can select your doctor for this first checkup so that he or she can get to know your baby and continue on with your child's care.

The best way to find a doctor is by referral from a friend, a relative, or your obstetrician. Start asking around *before* you know you're going to need a doctor. You want to have plenty of time to do your research.

When someone does refer someone to you, ask these questions (and use the form in Appendix D to write down the answers):

✔ What do you like about this doctor?

✔ What do you dislike about this doctor?

✔ Does this doctor seem open to your questions?

✔ Is this doctor kind and gentle to your children?

✔ Do your children like this doctor?

✔ Does this doctor take the time to listen to your concerns and discuss problems with you?

✔ Does this doctor have experience with mothers who have successfully breastfed?

✔ Does this doctor share your points of view on nutrition, starting babies on solids, weaning, and so on?

If this referral business doesn't work, it's time to get out the phone book. Start with those doctors who are located close to you. The less travel time the better.

Call and do some research over the telephone first. You want to spend a few minutes talking to the receptionist or nursing staff because you'll be working with them also. If they seem unfriendly or uncooperative, take that into consideration. Do you want to hear that kind of attitude over the phone every time you call them?

You can call the national office of the American Academy of Pediatrics for names of doctors who are certified by the American Board of Pediatrics (800-662-2797).

Plenty of questions to pose

Here are some questions you can ask the doctor's office staff. (Use the form in Appendix D to write down their answers so that you can compare them later.)

What are your open hours?

Do they have extended hours so that you can get to them in the evening after work or on Saturdays for minor emergencies? Kids can be pretty inconsiderate at times and get sick on the weekends, too. And there's the curse of the *midnight boogers*, which may require some late-night professional nose cleaning.

Midnight boogers are when your baby gets a stuffy nose and has difficulty breathing (because babies insist on breathing through their noses, even if they're stuffy). The only way to help the breathing is to clean out the nose.

How do you handle follow-up visits?

Kids get a variety of illnesses that require follow-up visits to make sure they are over their sickness. Find out what the procedures are for follow-up visits and if you're required to pay full price for the visit.

Do you have bench checks?

Look for a doctor who has what some refer to as *bench checks*. Bench checks don't require an appointment. You come in when your child is finished with the recommended dose of medicine and the doctor will quickly check out the medical problem to see if it has improved. Typically these bench checks are less expensive than normal checkups. Doctors do this to encourage parents to bring their kids back without having to worry about paying full price — which, as you may be well aware, can be quite pricey.

How do I pay?

Do you have to pay first, or will they bill your insurance company for you?

Ear infections demand bench checks

Ear infections are a common situation where your doctor will prescribe medicine and then want to see your child again when the medicine is finished. Many times these ear infections don't go away after the first dosage of medicine, so it's important to always have a follow-up visit.

What do I do in case of an emergency?

Is the doctor on call at night in case of an emergency?

Do you have additional doctors?

Does this doctor share office space with other doctors? If so, do you have the choice of only seeing one doctor, or do they do a rotation with the patients? If your child is rotated among other doctors, it's harder to develop a doctor/patient relationship. On the other hand, if there is more than one doctor, chances are good that you will be able to come in to see someone at the last minute.

Do you have backup doctors?

It's unrealistic to think that all doctors can be on call 24 hours a day, seven days a week. They need rest, too. It's important that they have a backup doctor in case of emergencies. It would also be nice if you and your child had a chance to meet this doctor. If you ever do need a backup doctor, it would be nice to go to a familiar face.

How is your waiting room arranged?

Some doctors' offices are large enough to have an area for healthy kids who are there for general checkups (or just tagging along with Mom or Dad), and then another special place for sick kids. Kids spread germs mainly by their hands. Those toys found around the doctors office are coughed on, sneezed on, and spit up on. If your kids are healthy now, they won't be after playing with those toys. It's nice to find a place that either separates the healthy and ill children, or has separate hours for the healthy children so they aren't around the ill children.

A family is a unit composed not only of children but of men, women, an occasional animal, and the common cold. — Ogden Nash

The ask-the-doctor interview

When you've found a doctor's office whose staff has answered the questions to your satisfaction (and they were nice doing it), make an appointment to meet with the doctor. Let the receptionist know that this meeting is just for you to meet the doctor and to ask some questions. Again, you want someone who is open and willing to be interviewed. If the receptionist says something to the effect that the doctor doesn't do this (but the receptionist is happy to answer the questions!), continue your search. You want someone who is going to respect your need to do research.

Once you meet with the doctor, you may want to bypass the questions about education and passing the medical board. After all, if the doctor graduated from Upper Thoracic State medical college, would that mean anything to you?

You want to ask questions about the things that concern you or about the doctor's thoughts on treating kids and dealing with illnesses. If you're a new mother, you can find out how your potential doctor feels about breastfeeding, nutrition, and so on.

Be perceptive to how the doctor handles your questions. Does the doctor take time to listen to you? Does the doctor seem understanding? These practices are important to your patient/doctor relationship. You don't want someone who doesn't seem to ever have time for you, or doesn't listen to you.

You want a doctor whose goal is not only to make your kids feel better, but also to educate you to continue the doctoring role at home. Your doctor should want to share information about your child's symptoms, illnesses, and any preventive care that you can do. Once you learn more about how to help your children, you'll be able to do more for your children at home and (hopefully) see the doctor less.

- ✔ Not everything can be perfect. You may find a doctor who has a marvelous personality but isn't thorough. Personally, I'd rather have a doctor who is thorough — yet has the personality of a vending machine.

- ✔ Don't forget your gut! You may find a doctor who seems to have all the right answers, the staff is nice, the facility is clean and close by — but you just don't feel right about the situation. Don't stop looking. You have to like and get along with your doctor, as do your children. If there's something about a doctor that bugs you, don't feel bad about continuing your search.

Call your local state medical board to find out if any doctor you're considering has been accused or disciplined for any offenses.

Don't forget the pharmacy

Almost as important as the doctor is the location of the pharmacy that you'll be using. Keep these things in mind (and use the form in Appendix D to write the information down):

Location: A pharmacy in the same building as your doctor's office is ideal. Anything that doesn't require taking kids in and out of car seats works great.

A drive-up pharmacy: These are rare, but wonderful. You don't have to leave your car; thus none of the car-seat thing again.

Hours open: Ideally, a 24-hour pharmacy is best. It does happen that your teething toddler wakes up at 2:00 a.m. screaming . . . and you're out of Baby Tylenol or Orajel.

Computer records: Many pharmacies now have all their prescriptions on computers that keep track of the medications your child has taken and what your child currently is on. This safety measure is designed to keep your child from receiving two different medications that may be harmful if taken together.

Medicine summary for the prescription: The medicine summary describes what the medicine is for and any possible side effects.

> ✔ Outside the United States, most English-speaking countries refer to a pharmacy as the *chemist*. Better still is the term *apothecary*, which you can use instead of pharmacy to sound snooty.

The Alternative Choice of Homeopathy

When your child gets an ear infection, a medical doctor will look at his ears and then prescribe a medicine to get rid of the infection. This doctor won't try to fix what caused the infection in the first place.

When you take your child to a homeopathic doctor, he or she will look at your child's body to figure out what the body is reacting to that produced the ear infection. This doctor then gives a remedy that will work to help your child's body to heal itself. Thus, no chemicals.

Homeopathy . . . cures a larger percentage of cases than any method of treatment and is beyond all doubt safer and more economical and the most complete medical science. — Mahatma Gandhi

Then again, Gandhi was supposedly obsessed with his bowel movements.

How homeopathy works

A homeopathic doctor's job is to educate you to the point where he works himself out of a job. (If only lawyers worked that way.) The more you know about the things that make you sick, the more you can do to prevent yourself, and your children, from becoming ill.

Homeopathic doctors treat the whole person, not just the infection, by learning about you and your relationship to food, hygiene, your environment, your health education — and a host of other topics.

Once they've discovered your background, they then prescribe a *remedy* that will strengthen your body so that it can heal itself. They use natural ingredients that are free of toxins.

Homeopathic medicine has been around for 200 years. It's less expensive than going to a doctor every time your child has a runny nose and fever. You can also keep the remedies at home and use them for prevention measures. That way, a runny nose and fever don't turn into a bad ear infection.

General stuff to know

Homeopathic medicine is not a group of wackos who sit around lighting candles, humming chants, and sticking pins into little dolls (although if you are someone who does this, I deeply respect your decision to do so). It is an honest-to-goodness science that works.

- ✔ We use both a doctor and a homeopathic doctor. We go to the doctor for the well-baby checkups, immunizations, and for sewing up deep cuts. We take our kids to the homeopathic doctor when they get sick.
- ✔ A 1990 estimate revealed that 2.5 million Americans use homeopathy, and 4.8 million visits are made each year to homeopathic doctors.
- ✔ Homeopathic remedies are available in most of the 43 national drugstore chains, including Kmart, Payless, Thrifty, and Walgreen's.
- ✔ Homeopathic doctors are also used for behavioral problems.
- ✔ Blue Cross of Washington and Alaska are trying a special program by offering insurance coverage of a group of homeopathic physicians in the Seattle area. If this program is successful, Blue Cross will expand its services.
- ✔ No, we don't own any Blue Cross stock.

The Child/Doctor Relationship

Your child looks to you to see how you behave in situations. So it's up to you to set a good example. The example you want to set is that you think the doctor is a good person even though he or she may do things that hurt or are uncomfortable (like shots, sticking cold things on your chest, flashing lights in your eyes). It's all for a good purpose.

Keep these rules in mind when going to the doctor (and check them off with the form in Appendix D to be sure you follow them):

- ✔ **Do be happy and relaxed.** If you're relaxed and comfortable, your child will be more relaxed.

- ✔ **Do greet the doctor cheerfully.** This lets your child know that the doctor is a person you like and are happy to see.

- ✔ **Do use the doctor's name.** People seem more like friends when you address them by name. This practice also teaches your child the name of the doctor.

- ✔ **Do thank the doctor after the examination.** This strategy again reinforces to your child the fact that the doctor is someone who is here to help.

- ✔ **Don't use going to the doctor as a threat against your child.** Avoid saying, "If you aren't good, I'll take you to the doctor for a shot." The next time your child does have to go to the doctor, the kid's going to feel in trouble for something and be worried the whole time about getting a shot.

- ✔ **Don't tell your child that something is going to hurt, or that it won't hurt if you really know that it will.** The best thing to do is keep quiet and let your child decide if it hurts or not.

Sit down with your child and read *The Berenstain Bears Go to the Doctor* by Stan and Jan Berenstain (Random House).

When to Go to the Doctor

The first few months of your new baby's life, you're going to feel that you're living at the doctor's office. Don't worry! The older your child gets, the less you'll have to go in for shots and well-child exams (these are general checkups to make sure your child is developing well). The following checkup list gives you an idea of when you'll be toting your little one off to the doctor, and for what reasons. The types of shots your child will receive are not listed here for a purpose. These shot schedules do change, and I'd hate to have to keep updating this book every time a new shot came out.

Appendix D has this same schedule for you to clip out and stick to your refrigerator (more refrigerator art) so you won't be guessing about when to take your child to the doctor.

Going to the Doctor

Age	Checkup
1 week	exam
2 weeks	exam and shots
2 months	exam and shots
4 months	exam and shots
6 months	exam and shots
9 months	exam and shots
12 months	exam
15 months	exam and shots
18 months	exam
2 years	exam
3 years	exam
5 years (or right before starting school)	exam and shots
every 2–3 years afterward	general exams
12 years	exams and shots
15 years	exams and shots

This shot schedule isn't chiseled in stone. Some doctors give you an option for giving your child shots at a different time. There are also parents who choose not to give their kids these shots.

- ✔ Your doctor may want to see your newborn more often than this chart shows, depending on your child's health.

- ✔ Don't overlook those times when your child gets sick. And never take cranky behavior, low fevers, or any other unusual behavior too lightly because it may mean that an illness is developing or an infection is brewing somewhere.

- ✔ Call your doctor or set an appointment for your child with a fever of 101° or more, or a low fever lasting for more that 24 hours. Also, read Chapter 23 for a list of signs of illnesses. Several things can indicate that your child is getting sick.

Hearing and Vision Problems (beyond the usual way they ignore you)

As you take your child to regular doctor visits, they'll check hearing, vision, and the development of your child's teeth. For the hearing and vision, these simple checkups are usually enough. Schools also offer additional hearing tests if you feel your child is developing a real hearing problem — other than the general ignoring when you announce it's time for bed.

Taking care of your child's vision is an important part of preventative health care. Your baby's eyes will be examined in the newborn nursery at the hospital, and by a doctor during the six-month well-baby visit. You need to make an appointment for your child with an ophthalmologist for the next visit, which should be between the ages of three and four, and then every year following that.

No matter what the age of your child, make an appointment with your doctor if any of the following happens (and use the checkbox list in Appendix D):

- Your child squints or rubs the eyes a lot (other than when tired).
- Your child's eyes move quickly either up or down or from side to side.
- Your child's eyes are watery, sensitive to light, or look different from the way they normally do.
- The pupil of the eye has white, grayish-white, or yellow-colored material in it.
- The eyes stay red for several days.
- Your child's eyelids droop, or the eyes look like they bulge.
- Pus or crust in either eye doesn't go away.

Starting a Good Dental Hygiene Program (happy teeth for kids)

Your dental program for your kids starts when they are babies. Their gums have to be kept clean as those sharp, little teeth start developing. You want them to have strong, healthy teeth so they can bite really hard when you foolishly stick your finger in their mouths to see how many new teeth they have.

To help them grow these really nice sharp teeth, they'll need a diet full of fruits and vegetables, dairy products, lean meat like fish and chicken, and starches like bread and potatoes. Any food that's high in calcium is good. Potato chips, fruit rolls, and ice cream do not exactly fall in these food groups.

In addition to a good diet, your children will need their teeth cleaned daily, fluoride (which they may get in their water), and regular visits to their dentist to make sure everything is going OK. (Be sure you can check all the boxes in the form found in Appendix D.)

✔ **Your children's teeth should be cleaned daily.**

Preferably twice a day. Clean a baby's gums with a wet washcloth. Use a baby washcloth and not one of your extra fluffy, extra absorbent Cannon cloths. You'll gag your kids and make them hate what you're doing even more than they're going to hate it anyway.

✔ **Flossing is important and should be done as soon as your children's teeth start touching, which will be their back molars first.**

You'll have to floss your children's teeth for them until they're about seven or eight years old. Once they start doing it themselves, be sure to supervise their flossing.

✔ **Give your kids, including your baby, water to drink.**

It's a great way to clean out their mouths. Babies will make an awful face when you first give them water but they'll learn to like it.

✔ **As soon as your children develop teeth, use children's toothbrushes and very gently brush their teeth.**

Be careful not to brush too hard around their gum area. Brushing too hard will push their gums back and damage their teeth.

✔ **Use just a tiny amount of toothpaste (like baby pinky fingernail size) when brushing your children's teeth.**

If the normal toothpaste is too strong for them, you can pick from a variety of children's toothpastes, or you can go to a health food store and buy toothpaste that is milder and doesn't contain artificial sweeteners. Make sure the toothpaste is ADA (American Dental Association) approved.

✔ **You'll still need to brush teeth until your children are seven or eight years old.**

Most kids have a hard time learning the up and down brushing motion that we use to clean the tops of our teeth near our gums. You may want to help them out only one or two days a week by the time they reach five or six, but always inspect their teeth after brushing and send them back for a second try if you see food stuck up around their gums.

> ✔ **Don't forget to brush the tongue (gag, gag, gag) and the roof of the mouth.**

Your kids should brush their teeth for about two minutes (and so should you!). Two minutes is an eternity for kids, so use an egg timer, play a song that's about two minutes long, or have your kids hum their favorite song several times.

When to go to the dentist

You can try to take your child to the dentist as early as two years old. Some children may be happy to sit in the dentist's chair and gladly open their mouths while some stranger with gloves on sticks his hands in. Some kids may not be able to handle this experience until much later. If you have a concern about your children's teeth, don't wait. If your children start to develop brown spots or places where it looks like the teeth are beginning to rot, if their gums are swollen or bleed during brushing, or if their gums or teeth hurt, make an appointment right away.

It's very important that you develop a relationship with a dentist and get on a regular, every-six-month check-up. Be warned, if you make an appointment for your children, the dentist will eventually lure you in, too.

> ✔ There are a small number of dentists who are pediatric dentists. They specialize in child development as well as in psychological and behavior management techniques.
>
> ✔ Shop around for dentists just as you would do for a doctor.
>
> ✔ You want to visit your dentist as soon as possible in order to determine if your children are getting enough fluoride. Some places (like where we live) don't have fluoride in the water, so you'll have to give vitamin supplements with fluoride in it.

Baby teeth come in pairs. Your child's gums will be sore during the whole teething process.

What's a dentist, and does it hurt?

Read the beginning of this chapter under "The Child/Doctor Relationship." It talks about the relationship you need to develop with your doctor. You also need to develop this same kind of open, trusting relationship with your dentist, too. Your children need to know that a dentist is someone who looks at their teeth to make sure they're healthy, strong, and are growing well. (Use the checkbox list in Appendix D.)

✔ **Do allow your children to go back to the dental chair by themselves.**

This is one more step in their independence, and they're more likely to do better without you hanging around. Besides, there's not that much space in those rooms, and you truly aren't needed. However, if this is a first visit for a young child, the dentist may allow you to go back until your child feels comfortable with the situation.

✔ **Do always thank the dentist after the appointment is finished.**

✔ **Do check out books on going to the dentist.**

Find one that has pictures of things your children may see in the dental office.

✔ **Don't use going to the dentist as a type of threat.**

✔ **Don't talk about any possible pain or anything hurting.**

It may not have even occurred to your children that there could be any pain. Leave the subject alone.

It's time to read again. *The Berenstain Bears Visit the Dentist* by Stan and Jan Berenstain (Random House) shows pictures of dental equipment that your child will see while in the dentist's office.

Your lesson for the day

You have a choice as to what medical professional you choose for your children, whether it be a doctor, homeopathic doctor, optometrist, or dentist. Take the time to do research and interview these people. You want someone who will always be there as your children grow.

Chapter 23
Health and Hygiene

*H*ygiene is something you must work at to maintain (as well as remember how to spell). It's the art of keeping yourself and your kids healthy by avoiding the things that make you sick. It requires effort and common sense, both of which seem to be lacking when it comes to a kid's regular mode of operation. This chapter is dedicated to the things that can make your children sick (other than eating *all* the jelly beans from the jumbo pack in one sitting).

The Nasty Elements (Sun, Heat, and Cold)

The sun, heat, and cold are harmful elements if you don't correctly prepare for them. Your children have very delicate skin, and those elements affect them more than they would you — someone whose skin has aged and been weathered, kind of like a really comfortable saddle. Ahem. But I digress.

Our Mr. Sun

If it's a nice, sunny day, your kids are going to want to be outside. And they should. The sun is a great source of vitamin D. But like most things in life, the sun is good only in moderation. Take these precautions when your kids are outside (and use the checkbox list in Appendix E):

✔ **Use sunscreen on your children anytime they're going to be in the sun (except for babies under six months old).**

This also means winter sun. Use a sunscreen with SPF 30 or higher, one that says it is waterproof and hypoallergenic, or non-irritating. These types won't have heavy perfumes in them and will be more gentle for delicate skin. Besides, you don't want the family dog hovered over your children licking off all the sunscreen because it smells like a coconut pie.

✔ **Apply sunscreen on all body parts that are exposed to the sun.**

This includes ears, behind the ears, noses, backs of hands, and the backs of necks. You will also want a lip balm with sunscreen so that your little ones don't get burnt or chapped lips from the sun and wind.

✔ **Lubricate your children with the sunscreen liberally.**

Really smear it on good. But don't apply sunscreen near the eyes — it can be very irritating. Also, don't use sunscreen on babies younger than six months old.

✔ **Read the directions on your sunscreen.**

You'll find that you'll have to re-apply it often. One slathering is never enough.

✔ **Don't let your children go out into the sun between the hours of 10:00 a.m. and 3:00 p.m.**

This is the time of day when the sun is the strongest. It's hottest during this time, and the sun can do more damage to delicate child skin.

✔ **Keep a hat on your children if they're going to be in the sun.**

A hat not only protects their skin from the sun, but it also will keep their heads cooler, which will help them avoid sunstroke. And a hat can be very fashionable.

The sun will burn a child's skin from reflective surfaces. This means water and snow. And a common mistake by parents is forgetting that the sun can be harmful and stronger than they think it is. Nine out of ten skin melanomas are linked to severe sunburn during childhood.

It's OK to let a child go all summer without a tan. It's sociably acceptable to be pale. After all, it's not like your children are in the back yard comparing tan lines.

If your kids get too sunburned, you can make a compress of equal parts chilled milk and cold water. Apply the compress to lip and eyelids to relieve the swollen, hot feeling. Cooled tea bags placed on the skin also help relieve sunburn.

It's too darn hot!

Kids will play forever in the sun without complaining. You or I feel that first drop of sweat and we're running off to air conditioning or the shade. But for some reason, kids just don't know temperatures. It may even take them a while to figure out what happened when you slide an ice cube down their shorts. Follow some basic safety rules:

✔ When it's hot outside, keep a close eye on your kids. If they appear too hot (red-faced, sweating, looking pale or faint), bring them in and cool them down.

✔ Don't let your kids stay outside for more than an hour at a time without having them cool down.

✔ Provide your kids with a lot of liquids. Cool water is the best thing you can give them on a hot day.

✔ Babies don't sweat well, so you must go through extra measures to keep them cool. Give them lots of liquids, and give them lukewarm baths to cool them. Don't put sun lotions on babies, and never put them in the sun without a hat — and never for more than a few minutes at a time.

Children get heatstroke just as easily as adults. Heatstroke is caused by staying in the heat too long; the body is unable to cool itself. If you feel your child may have heatstroke, call for help immediately, move him to a cool place, and — starting with the head — sponge him down with cool water (not ice water or rubbing alcohol). With heatstroke comes dehydration, so start giving your child cool liquids. Children commonly have strokes when they play outside in the heat for too long (and when they are overdressed for the heat).

Dealing with the c-c-cold

The best way to spend the winter is to be inside nestled in a big, over-stuffed chair, sitting by a big roaring fire, and drinking hot peppermint tea (with a bag of Oreos on the side). OK, so this is my opinion. Children think differently. Like they do with the heat, children don't seem to mind the cold. And also they can become overexposed to the cold. (Use the checkbox list in Appendix E.)

✔ **Never send your kids outside in the cold without proper clothing.**

This means long underwear, turtle necks, water repellent long pants, water repellent coats and shoes, cotton socks, hats that cover the ears, and mittens that are lined and waterproof (they'll keep your children's hands warmer than gloves). Always use cotton when dressing your children. Avoid polyester or rayon.

Look for signs of frostbite

Listen to your kids if they say they're getting cold. Bring them inside and look for these signs of frostbite: their skin feels very cold and they've lost feeling in that area; or the skin is pale, glossy, and hard. If you think your child has frostbite, call your doctor immediately. To help with frostbite, give your child warm liquids to drink, and put the child in warm water to start bringing warmth back into the frostbitten area (but not too warm — the water will feel warmer than it actually is). You may also try warming your child by wrapping him in blankets or putting the affected area in a warm washcloth or heated towel. *Don't rub the affected area.* Rubbing will not only be painful, but it may damage the skin. As your child begins to warm up, his skin may feel like it's burning or tingling, and the skin should start turning red.

✔ **Keep children's fingers and toes dry when they play outdoors.**

Wet clothing makes skin cold and increases the chance of frostbite. Buy waterproof clothing.

✔ **Make sure boots and other winter shoes are not too tight.**

Tight footwear affects the circulation and can lead to frostbite.

✔ **Limit the time your children spend outdoors.**

When the weather is windy or rainy, when the temperature is below 32° Fahrenheit, or when the wind chill reaches zero degrees or below, limit the exposure time.

The cold air of winter can cause children's face to get chapped. To prevent chapping, apply moisturizing cream on their faces before they go out. If they have a runny nose or are in the drooling stage, put petroleum jelly under their noses and on their chins. Petroleum jelly won't wash off as easily as moisturizing cream.

Sniffles and Sneezes

It's sad, but there will come a day when your child will get a cold and you'll wonder who feels worse — you or your child. You'll feel bad because there's really not a whole lot you can do for someone who has a cold. Your child will feel bad because that's what colds do to people.

When you notice the sniffles and sneezes coming on, immediately start to work:

> ✔ **Wash door knobs and toys that could be handled by other children.**
>
> Germs are mainly transferred by hands, and you don't want anyone else to get sick.
>
> ✔ **Wash both your hands and your children's hands every chance you get.**
>
> You don't want to catch the cold, and you don't want to pass it on to someone else. You also don't want your children to rub snotty noses, and then rub thier eyes spreading germs all over the place. This is how eye colds or eye infections start.
>
> ✔ **Be prepared to give your doctor a detailed description of your children's symptoms.**
>
> Can you describe how your children are acting, eating, feeling? What their bowel movements are like? If they are pulling at their ears? Coughing and producing anything (and what it looks like)? If thier noses are running? And what color (clear or green) the stuff coming out is?

Your baby will feel better when cool. Don't overdress a child in the hope of sweating out the cold. It doesn't work. A child will also sleep better when a tad cooler as opposed to a warm, stuffy room.

Give your baby frequent warm baths. Pour a cup full of water over his head (while also supporting his back because he may jerk back) and wipe away the phlegm that will come from his nose. Do this a cup at a time, until your baby's nose seems clear. If your child is too young, he can't blow his nose, and kids typically don't like snot-sucking syringes stuck up their nose — which is also a way to clean the nose out. Actually, I don't know anyone who likes to have things stuck up their nose.

I got the fever!

Fevers are a sign that the body has an infection, such as a cold or flu. There is nothing you can do to make a fever disappear other than healing the body to make the infection go away. There are medications such as acetaminophen, which will reduce the fever, but won't cure the problem.

> ✔ Ask your pediatrician about giving your child acetaminophen (like children's Tylenol).

If your child has a fever, there's an infection somewhere. This usually means that your child is contagious. Wash your hands as often as possible until the fever is gone. Germs are passed by the hands, and you don't want whatever is making your child sick — and you don't want to pass it on to other family members.

To help your child feel more comfortable at home, give plenty of water and juice, and dress your child lightly. You'd make a sick child feel even more uncomfortable if you over-dressed your feverish patient .

Always ask your doctor about brand names, amounts of medicine, and the times to give it *before* you give your child any medication. Never, ever give your child aspirin unless your doctor has prescribed it.

When to call the doctor

Fever means infection. Never take a fever lightly and never assume that giving children's Tylenol is going to make it all better.

Breaking down fever according to your child's age makes it easier to decide what to do:

- **Babies under three months old.**

    Call your doctor if your baby has any signs of fever. Their little bodies have to work very hard to fight off infections.

- **Babies three to six months old.**

    Call your doctor if your baby has a temperature of 101° or over.

- **Babies, toddlers, and older children over six months old.**

    Call your doctor if your child has a temperature over 102°.

Keep a close eye on your child's temperature. Check it two to three times a day so you'll know if there are any drastic changes. If there is a drastic increase in temperature, call your doctor.

Those annoying ear infections

It's very sad that many babies and small children get ear infections and never seem to get rid of them: Their ear canals are very small, so liquid gets caught, and an infection starts.

Your doctor will prescribe a medication for the ear infection, and it should clear up within seven to ten days. Always go back for the recommended check up because these infections don't always clear up easily. Lingering infections are common and can cause damage.

Don't take these ear infections lightly; they can lead to other, more harmful, things. If you find that your child starts pulling at an ear, take him to the doctor. A child with an ear infection may also be irritable, run a fever, or have other signs of illnesses.

The signs of illness

Don't wait to call your doctor if your child acts very ill but has only a low fever. Other signs of illness include:

- difficulty breathing
- screaming loud with knees drawn up
- pulling at ears
- swollen glands
- sleeping past feeding times or not eating as much as normal
- changes in sleeping schedules
- difficulty in waking up from sleep
- looking pale or gray
- dark circles under the eyes
- blue lips
- acting limp and without any energy
- bad breath (other than the fact that your child just ate three hard boiled eggs)
- smelly private parts, even after a bath

These are all problem signs. Get your kid to the doctor; don't ever take chances on your child's health. (Use the checkbox list in Appendix E.)

Be wary of doctors who suggest you get tubes put in your child's ears. This solution isn't always necessary. Go to a homeopathic doctor or a family practitioner and get a second opinion: They will most likely give you another alternative to tubes. Read Chapter 22, which contains a section on homeopathic doctors.

Preventing the spread of germs — yucky, yucky

Germs are *rarely* spread by them flying through the air with the greatest of ease. They're transferred by hands or by some sort of touching. Keeping this in mind, read these suggestions on how to keep the spread of germs down to a minimum (and see if you can check all the boxes in Appendix E's form):

Don't share towels. Especially if you dry off one child with a runny nose and then use that same towel to dry off your other children. See how this spreading thing works?

Don't share cups. It's an easy habit to give your child a drink from your cup, but try to avoid this type of sharing as much as possible. You can have a designated cup for each family member who can use the same cup all day. This way you're not using every cup in the house, and you also aren't sharing each other's coughs and colds.

Don't kiss your pets. As much as we love our pet cats, dogs, iguanas or whatever, we need to reserve the affection to petting and giving proper care to them. Save the kissing for your family. Pets carry germs around, and you don't want to get anything they have.

Don't sit on a dirty toilet seat. Toilet seats can be pretty nasty. That's why someone developed for public restrooms those paper butt gaskets you have to sit on — which eventually stick to your rear or get caught in your clothes.

Don't eat raw meat or eggs. As much as I love sushi, this is hard to write. (Of course I only eat the cooked stuff.) Raw meat and eggs can carry bacteria with them.

Don't smoke. It's no longer a myth that the results of cigarette smoking are severe. If you smoke, get out of denial and into the real world. Second-hand smoke increases the amount and severity of colds, cough, ear infections, and respiratory problems in those around you. If you smoke around your kids, they're smoking, too.

Don't touch your face. It's a hard lesson to try to teach, but little hands must be kept off little faces. Consider the following basic math problem:

Touching a runny nose + wiping something out of your eye = eye infection.

Do wash your hands. And everyone else's hands, too. Wash them after using the bathroom, changing a diaper, after you sneeze or cough, before and after handling food, before you eat, after working in dirt, and after cleaning. Wash your children's hands before and after they eat, after they go potty, if they grab themselves during a diaper change, after they play with friends, when they get home from school or day care, and if you see them wiping or rubbing their eyes or nose. Basically, you'll spend all day washing hands.

Do disinfect your house often. This will be a life-long process for you. Wash everything, including door knobs, anything and everything in your kitchen, and anything to do with your children — like toys and diaper changing stuff. (Just give up and by some Lysol stock right now.)

Train up a child in the way he should go and when he is old he will not depart from it. — Proverbs 22:6

Is Your Medicine Chest Okee Dokee?

You don't want to have a sick child on your hands, look in your medicine chest, and see bare cabinets. Prepare for the worst beforehand. When your children do catch a cold, a flu — or use their heads to stop the floor — be prepared to take care of things. Look for this checklist in Appendix E, too. You can cut it out and take it with you to the store so you don't forget anything.

✔ **thermometer**

Rectal thermometers are supposed to be the best to use for babies. I've personally never been able to keep my kids still enough to perform the delicate deed of placing the thermometer where it belongs. The thermometers that require placing a plastic tab on the child's forehead are also difficult to use. Again, kids don't want to sit that long. The thermometer in the armpit and those stuck in the ear (and these are two different kinds) are fairly accurate and easy to use. You may have to experiment with your children to see what they'll stand for and what they won't.

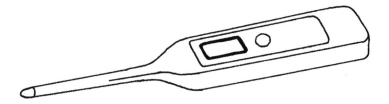

✔ **suction syringe**

These devices are used to clean baby's tiny little nostrils, nostrils that tend to fill up with snot and can make gross sucking noises that don't seem to bother baby — but bother you a lot. The best syringes are the ones they give you after you've had your baby in the hospital. The syringes sold on the market aren't nearly as effective.

To make the syringe more effective, place it in one nostril and close the other nostril with your finger. This is sort of like when you blow your nose and you close off one side. Things come out easier.

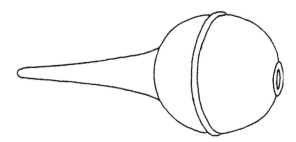

✔ **eye dropper**

Children occasionally get eye infections along with a cold. They rub their faces and smear the germs all over, including into their eyes. Eye droppers are good for dropping mild salt water into a child's eye to help clear up the infection.

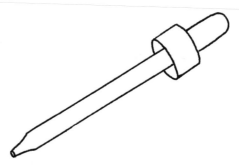

✔ **medicine dispenser**

You'll need something to give out medicine. Drug stores usually have a dispenser that looks like a large eye dropper with measurements on the side. Remember to clean the medicine dispenser after every use.

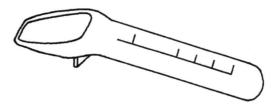

✔ **children's or infants' Tylenol**

Only use Tylenol (or any other type of acetaminophen) when your doctor recommends it. Keep in mind that this medicine should be used sparingly, and only if your children have a lot of discomfort from a cold or flu. Tylenol, or any medicine of the same nature, will not cure a cold or flu. Its only purpose is to hide the symptoms of an infection and make your children feel better.

✔ **ice packs**

Gravity and your children will become very well acquainted. The end result will be several bumps on the head and a few bloody lips. This is when you need your ice pack. You can buy ice packs that look like bunnies that you keep in your freezer, or you can make one by putting ice and cold water in a baggy and wrapping it in a wash cloth. Never put ice directly on child's skin. Not only does it hurt when you do this, but you can damage the skin.

If your child gets a deep cut, put an ice pack on the cut and go to the doctor. Doctors are better equipped for this kind of injury.

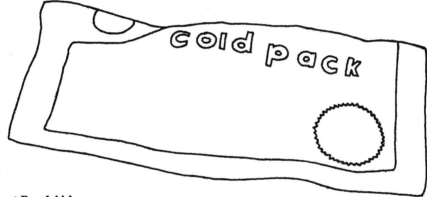

✔ **Band-Aids**

If your child falls and skins a knee, the best thing is to wash the cut with soap and water and then leave it alone. It's best for cuts to be open to the air. But sometimes kids won't leave a cut alone. They're too interested in it and will want to touch it and mess with it. This is the time you'll need a Band-Aid (simply to keep their hands off of it). Put the Band-Aid on very loosely so that it can still get some air — then sit back and watch the fun as your child sits and tries to pick off the Band-Aid.

✔ **Pedialyte**

A baby with diarrhea or a high fever, can easily become dehydrated. Pedialyte is one of the best ways to prevent dehydration, whereas water and juice don't always help. In fact, if you give too much juice when your child is sick, that alone can cause diarrhea. Ask your doctor about Pedialyte, and when and how much should be given.

✔ diaper-rash ointment

The diaper-rash ointment needs to contain zinc oxide.

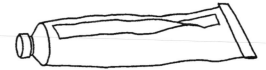

✔ petroleum jelly

Petroleum jelly is for chapped lips or faces, to put under runny noses so your kids' faces don't get sore from wiping their noses, to prevent diaper rash, and also for those ever-so-popular rectal thermometers.

✔ lip balm

If your children ever get a cold, their lips will get chapped because of breathing through their mouths. If lips get too chapped, they'll crack and bleed, so keep these tender little lips nice and lubed.

✔ anti-itch lotion

This lotion is for when your children become the main course for hungry mosquitoes. It's also good for rashes, insect bites, and poison ivy.

✔ Syrup of Ipecac

You give this syrup if your children have swallowed something poisonous. *Only give this to your child if you have been instructed to by your doctor or the Center for Poison Control.*

✔ flashlight or penlight

These items are for looking down sore throats as well as removing splinters.

✔ pad of paper and pen

Use this stuff to write down symptoms of illnesses, along with times and amounts of medicines given. This information is helpful to your doctor or homeopathic doctor when you call them.

✔ moisturizing soap and lotion

Lotion is especially needed during the winter months when our skin tends to dry out. Don't use lotions on children too often during the summer because it will only make them feel hot.

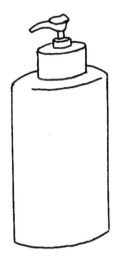

✔ tweezers

A definite must for pulling out splinters.

✔ cool-mist humidifier or vaporizer

This type of vaporizer (even if you *can't* fit it in your medicine chest) is great for when your children have colds. The cool, moist air is easier to breath than dry, warm air. It also loosens the mucus in their nose. You must clean the humidifier daily so it doesn't get moldy.

✔ **scissors**

For cutting bandages, gauze, or tape to size.

Your lesson for the day

Medicine is not an exact science — heck, it's an *art*. There's usually more than one way to solve a problem. Use your gut instinct. If your doctor is prescribing a medicine or doing something that doesn't sound right to you, don't hesitate to question what's going on. Remember, you've hired this doctor. You are your doctor's employer. If you don't like what your employee is doing, you can fire him or her just as easily.

Chapter 24
Punishment and Discipline

· ·

In This Chapter

▶ The differences between discipline and punishment

▶ Setting the guidelines for discipline and punishment

▶ What to do when your child repeats a *crime*

▶ Some basic stuff to keep in mind

▶ Guidelines to follow to keep within the purpose of punishment

▶ A nice variety of punishments

▶ Making discipline and punishment decisions with your partner

· ·

*I*t's hard to fathom, but at some time or another, your dear, sweet child is going to do something that will make you want to pull your hair out and scream at the top of your lungs. You don't ever want to get to that point. You also don't want your kids to be brats, so that involves some strong decision making and pretty strong parenting on your part. Your children will protest your saying "No," and then they'll do stuff that, well, infuriates you. So it's a vicious circle. You don't want brats. You also don't want to beat your kids (really, you don't).

This chapter covers the things involved in disciplining your child. It also covers punishment — which is what you do when your child chooses not to follow what's right.

The Big Diff Between Discipline and Punishment

Some parents are afraid to discipline their children. And some parents feel that discipline is a parent's way of pushing their will on their child, regardless of what the child wants. Both attitudes are wrong.

The whole point of discipline and punishment is to *teach* your children. It's a learning process. You can be a good parent with definite discipline and punishment ideas without being afraid that either your children are going to hate you, or that you'll mess up their lives forever.

Crime and punishment

Discipline is about setting ground rules and boundaries — and making your children live and follow those rules. Sounds easy enough. The only problem is that your kids, for their own reasons, aren't always going to want to follow those rules and boundaries. They'll always seem to have their own agenda, and it may not match yours.

It's hard, but you must be tough and not give in to whining, crying, and big puppy-dog eyes filled with tears. If your kids cry because you don't let them jump on the couch, well, that's OK. They're crying because they're mad, not because they're physically hurt. There's a big difference. You should know the difference between the two cries.

If your children are mad and start to cry, you have these options:

✔ **Accept the crying.**

Don't get mad and spout the ever-so-popular line, "I'll give you something to cry about." Just because your children are mad doesn't mean you have to be mad. One mad person is enough.

✔ **Try to console your children.**

Let your children know why you don't want them doing something (which doesn't always work when kids are mad). If you can, simply hug, kiss, and hold them. Just because they're mad, or you've not let them do something, doesn't mean you can't be affectionate. Sometimes crying children will continue to cry longer and louder if you're hugging them. So listen closely and know when to let them go, when tell them they're OK, and when to send them on their way.

✔ **Ignore or tune out the crying.**

Some kids will scream louder and longer if they know that you're listening or that it's bothering you. You can give your children the option to go to their rooms and come back to you when they've gotten control of themselves, or you leave. Tell your children you'll be back after you feel they should have been able to calm down.

✔ **Take their minds off it.**

This strategy works great for babies and toddlers who are easily distracted. If your children are mad, take them outside for a walk or hand them a toy. Sometimes this distraction works like shutting off the water valve. Instant happiness.

Please, oh please, don't say this . . .

You've just scolded your kids for jumping on the couch. They're upset, maybe mad, and are crying. Please don't say, "You stop that crying or I'll give you something to cry about." Don't you get it? They already have something to cry about. They're mad. For kids, that's as good a reason to cry as anything. Beating them for crying is really not going to stop the crying. Never has, never will.

Kids will test your rules. Some kids will get the idea after only a few times of saying, "No, don't sit on the cat." Some kids will think it's just too fun to resist and will keep sitting on the cat, so you'll have to be just as stubborn as your children and keep pulling them off of the cat, telling them again and again "No, don't sit on the cat."

Discipline and torture techniques

As you go about disciplining your children, you may start to sound kind of naggy. No one likes to listen to someone nagging. As a defense to this annoyance, your children may start to tune you out. Sort of like your husband who tunes you out when you start talking about him throwing his dirty clothes *next* to the clothes hamper instead of *in* the clothes hamper or your wife when you describe the big fish that got away.

Humor (the Ha, Ha, Ha's of life)

Anything approached with humor will go over better than when you don't use humor. When you discipline your children, it's usually not going to be a life-or-death situation, and a little humor may get your point across better. It's easier to remember a funny situation than a direct Marine drill-sergeant type of command:

What you want to say:

"Put your shoes where they belong."

What you should say:

"Your shoes snuck out of your closet. Can you help them find their way home?"

What you want to say:

"Eat with your mouth closed."

What you should say:

"Does your mouth know how to chew and stay closed at the same time? I'd really like to see that happen."

What you want to say:

"Who left the milk out?"

What you should say:

"Why don't you be the milk police. It's your job to make sure everyone follows the milk rules. Arrest whoever breaks this law!"

What you want to say:

"Stop hitting your sister."

What you should say:

"I know your sister does things that make you want to clobber her, but why don't you just hit your bed instead of her when you get really angry?"

What you want to say:

"Did you break the knob on the TV?"

What you should say:

"Oh, oh. The knob on the TV is broken. Did the TV *blow* the knob off, or did you have something to do with this?"

Put it in writing

The goal of discipline is to educate your kids about right from wrong, and to teach them rules about proper behavior. But if they're tuning you out because you're beginning to sound like a broken record, your whole goal of trying to teach something is gone. Chapter 2, "Communicating with Your Child," talks about alternative forms of communication to get your point across. Writing notes and letters, for example.

If you're tired of telling your children every day to shut the lid to the toilet, simply put a sign on the wall behind the toilet. This gentle reminder will keep you from sounding like you're nagging, and your kids will get the message — if they can *read!*

> Please, close me when you're
> done with your duty!
> Thank You,
> Mr. Toilet

The Ordeal of Punishment

After you've set your rules and boundaries, but your children make the decision not to follow them, it's the time for punishment. This situation is different from your ten month-old leaving toys scattered all around. A child this young hasn't learned to pick up toys yet. (For some kids, that day may never come.)

Punishment is the penalty inflicted upon your children when they break rules or guidelines that you've set for them. It's an *educational tool* used to teach your children about these rules. (It comes when your eight-year-old decides to throw rocks at cars, for example, even though the kid already knows that it's wrong.)

You can't give punishment, however, if your child doesn't know or understand the rules.

Make the punishment fit the crime

So Junior just broke your car window with a rock. Actually, it was one of several rocks. Now what do you do? Look at punishment as a great learning device. The point here is not to physically beat your children every time they look the wrong way, but to teach them to make good choices. If they don't make the proper choices, there are consequences. Keep these things in mind when setting punishments:

✔ **Be realistic when setting the punishment.**

   Don't *ground* someone for a year if you know that you'll never keep the punishment going that long.

✔ **Don't be too lenient.**

If a punishment has no effect on your children (other than just taking away some time), you're being too lenient. It has to mean something to children in order to be a learning experience.

✔ **Consider your punishment carefully.**

Sometimes just hearing a parent get upset and then being scolded by the parent is enough to crush any child.

To apply the punishment to the car window breaking incident you'll have to assume a couple of things. First, consider if your child is old enough to be outside throwing rocks — say, six years old. And second, consider if your child understands and has been told not to throw rocks around the cars. If these two assumptions aren't true, you have to question the punishment.

For example, if a two-year-old threw the rock and just got a lucky shot in, you can't do a whole lot other than scold. But a two-year-old won't understand what he did was wrong — and probably has never been told not to throw rocks around cars.

For the window-breaking punishment, you have several options:

Punishment: Time out

Result: The only thing a six-year-old would learn from a time-out for breaking a window is that he got off really easy. This kid wouldn't learn a thing.

Punishment: Spanking

Result: Spankings don't last that long and aren't good for teaching. Again, your child would probably look at this as getting off pretty easy.

Punishment: Working to pay for the window

Result : Doing extra chores to pay off the window has a lot of learning potential. To really drive the point home, make a chart with the list of chores, the price paid per chore, and the total price it's going to cost to pay for the window. This chart, along with the chores, is a good reminder to a child who made a wrong decision.

Punishment: Loss of a privilege

Result : This punishment would be good in combination with the punishment of working to pay off the window. Instead of getting to go roller skating, the child would spend that time doing the extra chores.

The idea here is to combine different punishments to drive your point home. But apply a punishment only where your children are going to *learn* something from it. When that works, your children will think twice about breaking the rules in the future.

Making punishment a learning exercise

Discipline and punishment should be times of learning. When your children break a rule and you feel punishment is deserved, make sure they fully understands *why* they're being punished.

For example, if you see your son doing something horrid, don't grab him by the arm and shuttle him off to his room. If you do that, you've passed up a very important discipline step. You forgot to let him know why he's being punished — that what he did you consider to be wrong. Say, "Since you did *whatever*, I'm going to send you to your room."

At some point, be sure to remind him of why he's being punished. Go visit him *in prison*, and explain your thinking. "You have to sit up here while all your friends play outside because you called Marilyn a bad name. Do you understand?"

If the punishment has a long duration, ask him from time to time why he's being punished. "Do you remember why you can't swim in the pool this week?" He should be able to tell you exactly why. If he says "I forgot," remind him. Keep to these simple guidelines:

- ✔ Make the punishment memorable.
- ✔ Make the punishment appropriate to the crime.
- ✔ Make sure your child learns from the punishment.

Have you ever spoken with children whose parents spank them all the time? When you ask why they got spanked the last time, they usually reply "I dunno." This response really drives home how effective that type of punishment is; if they can't remember the crime, what good is the punishment?

Whether you're trying to teach your children what the household rules are, or punishing them for breaking those rules, always stop and let them know why something is not allowed. It will mean more to them, and so they're more likely to remember. If they understand that jumping on the couch will break the springs and then they won't be able to sit on the couch again, they're less likely to do it again in the future. If you can, stop and show them the springs in the couch so that they can see what it is you're talking about.

Guidelines for Discipline and Punishment

Don't take lightly the idea of disciplining or punishing your children. It's not easy to always be on your toes to make sure your kids are following the rules of the house. It's also not easy to decide on what kind of punishment you are going to give your children, which is never a pleasant task.

To make this easier, your decisions about what is allowed in the house and what's not must be crystal clear. You can't have double standards (letting one child get away with something while punishing another child who does the same thing), and you have to follow through with your kids.

How to be lovingly unbending (the art of consistency)

Once you set your household rules and guidelines, you can't be inconsistent about these decisions. You also can't punish children for something and the next time act like it's no big deal. This inconsistency will cause you more trouble than it's worth.

Be tough. Be strong. If your children cry because you've not allowed something, that's OK. They're crying because they didn't get their way. This isn't a sign that they're going to hate you or that you did anything wrong. It means that your children are mad. They'll get over it.

Read Chapter 3, "Being a Consistent Parent."

Don't forget your follow through

Follow through comes when your children have broken a rule on purpose. When your children do such a thing, consider it a test. They're testing to see if you're really going to do something. This is not a test you can afford to fail.

If you have set a rule that your kids can't throw balls in the house, and they do, your follow-through is the punishment you set forth. If you make a rule and you don't follow through with a punishment if the rule is broken, your kids won't think anything about breaking other rules. They'll consider your rules *bogus*.

Follow through also means that if you've set a punishment where your children have to do to something (such as write a report or clean something), make sure it's done. If you fail to follow up with the punishment, you're setting a bad example for your kids. You're letting them know that even though you say something, they don't need to take it too seriously because chances are your won't check to make sure something was done.

WORDS OF WISDOM

Read Chapter 4, "Follow Through."

Anger is to be specially avoided in inflicting punishment.— Cicero

The Repeat Offender

Discipline is simple. It's making your kids learn and follow rules so they can grow up to be nice people. Punishment is a little more difficult. When a child still repeats the same *crime* over and over, you may want to stop and think about why this child seems so determined to do so.

Have you explained why he isn't supposed to do whatever it is he does? If you have — and he seems very aware that digging in your plant not only causes a mess, but may also kill the plant — maybe something else is going on.

You may want to ask yourself these questions:

✔ Are you giving your child enough attention?

It's always been understood that children prefer to get positive attention. They like playing with you, getting hugs and kisses. But if they aren't receiving that, kids will go for any attention they can get. Negative attention is better than no attention at all.

✔ Is your child bored?

Have your child help you with laundry or cooking. Play games together. Give projects that he can do on his own, but be sure you check on him often and give him praise for what he's doing.

✔ Is there a pattern to the crime?

Does your child only dig in the plant when you seem to be putting his little sister to bed or when you're sitting down to pay bills? If this is the case, he may be letting you know that he doesn't like you giving your attention to someone or something else. Let him know that as soon as you're done with what you have to do, the two of you can do something special together. Then give him something to keep him busy while you're doing your chore.

Be in Charge without Being a Tyrant

The fact that you need to discipline your children is not an open invitation to treat them with a lack of respect or decency. It also doesn't meant that you take on the role of Czar with your children as the peasant slaves.

Let kids be kids

Kids will be kids and should be allowed to make mistakes. You can't expect miracles from people who may not be as old as your favorite suit. Kids are awkward at times, spill and drop stuff, knock things over, and generally do things that are goofy without being malicious or evil.

Don't make words less meaningful by using them over and over

Instead of always saying "No" or "Stop," offer alternatives to whatever it is your children are starting to do. If you see your children starting to color on the walls, say "Don't color on the walls. Here is a piece of paper. We can color on the paper instead." If you always yell out "No," "Stop," "Don't," "Quit," or "Help me, my children are taking over," your words will lose their effectiveness after a while.

You don't always have to win

Discipline shouldn't be a series of wins and losses between you and your children. Discipline can sometimes leave room for compromise between you and your children as long as you get your point across.

It's not important that you always win the clothing selection war, for example. This may be one of the first areas where you find yourself coming to a mutual compromise with a child. Your goal is to get your child dressed, and your child may want to exert his independence by helping to choose the clothing. This is where you compromise and come up with an outfit you both can live with.

Parents tend to think that if they don't always get their way, they're letting their child run over them. Think about the getting-dressed scenario. Your goal is to get clothes on your child. Does it really matter if your child wears the pink button-down Oxford shirt or the Mario Brothers T-shirt as long as you get the kid dressed? No. It doesn't.

It is better to bind your children to you by respect and gentleness, than by fear. — Terence

Handle situations with gentle guidance

It's just as easy to get your children to do something, or not to do something, and be gentle about it as it is to yell and scream. Remember, your goal is to teach when you discipline. Your children will be more open to listening to you and *hearing* you if express what it is you want in a kind and gentle manner. Don't be surprised if you can't always accomplish this, however. You may quickly lose your temper and yell if you walk into a room and find mud all over your white carpet. The goal here is to *try*.

With soft words, one may talk a serpent out of its hole. — Iranian proverb

Use enthusiasm to guide your children

If you're trying to get your children to do something they don't necessarily want to do, approach the situation with a lot of enthusiasm and make it sound like fun. If you make the process of getting shoes on fun and like a game, your children will think it fun — and maybe forget to scream, kick, and throw the shoes across the room.

Don't harass your children

You should always have faith that your children are going to do what's right. You can't sit and wait, like a cat waiting for a mouse to come out of its hole, for your children to do something so that you can pounce on your prey . Don't fall into the trap of scolding your children before anything has happened, just in anticipation that they *may* do something. This behavior is nerve-racking.

The Purpose of Punishment

Punishment should be a positive action. It's impossible to predict every possible scenario and then handle it a certain way, but keep these guidelines in mind:

✔ **What will the punishment teach your children?**

If you fall into the habit of giving the same punishment for the same crime, this punishment may lose its effectiveness and not teach anything. If that's the case, change the punishment.

✔ **Your children should always know the reason for the punishment.**

If you send children off to their rooms and they have no idea why, you've lost the opportunity to teach. The punishment will mean nothing. Explaining punishment may be difficult with toddlers and preschoolers who require clear and specific explanations.

✔ **Don't set punishments when you're angry.**

Decisions are never very good if you make them quickly or in anger. You're also more likely to set a punishment that is more out of retaliation than out of the idea of what it will teach. Set the punishment when you've taken a few seconds to cool down and think about what it is you should do.

✔ **Give your children a chance to fix the error.**

Everyone should have a chance to correct whatever they did wrong. Your goal is to resolve the problem, not to punish whenever possible. Punishment should be the last straw. Lying is a good example. If you catch a child in the process of *stretching the truth*, but can stop him before it turns into a Paul Bunyon-sized lie, you've given your child a chance to correct the error.

✔ **Forgive and forget.**

Don't hold grudges against your children. After you've had to punish them, tell them you still love them — then forget about the crime. There's no need to bring it up again or use it against them at a later time.

We can not be forgiven if we refuse to forgive. — Janette Oke

Punishment is not fun. If you enjoy punishing your children, you need some serious psychological help. The only way to avoid punishing your child is to consider it as a last possible resort. Look at the following examples of ways you can handle the problems while avoiding punishment:

Remove the temptation to get into things. If you spend all your time putting your china back into the cabinets, put childproof locks on the cabinets. Make the things you don't want your children to get into out of their reach or not accessible to them. Of course, this isn't always possible. After all, it's a little difficult to remove all the cushions from your furniture just so that your toddler will stop throwing them on the ground for an extra bed.

Reconsider what's important. Did you set a rule before you really thought it through? Like the preceding example, do you really mind if your child throws the furniture cushions on the floor to play with them? Is it so important that the cushions stay where they belong? Think long and hard before you set a rule.

Let your children help you solve problems. If your son can't keep from throwing the shirts he doesn't want to wear on the floor rather than put them back, ask him to come up with a solution to the problem. He may suggest changing the drawer with one that is lower so that he can reach his shirts better and be able to put them away.

Get in your children's way so they can't get into trouble. Physically stand in a child's way so that he can't push the tree over in the living room. Tell him he has to leave the tree alone, and then get him interested in something else.

Stay calm and don't yell. Your kids will most likely tune you out if you yell. Even when a child is yelling at you, don't fall into the trap and yell back. Gather your patience and keep your voice calm, cool, and relaxed. This strategy will not only calm your child down, but also teaches that staying calm is the best way to communicate.

Explain why and what you're doing. Knowledge is powerful. If your children understand why you do something, or why something is not allowed, it'll make more sense to them, rather than their having to obey random rules that don't mean much — sort of how I feel about accounting. Your children may not learn at first, but don't give up hope. Eventually what you're saying will make sense.

Have your child start over. When your children talk or behave rudely to you, ask them to start over. Even have them leave the room and come back in to approach the situation again, but this time ask them to think about what they're saying and how they're saying it (or ask them to think about what they want to say and how they should say it).

Types of Punishment

So it's happened. You're really going to have to punish a child for doing the unspeakable. The list below gives you some options for punishment. Alter your punishment so that one type doesn't become habit and lose its effectiveness. We must be *creative* disciplinarians.

Every child is different and handles punishment differently. You can't always apply the same punishment to every child. — Shirley Hardin

Time-Outs

Time-outs seem to be a popular method of punishment. A time-out is where you physically remove a child from a situation and have him sit somewhere, alone, for a specific period of time. The thought here is that if your child is hitting, screaming, or just throwing a fit because he didn't get his own way, this time alone will allow him the opportunity to *get in touch with his inner-most feelings*. Actually, it's a time for him to get control of himself. And the act of taking him away from his play group can be very *painful* to a young child.

Like most situations when it comes to children, however, you have to gear it to a particular child and the situation. You also have to take two things into consideration:

- **The place:** Is your child's room really the most effective place for time-out? Will it help make him sit and think about what he did? Isn't his room also the place where he goes to play, read, perhaps even watch TV? If you're going to take the time to punish your child, don't send him to the place he most would like to be. It'd be like saying, "OK. You've really done it this time. Boy are you in trouble. Your punishment is to take this $20 and go to Baskin-Robbins."

- **The time:** Don't set a strict guideline on how long, time-out should be. If you tell your child that the designated time out is for five minutes, but after five minutes the crying and temper tantrum are still going on, the time-out hasn't been long enough. It won't be effective if you let the out-of-control-kid off the hook. Nothing will have been learned. The five minutes would not have been long enough for your child to gain control.

You should put a disclaimer at the end of your time-out rule: "You'll have time-out for five minutes. If you can control yourself by then, I'll let you out. If you haven't calmed down by then, you'll have five more minutes of time-out."

If the time-out is just to have him sit and contemplate what he's done, the rule usually is to make him sit out for one minute per each year. A four-year-old would sit out for four minutes. A thirty-year-old would sit out for thirty minutes. My mother would be sitting out for hours!

Take away privileges

Punishment is most effective if it's a learning tool that can be emphasized over and over. For example, taking away a privilege — like no videos for a week — is something that will make an impact on your children every day of the week. Unlike a punishment of spanking or time-out, which is over quickly, taking away something of importance has a greater opportunity to make an imprint.

I like to take privileges away from my kids if they've done something to deserve a punishment. I do so for a length of time that I feel will really make an impact. My oldest son took a hammer and dug chunks out of our deck. He was five. Rather than spank him (I knew he would forget why he was spanked 20 minutes later), I took away the privilege of watching *Batman* for one week. I'm sure I would have seen fewer tears had I spanked him. But for five days, every time he asked to watch *Batman*, I was able to reinforce that he made a poor decision (the hammer and the deck), and because of that decision, he couldn't do something he really enjoyed. Needless to say, we've never had a hammer problem again.

Taking away privileges doesn't work on kids who are too young to remember or know they did something wrong.

Give extra chores

Your children should have chores that they have to do on a daily basis, such as make their beds, hang up their clothes, take out the trash, whatever. And your children should be taught that everyone has to do chores: It's a part of life. But if a child has done something that requires a punishment where chores are involved, divvy out extra chores. For example, if your children have played outside all day and spread trash all over the yard, the punishment could be to clean up the yard — and while they're at it, rake up the leaves and pull weeds from the garden.

Use this punishment sparingly. Your kids should have to do their own set of chores anyway, and you don't want to them to always think that they're in trouble just because they're asked to do extra chores. But, if used on occasion, this type of punishment is very effective.

Punishing by educating

Kids *generally* aren't evil beings sent here from another planet just to make your life miserable. Honest! And so when your children do things that you consider to be wrong — like breaking household rules — keep in mind that these acts aren't *usually* done out of spite. Many times kids break rules because the outcome of breaking these rules isn't known, or they don't know the rule in the first place. Since your kids truly want to do what's right, education can be a powerful tool so the same *crime* isn't repeated.

For example, if a child is caught breaking a rule, such as stomping on your flower garden, turn the punishment into an opportunity to teach something. Have him research and write a report about flowers, or roots. If he's too young to write, have him draw a picture of flowers and their roots. Take the time to go out and look at flowers and other plants and talk about how roots work. Go to the library and read about roots. The more your child knows about the consequences of what he's doing, the less likely he is to repeat what he did.

This kind of punishment/lesson learning doesn't work for children under three years old. They're too young to understand the relationship between what you're reading in a book and what they did.

Spanking — yikes!

A large percentage of people still believes spanking is an acceptable form of punishment. Their reasoning is, "I was spanked and I turned out OK," or "I only spank to really make my point." I'm not going to say if spanking is good or bad, I'm just going to put some ideas in your head.

Punishment is a learning tool. You're using it to teach your kids something. Does spanking accomplish this? No, not really. Besides, if you hit your child, what does that teach?

Isn't spanking just a quick and easy way for you to resolve your own frustrations with not being able to handle a situation? After all, it's simple to whack a mouthy kid. It takes much too much time to be patient and explain things — which, of course, has more positive results.

You're setting an example of how to behave with every one of your actions. If you pout when you don't get your way, your children will pout, too. If you yell when you get frustrated, your children will, too. If you hit (or spank) when you get mad, your children will, too. Don't rely on the old saying, "My kids know better than to hit," because your spanking is teaching them something different. They can't distinguish between *hitting* and *spanking* — and the situations that make the distinctions.

Punishment should have an impact on your children. It should be remembered for as long as possible. If you spank your children, how long are you able to remind them of why they were punished? The whole spanking process doesn't really last that long, so it's usually quickly forgotten.

Team Decision Making

Both parents have to be in agreement on the rules of the house. Mom can't believe that the kids can't jump on the couch while Dad goes in and jumps with them. You both have to agree that the couch is for sitting on, not jumping on. You both also have to enforce this rule if you see the kids breaking it. Mom can't be the one who always has to set punishments while Dad pretends he doesn't see what's going on.

Chapter 19, "Guidelines for Co-Parenting (The Two-Party System)," talks about working together as a couple when it comes to parenting. Discipline and punishment are areas were you both have to agree. You can't have two different set of standards and try to enforce them.

Behind-the-scenes decision making

As you and your partner encounter situations that require decisions about punishment, sit down and discuss how you both feel are the best ways to handle these situations as they come up. Don't be surprised if your opinions differ. You are coming from different backgrounds (unless you're marrying your cousin) and may have different points of views on things. Listen to each other, be respectful of each other's point of view, and then come up with a mutual decision on discipline and punishment.

Learn to be flexible

If you start making discipline and punishment decisions before you've had kids, you may find that, in reality, what you've decided doesn't work. Give yourself enough room so that you and your co-parent can re-group and think about the decisions you've made. Always discuss these changes. You don't want to upset your partner by making changes without talking about it.

Your lesson for the day

Discipline and punishment should be used as a form of *educating* your children about right and wrong, household rules and guidelines, and making good choices.

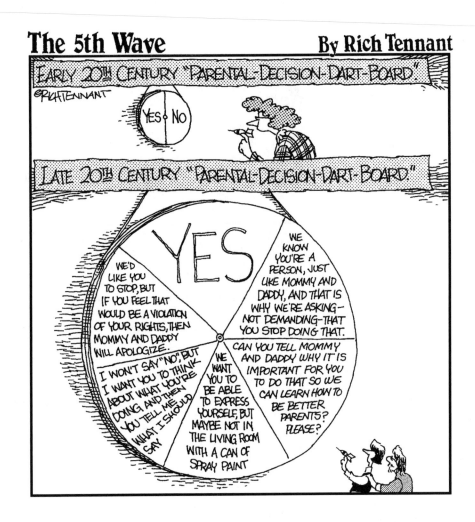

Chapter 25

Squelching Squabbling Siblings

Hey, Joey, did you see what Mom and Dad brought home? It's a really small kid. He doesn't seem to do much. Why don't you toss something into his cage and see if you can wake him up. Here, try this Tonka truck.

Brothers and Sisters Living In Harmony is not the title from an old *Star Trek: The Next Generation* show, but a reality. It's your job to make it happen. This chapter is dedicated to brother and sisterly love — and the path you must lead your kids down to get there.

sib•ling \'sib-ling\ *n.* A brother or sister. The *gender neutral* for a brother or sister when you don't know which one it is.

I don't have any siblings. My parents never sibled. — Hawkeye Pierce in *M*A*S*H**

There's a New Sibling in Town

You may be at the time in your life to expand your family. Oh happy, happy, joy, joy! But you may be wondering how your only or other children are going to respond to a new family member. It's a very good question, and one that deserves special attention on your part.

Hearing that there is going to be a new baby in the house is going to bring up a lot of interesting questions. Don't be shy about answering them. Also, read the section, "Answering Questions," in Chapter 2.

Here are some suggestions about how to handle the arrival of a new baby:

✔ **Don't tell your children that they'll be getting a new playmate.**

This may be true sometime in the future, but not for a good year or so. Don't give them the expectation that as soon as their little brother or sister gets home, it's instant fun — because it won't be. Newborns don't do much to entertain, other than spit up every now and then.

✔ **Don't forget to recognize that your children are special to you, just like the new baby will be.**

Do something special. Give them a gift "from the new baby," or make them a special T-shirt so that they know they're still special in your eyes.

✔ **Don't neglect your older children.**

Make an effort to do something with them after the baby comes. This activity is something you'll have to schedule. Having a new baby in the house can swallow up a lot of time before you know it. Continue to share "dates" with your children.

✔ **Give them an honest idea of what it will be like when the baby comes.**

Let them know that, at first, the baby will demand a lot of time, and will mostly just cry, eat, and sleep. Not a whole lot more. Also let them know that Mommy will be very tired and will also have to take naps to rest.

✔ **Call your local hospital to see if there is a sibling class that your children can take.**

These classes go over what babies like and dislike, what it's like to change a diaper, and other basic information that your children will need to know. They have to learn that it's *not* OK to toss a Tonka truck into the crib with baby.

✔ **See if your local hospital has a sibling class that you can take with your children.**

These classes give you a general idea of how your children may act with a sibling around and some things you can do to prevent them from being jealous.

✔ **Get your kids involved with the preparation and arrival of the new baby.**

Ask for their help. Have them draw pictures to put in the baby's room, pack the diaper bag (after you lay all the stuff out), and fetch diapers or bottles for you. Getting your kids involved with the baby will help them feel more like a part of the baby's life.

After you've done this preparation, how are your children going to act toward the new sibling? It depends on your children and their maturity level. If you take the "new sibling" classes previously suggested, you'll find that behavior is usually broken down according to age. I think it depends more on the maturity of your children. Normally, a two-year-old would be expected to show anger or jealousy to a newborn while your eight-year-old may be exhilarated. But that's not always the case. You may find that you have to keep an extra eye on your two-year-old who wants to *help* you by carrying or picking up the baby — while your eight-year-old suddenly seems to be very angry at you for no apparent reason. Whatever the age of your children, they may experience increased crying bouts, temper tantrums, and regressions (such as bedwetting, acting like they can't feed themselves, wanting to be carried when they are fully capable of walking, and so on). You may find that your younger children actually try to take the baby out of your hands so they can crawl in to your lap. These actions are usually signs that your children are insecure and need your attention.

How to Handle Siblings

When you have more than one child, you have to take on some new roles. You instantly become a mediator, negotiator, referee, and judge. You'll find yourself walking into situations, and it'll be your job to listen to both sides of the crying and sobbing to determine what happened. Most of the time you won't have a clue. Both sides will sound convincingly right. And they both will *feel* they're right.

Here are a few general guidelines that will help you keep your sanity while you mold your children into loving, kind siblings.

✔ **Don't compare your kids.**

It's very tempting to say, "Why don't you sit quietly like your brother?" That's the wrong thing to say. Your kids will start resenting each other if you always make them feel like one is better than the other. If you want your children to be quiet, ask them to sit quietly — of course, it always helps to tell them why they should be quiet. Don't mention that your other child is already doing so. That's really not important to bring up.

✔ **Don't take sides.**

You need to be the neutral party everyone can come to. If you always seem to take sides with someone rather than help solve the problems, your children may decide they would prefer to punch it out than come to you.

Sometimes it's better just to put your head down and let them try to work things out. And usually they will work out their own problems. Besides, you won't always be there to help them work out their differences. Of course, you should intercede if the conversation becomes physical. Your children should never be allowed to solve their problems with knock-down-drag-out fights.

✔ **Stay calm.**

When your kids are upset and all rational thought and action seem to be gone, your job is to stay calm. You need to be the one who can walk in and quietly help everyone else to get control of themselves. If you get upset too, you won't be much good at helping to solve differences.

✔ **Keep a sense of humor.**

Laugh. And do it a lot. Sometimes it's the only solution to conflict. If you can help your kids see the humor in situations, it will diffuse the problem. Besides, how can you take an argument over who touched whom first seriously?

✔ **No name-calling.**

This is a big rule in our house. Name-calling can be very hurtful, and it's harder to fight if you can't call someone Rhino Nose or Big Butt. Once someone starts to call names, stop it immediately. It should be a rule from the beginning. That old saying, "Sticks and stones may break my bones, but words will never hurt me," is not exactly true. Sticks and stones do hurt, but words hurt, *too*.

✔ **No hitting or pushing.**

This is the hard one. It's a natural instinct to want to lash out at someone who makes you mad. I've seen kids as young as ten months old lash out at their older sibling when they got fed up having a toy ripped from their hands. It's a constant lesson, and one that isn't easily learned. You have to consistently teach that hitting or pushing isn't allowed in the family. If children can't touch someone in a loving way, they shouldn't touch them at all.

✔ **Give your kids time alone.**

If your kids seem to be always *attacking* each other, they may just need some time alone. If you can separate your kids — have one child play in the bedroom, the other in the living room — they won't get on each other's nerves as much and will be more tolerant with each other. It's just like cabin fever for kids: If they're always around each other, they sometimes need to get away and have time alone.

Teach Siblings How to Play Together

The main problem with kids playing together is that, at some point in time, they all will spot the same book or stuffed animal — and the fight is on. Or a different version to that scenario is when one child has a toy and his older brother decides that it's time for him to play with it *instead*.

When play turns into fights

No matter how much you read about how to get siblings to play nicely together, there will be a time when little battles occur over who gets to play with what first. Your children aren't always going to have you around to break up fights and be a mediator, so you need to stay out of their way and let them work out their problems on their own.

Keep a close eye on the situation, though. It's your job to jump in if the arguments turn physical, and punching, kicking, or name-calling gets started. This is where you become a teacher again. You'll need to let your kids know that fighting and name-calling are not allowed, but they can use *words* to work out their differences.

Sharing is hard to teach. When I get a box of chocolates, I've got to tell you, I have a hard time sharing. If someone else reaches for that one and only cherry cordial, I go crazy!

The thing that you'll want to do — but shouldn't — is buy duplicate toys for all your kids. If it's something like bicycles, well then *yes*. It's more fun for kids to have their own bicycles so they can all ride together. Any toy that is more fun if everyone has one (such as Barbies) is great. If it's a game, *no*.

Your kids have to learn to share. They can't go through life thinking that everything they own is theirs and only theirs. The next thing you'll end up doing is buying them their own box of cereal because someone keeps eating all the marshmallows out of the Lucky Charms.

You can handle sharing toys by teaching one child to offer a toy in exchange for the toy that another child has. Sometimes this works, sometimes it doesn't. The hard part is teaching your children that if someone doesn't want to exchange toys, they'll just have to wait until the toy has been set down. Of course, they'll watch the toy like a hawk until it's down, and then they'll pounce on it.

Teaching Siblings How to Have a Loving, Caring Relationship

I've met enough families in my life to know that being loving and kind to your siblings is something that doesn't come naturally to everyone — or at least hasn't been encouraged. You have to teach kids to be loving and kind to each other. Make sure that your actions are also a part of teaching. These actions show your kids how they should behave towards each other.

✔ **Don't gang up on a child.**

Teasing can sometimes be fun, unless you're on the butt end of the teasing. That's never any fun. Don't mistakenly join in teasing someone, teasing that you may think is harmless joking. Not only are you confirming the fact that teasing is OK (and as adults we take it pretty well; kids don't), but joining in on a tease makes it look as if you're ganging up on someone. If that *someone* happens to be your own child, that's doubly bad. You're supposed to be that child's best cheerleader and supporter.

✔ **Don't talk bad about others in front of their siblings.**

Again, you need to be your children's best supporters. You should never talk bad about your children anyway, but especially never in front of your other children. Your children need to hear that everything you say about them is positive and in a loving manner.

✔ **Don't pit your children against one another.**

Your job as a parent is not to instigate fights or arguments, and then sit back to watch the excitement begin. Some parents do this — and it's wrong. Your kids are going to have enough confrontations with each other without having you add to their fire. This type of confrontation can also be accomplished when you compare your children with each other. Each of your children will have individual strengths and weaknesses. No one likes to hear, "Why can't you be more like your sister/brother?"

✔ **Encourage hugs and kisses between siblings.**

Young children naturally pick up on affection if you're liberally passing out hugs and kisses. When you see your young ones showing affection to each other, let them know how happy you are that they're giving out hugs and kisses. Encourage them to do so often. This positive re-enforcement will let them know that giving affection is a natural and good thing.

✔ **Teach children how to be gentle.**

When you see your toddler belting the baby, take the toddler's hand and gently caress the baby with it. Let your toddler know that this is how we touch others. You may also have to teach gentleness to older children who may not have been around younger children or babies.

✔ **Teach family togetherness.**

Your actions are an important way to teach this. There are several chapters in this book that emphasize your family doing things together. Getting everyone involved in housework, cooking, and playing together is an excellent example of how family togetherness works. This is one of the most important and valuable lessons that you can teach your children. And don't forget the power of story books that you can read to your children — books that emphasize family togetherness.

Don't leave siblings under the age of four alone together. They can easily hurt their siblings by hugging them too hard or by trying to pick them up.

Sibling Communication

Everyone is going to be an example to your young children, especially older siblings. Listen closely to how they communicate together. If you find that an older child is losing patience and beginning to yell or be hateful to a younger child, step in and remind them that the best way to talk is calmly and nicely.

All your children are also going to look to you as an example. If you remain calm, don't yell, and leave sarcasm out, your kids will pick this behavior up from you. Your older children will try to imitate you and your actions towards your kids. Make sure you portray a loving, kind, and gentle person.

Otherwise, this is what your children will learn from you and their older siblings:

- **ignoring**

  Too many parents ignore their kids when they talk. It's a bad habit that not only frustrates the kids, but is also a bad trait to pass on to someone. Make sure that you listen when your children are talking to you. Acknowledge what they're saying. If you hear your children playing and one child is ignoring the other, point it out.

- **sarcasm**

  My family excels at sarcasm. As a result, I have to watch myself carefully not to be sarcastic in front of my kids. Sarcastic children are the worst to be around; they appear to be disrespectful and hateful. If your family has a reputation for sarcasm, try to curb it as best you can. Answering children's questions seems the *perfect* opportunity to use sarcasm, but the children won't get it — and they'll learn an awful trait.

- **bullying**

  You'll witness bullying when your older child realizes that he is bigger and stronger than the younger child. It's like a hidden gene that we all have, but we don't get the opportunity to use it. If you see your older child bullying a younger child, point out what he is doing and why it's not something that should happen. This is a good opportunity to teach kindness to your children. Children need to learn that just because someone is smaller, they can't force someone to do something or take advantage of this person. Children need to be kind, gentle, and helpful whenever possible.

Your lesson for the day

Sharing is a hard lesson to learn. Tears are usually involved, along with temper tantrums, but kids will get over it. The important thing is for your kids to learn that toys — as other things in life — are to be shared.

Part V
The Part of Tens

"Mr. Klein, would you mind telling me the next time you plan to smash your thumb with a hammer?"

In this part...

Lists of things can be amusing: the ten tallest mountains, the ten biggest diamonds, ten vegetables that resemble former presidents, ten people named Ned who have phlebitis, and so on. Of course, lists of ten don't always have to be corny. There's a lot to learn that can be presented in lists of tens (such as do's and don'ts). That's what you'll find in this section — some last lists of tens to help you become a better parent.

Chapter 26
Ten Things to Do Every Day

*B*eing a parent means there's a lot of stuff you should be doing every day, but I had to keep this list to ten (hence the name of this section, *The Part of Tens*). So I picked out the ones that came to my mind first. Most of these things I would consider to be at the top of the *really important* things you can do.

Give lots of hugs and kisses

Your whole family needs to feel your love every day. Not only your kids, but also your parenting partner. Don't hold back on all those hugs and kisses. Affectionate people live longer. Or, at least, they should.

Tell your family members you love them

Everyone needs to feel loved. Even though you may show your love by the special things you do for your family, it's also important that they hear those ever-important words, "I love you."

Children need love, especially when they do not deserve it. — Harold S. Hubert

Tell your family they're special

Along with the need to feel loved, your family needs to know they're special. You can let them know this not only by telling them, but also by doing special things for them. Send notes to your children in their lunches, or send a note in your partner's briefcase or purse. Or leave a message on the phone at work. You make people feel special by the special things you do for them.

Feed your family nutritious food

It's not only important that your kids eat the right foods, it's also important that you take care of yourself, too. Not only are you setting a good example by grabbing a banana for dessert instead of the piece of fudge (*ummm, fudge*), you're also teaching your children about making good food decisions.

Read to your kids

Reading to your kids not only gives you quiet time to be alone with them, but it also starts them on a good habit and a beginning love for books. Kids who are read to (*and who read*) are associated with higher IQs, better vocabulary, and increased language skills.

Talk to your kids

Every day you should know what your kids are doing, where they've been, and who they've been with. Talking to your kids also starts a habit of open communication between you and your family. You all need to practice open and honest communication with each other.

Have a special time with your kids

Spending individual time with your kids is essential if you have more than one child. Each child should be made to feel special and important. By spending time alone with your kids, you'll help them not to feel lost in a large group; they'll feel more like a member of a family.

Practice good manners at every opportunity

The best way to teach manners is by example. If you make a habit of always saying "please" and "thank you," your kids will naturally pick up on your good manners.

The first quality of a good education is good manners — and some people flunk the course. — Hubert Humphrey

Be patient even when you don't want to be

Oh Lordy, this is a hard one. Your patience may not be tested every day, so it's good to store it up for those days when you really need it.

You can learn many things from children. How much patience you have, for instance. — Franklin P. Jones

Be approachable at all times

Chapter 1, "Winning *The Parenting Game*," talks about the different roles you play as a parent. One of those roles is that of friend. If you act as a true friend to your children, you will naturally be approachable. You want your children to be able to talk to you about anything, ask you questions that are bothering them, and never feel like you're too busy for them.

Chapter 27
Ten General Household Rules

*T*hese household rules are to be followed by everyone. Double standards or special allowances shouldn't be made. That means you too, parents, must follow these rules. You must be consistent and follow through when these rules are broken. Be strong, be tough, be one of the few, the proud, the Marines.

Be proactive toward your children, not reactive

Being proactive toward your children means being an active part of their lives. If you're just reactive, you're just responding to the things they do and say. Play games with your children instead of just hearing about who won. Read books to your children instead of just putting the books away when they're done.

No name-calling

"Sticks and stones may break my bones, but words will never hurt me." This is so untrue. Some of the most hurtful things that we remember in our lives are unkind words. Make a rule in your house that if nice things can't be said, nothing should be said.

If you can't say something nice, don't say anything at all. — Thumper in *Bambi*

No hitting or pushing

Touching in any household should be kind and gentle. If any situation turns to hitting or pushing, stop it immediately. You'll usually find such situations when siblings are trying to work out their problems on their own but things just don't seem to be going their way.

Don't hit your sister 'cause you'll always get caught. — from cousin Justin, age 16

No ganging up on someone

Playing as a family is fun, until *sides* are chosen and everyone seems to be *ganging up* on someone else. Teasing typically starts this way. Someone says something jokingly, and then someone else pitches in, and finally everyone is involved. This situation is OK if the person on the butt end of the teasing is taking things well — but if not, stop it immediately.

Your children should come first

Television, work, Saturday sports, over-zealous hobbies. These are all things that can affect your time with your kids. It's OK to have a life outside your children, but balance that time. Spending time with your family should be more important than anything else you have to do. Someday your kids will grow up and you'll wish they could make more time for you. Harry Chapin captured this thought in his song "Cats in the Cradle." Listen to the words. But don't play it backwards because it doesn't say anything when you do it.

Be kind and respectful to others

This is simple. It means being nice and treating your family like you would treat a house guest. Don't ever take your family for granted. When you do, you forget to say "please" and "thank you" or to do nice things.

The only reason I always try to meet and know the parents better is because it helps me to forgive their children. — Louis Johannot

Keep to schedules

It's OK to vary your day-to-day routine on occasion, but children need to have schedules. They need to eat at the same times during the day (at least close to the same times) and go to bed at the same time. They rely on these schedules and will be in better moods if they stick to these times.

Always use safety precautions in the house

Your kids will roll over, walk, talk, and jump before you know it. Their tiny fingers will peel and pry things open so they can stick whatever they find in their mouths. Prevent accidents by using every safety precaution and safety device available. You don't want your children to have an accident that could have easily been prevented.

Everyone helps take care of the house

It's not written anywhere that Moms cook and clean, children play, and Dads take out the trash and read the evening paper. It's a myth. Everyone should have responsibilities that help take care of the house and family. The less time you have to devote to chores, the more time you can devote to doing fun, family things together.

Everyone must let everyone know where they are

It should never be a secret where your kids are. You should always know where they are and who they're with. And they, too, should know where their parents are. It's safer if everyone can be accounted for.

Chapter 28

Ten Things for Your Conscience to Whisper into Your Ear

● ●

In This Chapter

▶ Are you working too much?

▶ Are you prepared for the worst?

▶ Are you yelling?

▶ Do you think about what you're doing?

▶ So your name is . . . *Jordan*?

▶ Are you talking about me?

▶ Are you telling the truth?

▶ Do you know where your kids are?

▶ Great habit — not!

▶ How safe is your house?

● ●

Don't, don't, don't! There's nothing more annoying that to see a list of *Don'ts*. But instead, think of these as the things that little angel sitting on your right shoulder would whisper into your ear. Just subtle reminders on walking that straight and narrow path to the truth.

There's no one out there who is going to reward you for listening to your conscience. You won't get a government grant. There are no commemorative tablets. And, since you're following the rules, you'll probably still pay a lot in taxes. But you will be rewarded by raising a fine crop of children. Often that's more important than anything else.

Don't be a workaholic

There aren't a whole lot of people who admit to being workaholics; most folks are too busy to care! They just make up feeble excuses to be at work, excuses that everyone in the free world can see through.

Work is important because it provides you with money so that you can take care of your family. Your family, however, is much more important than any outside job you could ever possibly have.

Don't be unprepared

Asking someone to always prepare for the worst possible situation sounds so doom and gloom, but it's part of being a parent. The way to prepare for the worst is to have your house as safe as possible. Have your medicine cabinet stocked with everything that you need (read Chapter 23, "Health and Hygiene"); get smoke detectors and fire extinguishers; have fire drills. If you prepare for the worst, you'll be ready should anything happen.

Don't yell or scream at your children

The way you communicate to your family is very important. It's one of the foundations on which your relationship is being built. If the only way you talk to your children is by yelling and screaming, you're missing out on some valuable communication time with them.

If you catch yourself starting to yell or scream, stop! Think about what you're doing and re-approach the situation. Then go back to Chapter 2, "Communicating with Your Child," and read it thoroughly.

Don't let them start something that you don't want them to continue

We watch our kids climb on top of the table and dance to the stereo. We laugh, *ha, ha, ha!* But, as parents, we've made a mistake. We've allowed them to do something that they really shouldn't do. Now that they've received positive feedback from what they did, they'll do it again.

If you don't want your children to develop habits that you eventually will have to stop, don't ever let them start such habits. Kids get into habits very quickly, *especially* if they get a positive response from you.

Don't put your children's names on their clothing

Bad, boogie-men type of people use names on clothing as one way to lure kids into their cars or houses. Don't supply them with this information. Kids are more likely to think that if someone knows their name, that person must be OK. Don't write names on your children's clothing. (Of course, bad, boogie-men are also stupid: "So your name is . . . *OshKosh B'Gosh?*")

Don't talk bad about your children

Talking bad about anyone is a *nasty* habit. Speaking unfavorably about your kids is especially unforgivable (and should be punished by caning). Your kids should always know that you support them and think highly of them and what they do. If you're talking negatively about them (like telling your friends about their bad habits), you're not supporting them the best way possible. Besides, your friends could really care less about your kids' habits.

The young do not know enough to be prudent; and, therefore, they attempt the impossible — and achieve it, generation after generation. — Pearl S. Buck

Don't lie to your children

At no other time in your life is someone going to love you and trust you unconditionally more than your children. Don't lessen your children's trust in you by lying to them. There's really no need for it.

Watch out for the unintentional lies, such as telling your kids that the taste of medicine is good, you'll only be gone for a minute (when you're gone for an hour), and so on. Think about what you say before you say it.

Don't leave your children alone anywhere

Don't leave your kids alone in the house, car, on a couch, changing table, or bed. All of these situations are dangerous and are the basis for children being hurt.

Don't keep your bad habits

"Anything you can do I can do better." Your kids will live by this motto. So, do you really want your kids trying to outdo how much you smoke, drink, spend too much time out in the garage piddling with your tools, spreading "F" words like they are smiles, eating Oreos for breakfast? Take a moment to reflect upon your life (elevator music should be playing here). Stop or change anything you don't want your kids to do. They're sitting there looking — waiting for you to do something so they can copy it.

In short, the habits we form from childhood make no small difference, but rather they make all the difference. — Aristotle

Don't leave your house unsafe

We're fortunate to live in a country where someone has thought of every worst-case scenario as to what your kids can do and made a gadget for us to buy. Don't overlook these gadgets. They do help. Invest in some cabinet locks and electrical plug guards so you have one less thing to worry about your kids doing.

Chapter 29
Ten Choking Hazards

In This Chapter

▶ Ten things babies can choke on (sorted by taste)

Kids are amazing. They'll stick anything in their mouths. Some kids suck up anything on the floor, and they do it so well we might as well call them Hoovers. What's the point? Who would want to try to taste such exotic things for the culinary virtues, save for maybe the French? (Let's be serious here: goose livers? I mean, "Mon Dieu, Marie! Quickly! A goose is passing. Let's kill it and eat its liver!")

The following list is the top ten items kids generally will stick in their mouths and choke on. Try to keep your kids away from these things.

Hard candies

You and I know not to swallow hard candies whole. Hard candies could lodge in a child's throat and cause suffocation. This is even true for Life Savers; the little hole isn't there for you to breathe through should they get stuck in your throat.

Popcorn

Not for anyone without teeth, except for Grandma and Grandpa at the movies.

Grapes

Babies just suck on them, so it's like sticking a marble in a baby's mouth; a no-no. Wait until your kids have teeth and are eating well on their own before you give them grapes. And always keep a watchful eye on them. You never know when a wayward grape will slide down an unsuspecting throat.

Raw vegetables cut in circles

Carrots are the worst. Cut your vegetables in long strips rather than circles.

Hot dogs cut in circles

Don't bother cutting the hot dog into strips. Cut them into teensy tiny pieces or give your kids something else.

Nuts

Here, Binky, have a cashew. Not!

Small toys and toy parts

Just because they give you a Mickey Mouse car in the Happy Meal bag doesn't mean it's food. (Actually, McDonald's is quite specific about their toys *not* being for small children.) Be especially alert for older children's toys that have small parts. Action heroes, for example, are famous for coming with dozens of small parts — perfect for grinding into the carpet and for baby to find later. Make it a habit to read warning labels on all toys for the age guideline.

Miscellaneous small stuff

This category includes pins, coins, and other small items that you find under seat cushions and in the back of old drawers. It's amazing how much of this stuff can cause choking.

Buttons

Buttons are easily pulled off clothing or stuffed animals and popped into small mouths before you know it. When you think about it, some of those buttons really do look appetizing.

Deflated or bursted balloon pieces

That balloon may be fun for baby to chew on, but when swallowed the rubber creates a hermetic seal between the lungs and the air. A severe danger. Kids love balloons — but when balloons pop, clean them up right away. Also, toss out balloons that deflate and lurk under sofas and in corners.

The best thing you can do to prevent choking is to be very observant of your children, and to keep your house clean. Clean, not only as in sterile, but also keep things picked up off the floor. Check under seat cushions, furniture, cabinets, and beds for small stuff that could be popped into mouths. Also, take a first aid class to learn about choking and how to get things *unstuck*.

Chapter 30
Ten Time Savers

"If I could save time in a bottle . . ." I'd probably lose the bottle.

Anything that we as parents can do to make our lives easier, which includes saving time, is better. Here are ten time savers that will give you a few extra minutes throughout your life to spend with your kids.

Keep the refrigerator stocked

Prepare extra juice and milk bottles and keep them in the refrigerator for quick access. This strategy is especially helpful for middle-of-the-night feedings. Also, keep easy-to-grab snacks at finger's reach for older children. Good examples are cheese slices, carrot sticks, fruit, and individual servings of yogurt and applesauce.

It's hard to get your kids to eat food if it hasn't danced on TV first. — Linda Mullen

Diaper bag on the go

Keep a packed and ready diaper bag for trips out. Make it a habit that every time you come back from a trip, you clean out the diaper bag, then re-stock it for your next trip. (Except for bottles and juice. Grab those on your way out.)

Be first to shower and shave

Get up, shower, and dress before your children do. If you don't have to try to get showered, shaved, and dressed while also taking care of the kids, you'll spend less time getting prepared.

Plan the night before

For kids who like to pick out their own clothes, have them pick the clothes out the night before. Have a special place for these clothes so that there's no mistake as to what the children are to wear the next day. This approach will make your mornings go smoother, and you won't have a daily Clothing War.

Bath preparedness

Have all your bath supplies together so you don't have to spend the time gathering wash cloths, towels, soap, and so on. The best place to keep these supplies is in a large basket that you can tote around in case bathtime ends up being in a different area than usual.

Manicures and pedicures

Cut your children's toenails and fingernails while they're sleeping. You'll spend a lot less time wrestling. You're also less likely to cut a child who isn't wiggling around. You can end this practice once your children get to the age when they can sit still for this *torture*. This *age* depends on your child. Some can handle it as early as two years old. Some (usually the more ticklish ones) have to wait longer. You'll just have to test out your own kids.

Cook more, more, more

Double your recipes when you cook dinner. Eat half of the dinner, and freeze the other half. When you're ready for a quick and easy meal, just defrost and you have a complete meal waiting for you. It's better than Hamburger Helper. (Prison food is better than Hamburger Helper — in my opinion!)

Every meal tastes better if you end it with a peanut butter sandwich. — John Coppernoll

Make lists upon lists

Make a chore list for everyone. If chores are written down, you'll spend less time reminding your family to *do* their chores. The family will eventually take less time doing them, too, as the chore becomes a good habit.

Clean as you go

Make a new family rule that you clean up after yourself. It saves you cleaning time later on. For example, if you change a diaper, immediately throw the diaper away and clean up any mess you make. If your child has dug into the cookie jar, have the little mess maker wipe off the counter.

What is learned in the cradle lasts till the grave. — Hungarian proverb

Keep everything in its place

Have a designated space for *everything*. Teach your kids that their coats can go only in one place; shoes go in the closet when taken off; extra diapers are stored in a certain cabinet. Also, make sure coats and clothing are put in their place the second they're taken off. Even though everyone may strip down in the foyer, they should *immediately* take their coats and shoes to the proper storage facilities.

If you have to constantly play *hide and go seek* every time you need something, you're wasting time.

Chapter 31

Ten Things You've Heard Your Parents Say

· ·

In This Chapter

▶ Quotables from parents (arranged in random order)

· ·

Parents say the darndest things. This final chapter is dedicated to the parents throughout history who have come up with these ever-so-clever sayings. At one time or another, we may have been on the receiving end and heard these things. And we may fall into the same trap as our parents and use these expressions ourselves. Only time will tell. . . .

Also included are some fancy and logical retorts that we as adults would want to use if someone told us this stuff today. Obviously, we wouldn't have done this as kids! Can you imagine the kind of trouble we would have been in? Yikes!

"I'll give you something to cry about."

As if the fact that I'm crying already isn't enough for you.

"You just wait until your father gets home."

Now I have three more hours to live. Maybe he'll take her out to dinner, and then I can harass the sitter.

"If your sister jumped off of a cliff, would you?"

Why? It would be the happiest day of my life!

"If I've told you once, I've told you a thousand times . . ."

So this makes it 1,001 . . . and counting.

"Children should be seen and not heard."

But what if I have to go to the bathroom? Or if I have a *really* important question? Or what if aliens came down and tried to kidnap me?

"I don't want to hear another word."

Fine. I'll sit here and make animal sounds.

"Do as I say and not as I do."

Yeah, like you'd ever catch *me* playing bridge with a bunch of 40-year-old women.

"Clean your plate. There are children starving in China."

Great, send this green pile of yucky goo to them and don't make me eat it!

"Tell me when you have to go to the bathroom."

But then I'll get in the habit of telling everyone when I have to go to the bathroom. I'll be attending a board meeting when I'm 52, and I'll stand up and announce, "Excuse me, but I have to doody."

"I hit you because you were closest."

Does this mean I can *pass it on*?

Part VI
Appendixes

The 5th Wave   By Rich Tennant

"The nice thing about having kids at our age, is that we've nearly got the same nap schedule."

In this part...

Here's the extra-value stuff you love finding in books. It's like sticking your hand in the pocket of an old coat and finding a $10 bill wadded up inside. You didn't know it was there, you're overjoyed that you found it, and it's worth something. That's the same feeling you'll get after reading Appendixes A through E — where you'll come across check-box lists and questionnaires that you'll find very useful.

Appendix A
Safety

• •

*T*rying to keep the world a safe place for your children may make you feel like you're being paranoid or overprotective. So be it. It's better to feel that way than to feel sorry that you didn't spend the extra time and money to make your house or car safe. Use these checklists to verify that you've got everything you need — or that you do everything necessary. Also, refer to Chapter 9 for more information on safety.

General Fire-Safety Devices

❏ smoke detectors

❏ fire extinguishers

❏ escape ladders

❏ carbon-monoxide detectors

Bedroom Safety

❏ Don't use homemade or antique cribs.

❏ Keep bedding simple — sheet, blanket, and bumper pads.

❏ Don't use pillows (until a child is three years old).

❏ Get rid of bumper pads when your baby is old enough to pull up.

❏ Don't put cribs or toddler beds near blinds, drapes, or wall hangings with cords that hang down.

❏ Put plastic covers on all the electrical sockets, and plastic boxes over the cords that are already plugged in.

❏ Make sure the toys in the bedroom are appropriate for the age of your children.

❏ Wash and dry all toys on a regular basis.

❏ Don't put toy chests or children's furniture near windows.

❏ Use toy chests made of light material, like plastic, with a lid that either comes off or hinges and stays up.

❏ Make sure purses and fanny packs are out of reach.

❏ Don't let babies sleep with plastic covers on their mattresses.

❏ Babies should never sleep on waterbeds, cushions, beanbag chairs, adult comforters, or pillows.

❏ Never, under any circumstances, do you walk away from, or turn your back on, a baby who is on the changing table.

Children's Accessories Safety

❏ Check toys for missing parts.

❏ Check pacifiers to see if the plastic nipple is still in good shape. If a pacifier is cracked, throw it away.

❏ Wash pacifiers often.

❏ Never tie a pacifier around a child's neck.

❏ Remove crib mobiles when your children are old enough to pull up on their hands and knees.

❏ Don't put your children to bed with toys in the crib.

❏ Don't use a baby carrier or a baby swing as a car seat or as a seat when riding bicycles.

❏ Follow all manufacturers' directions for assembly when using a baby swing.

❏ Don't put high chairs too close to walls, counters, or tables.

❏ Use your strollers with all the safety equipment provided.

❏ Watch out for little fingers when setting up the stroller or folding it.

❏ Don't hang heavy bags, purses, or diaper bags from the handle of the stroller.

❏ Don't use a baby walker if you're not going to put gates on your stairs.

Living/Family Room Safety

❏ Put plastic covers on all the electrical sockets and plastic boxes over the cords that are already plugged in.

❏ Put gates on all the stairs going up or down.

❏ Take portable gates to place in the doorway of staircases if you're traveling to someone's home.

❏ Put breakable items either away or in a higher place (until your children are old enough to learn to leave them alone).

❏ Don't leave babies and young toddlers unattended on furniture.

❏ Scrape, sand, and repaint all old paint areas.

❏ Have furnaces, fireplaces, and gas barbecue grills checked for carbon monoxide leaks.

❏ Clean air filters from heaters and air conditioners once a month.

❏ Don't keep your car running in the garage.

❏ Keep blind or drapery cords tied up, out of the reach of children.

Kitchen Safety

❏ Put locks on all your cabinets.

❏ Use the back burners when cooking on the stove.

❏ Keep drawers locked.

❏ Keep small children out of the way when cooking.

❏ Lock up or throw away plastic shopping bags, garbage bags, plastic wrap, plastic sandwich bags, plastic dry cleaning bags, or plastic film of any kind (like those on toy wrappings).

❏ Keep alcoholic beverages away from children.

❏ Keep chairs away from counters.

❏ Keep important phone numbers on a list, displayed, and by the phone.

❏ Keep *Syrup of Ipecac* in your medicine cabinet, but don't use it unless you are instructed to by a physician or someone at the Poison Control Center.

Bathroom Safety

❏ Keep bathrooms blocked off with gates or install safety locks high enough so your children can't reach them.

❏ Keep lids to toilets closed.

❏ Keep shower doors closed.

❏ Never leave water standing in sinks, bathtubs, or buckets.

❏ Keep cleaners, perfumes, deodorants, and any other *foofoo* stuff locked up.

❏ Always keep medicines in the medicine cabinet and away from children.

❏ Use child-resistant packaging for anything and everything you use.

❏ Keep small appliances (like blow-dryers, curling irons, electric razors, and irons) unplugged and put away.

❏ Don't allow children to play in the bathroom.

❏ Never leave children unattended in the bathroom.

Car-Seat Safety

❏ Always, always, always use a car seat when traveling. It's the law.

❏ Use only the type of car seat that is age- and weight-appropriate for your children.

❏ Fasten the car seat down with the seat belt.

❏ Always use the car seat's safety belt.

❏ Read the directions on the car seat and FOLLOW THEM!

❏ Don't put rear-facing car seats in the front seat where there is an air bag.

❏ Children weighing under 20 pounds should always be facing the rear of the car.

Burning

❏ Put your coffee cup in the middle of tables or counters.

❏ Don't hold your children when you're holding a cup of hot liquid.

❏ Use your back burners to cook when possible.

❏ Turn pot handles toward the rear of the stove.

❏ Keep kids away from floor furnaces or area heaters.

❏ Hide your disposable lighters, or don't use them.

❏ Don't let your children use the microwave oven.

❏ Never hold your children while you're cooking.

Choking Hazards

❏ grapes

❏ hard candies

❏ deflated or bursted balloon pieces

❏ coins

❏ raw vegetables cut in circles

❏ buttons

❏ nuts

❏ popcorn

❏ pins

❏ small toys and toy parts

❏ hot dogs cut in circles

❏ plastic bags

Appendix B
Traveling

*T*raveling can be a relaxing, enjoyable event (if you're prepared) or a royal pain in the behind (if you're not). Use the checklists below when you plan for those days out. Also, refer to Chapters 17 and 20 for more information.

Important Baby-Bag Contents

❏ diapers

❏ baby wipes

❏ diaper-rash ointment

❏ burp-up towel

❏ changing cushion

❏ food

❏ eating utensils

❏ change of clothing

❏ pacifier

❏ blanket

❏ water

❏ bottles

❏ nipples

❏ bib

General Traveling Tidbits

❏ Allow yourself plenty of time to get to wherever it is you're going.

❏ Ask your travel agent about vacation sites that cater to children.

❏ Have snacks and toys close at hand.

❏ Take the phone number of your child's doctor with you.

❏ Take your medical insurance information with you.

Automobile Travel

❏ Make regular stops for rest, food, and gas.

❏ Clean up your car and bodies often.

❏ Exercise caution.

Airplane Travel

❏ Pack extra diapers and clothing.

❏ Be prepared for ear un-plugging.

❏ Take a car seat when you travel with your toddler.

❏ Take snacks and beverages with you.

❏ Limit your carry-ons.

❏ Don't let your kids walk the aisles.

❏ Reserve a bulkhead seat when flying.

Traveler's Supply List

❏ diapers

❏ baby wipes (or hand wipes)

❏ spit-up towel

❏ bottles and nipples

❏ light blanket

❏ eating utensils (cups, spoons)

❏ plastic bag for dirty diapers or dirty clothes

❏ change of clothing

❏ beverages (juice, formula, water)

❏ food

❏ entertainment for the kids

❏ current passport (if traveling outside the United States)

❏ name and phone number of your doctor and medical insurance

❏ medications

Family-Vacation Guidelines

❑ Don't over-schedule your time.

❑ Keep your kids on their eating and sleeping schedules (as much as possible).

❑ Have plenty of free time for goofing off.

❑ Don't eat too much junk food.

Food-on-the-Road Guidelines

❑ Have enough eating/drinking supplies.

❑ Keep enough food on hand.

❑ Keep plenty of liquids with you.

❑ Keep a bottle of water from home with you.

❑ Keep a supply of juice.

❑ Limit fresh fruit that you take with you (or buy it on the way).

Appendix C

Child Care

• •

*O*f all the things you as a parent need to research thoroughly, child care should be at the top of your list. Use the checkboxes and questionnaires in this appendix to make your search easier. More details on child care can be found in Chapter 21.

You don't want to leave your kids with a sitter of any kind without giving them permission to authorize medical treatment in case of an accident (unless your child has specific medical problems that only you can handle). Use the following slip. Fill it out and leave it with your sitter when you leave him or her alone with your children.

_____ has my permission to authorize medical
fill in the complete name of your sitter

treatment to my child(ren) _____
in case of a medical emergency.

Signed,

_____
sign your complete name

Sitters

Take time going over the following with your sitter:

❏ the evening schedule

_____

_____

_____

❏ the nap and bed time

_____

❏ the household rules

_____

_____

_____

❏ a list of emergency phone numbers and the phone number of where you are going to be for the evening

_____

_____

_____

❏ any food favorites or allergies

_____

_____

❏ favorite toys and the names your child uses

_____

_____

❏ fears, along with things to help calm your upset child

_____

_____

_____

❏ a list of *Do's* and *Don'ts*

_____

_____

_____

After-School Program Questionnaire

1. Is the afternoon organized? ❏ Yes ❏ No

_____

_____

2. Is there a scheduled time for kids to do their homework? ❏ Yes ❏ No

_____

3. Do kids get an afternoon snack or are they ❏ Yes ❏ No
   expected to bring their own?

_____

4. How are the kids released to their parents?

_____

_____

Child Care Hunting Questionnaire

1. May I have some names and phone numbers of ❏ Yes ❏ No
   parents who currently have their children attending
   here (or of parents whose children you have cared for
   in the past)?

_____

_____

_____

_____

2. Do you allow visitation during the day? ❏ Yes ❏ No

_____

3. What kind of snack or lunch program do you offer?

_____

4. May I see the play areas? ❏ Yes ❏ No

_____

5. What is the procedure for releasing the children at the end of the day?

_____

6. What are the rules regarding sick children?

_____

_____

7. Do you give out medications?   ❏ Yes   ❏ No

_____

What is your policy?

_____

8. What will you do if my child gets injured?

_____

9. If your caregiver calls only for an emergency, what constitutes an emergency?

_____

10. What are your fees?

_____

Do you have a late pick-up charge?   ❏ Yes   ❏ No

_____

What kind of payment schedule do you have?

_____

Do you allow time off for vacations?   ❏ Yes   ❏ No

_____

11. What is your teacher to child ratio?

_____

12. What are your teacher qualifications?

_____

_____

13. What is the turnover rate of your teachers?

_____

14. Do you do background checks on your employees?   ❏ Yes   ❏ No

_____

15. How do you discipline children?

_____

_____

16. What kind of communication will I have with my child's caregiver?

_____

_____

17. How well does my child have to be potty trained?

_____

18. What is your daily curriculum for the children here?

_____

_____

_____

_____

_____

_____

19. Do you have a nap time during the day?   ❑ Yes   ❑ No

_____

What is your policy on children who no longer take naps?

_____

_____

20. Can I see your last licensing report?   ❑ Yes   ❑ No

_____

21. Do you have NAEYC (National Association for the   ❑ Yes   ❑ No
Education of Young Children) accreditation?

_____

Rules for Child Care Drop Off

❑ Don't rush getting ready in the mornings.

❑ Spend some time together with your child in the morning at your child care.

❑ Never sneak out while your child is doing something else.

❑ Make your good-byes quick and to the point.

❑ Don't scold a child who cries because you're leaving.

❑ Don't be too hard on yourself.

❑ Don't be upset if your child isn't as *tidy* as when you left.

Appendix D
Medical Care

· ·

*p*icking the right doctor means you're going to have to do some research. Use the following questionnaires and lists as guidelines to find the right doctor for your family and to help remind you of other important stuff. You can read more information on finding medical care in Chapter 22.

Questionnaire For Your Doctor Hunting

1. What are your open hours?

_____

2. How do you handle follow-up visits?

_____

Do you have bench checks?   ❑ Yes   ❑ No

_____

4. What are my payment options?

_____

_____

5. What do I do in case of an emergency?

_____

6. Do you have additional doctors?   ❑ Yes   ❑ No

_____

7. Do you have back up doctors?   ❑ Yes   ❑ No

_____

8. How is your waiting room arranged?

_____

Questionnaire for People Who Refer You to a Doctor

1. What do you like about this doctor?

   _____
   _____

2. What do you dislike about this doctor?

   _____
   _____
   _____

3. Does this doctor seem open to your questions?   ❏ Yes   ❏ No

   _____

4. Is this doctor kind and gentle to your children?   ❏ Yes   ❏ No

   _____

5. Do your children like this doctor?   ❏ Yes   ❏ No

   _____

6. Does this doctor take the time to listen to your   ❏ Yes   ❏ No
   concerns and discuss problems with you?

   _____

7. Does this doctor have experience with mothers who   ❏ Yes   ❏ No
   have successfully breastfed?

   _____

8. Does this doctor share your points of view on   ❏ Yes   ❏ No
   nutrition, starting babies on solids, weaning, and so on?

   _____

Pharmacy-Hunting Guidelines

Location: _____

A drive-up pharmacy: _____

Hours open: _____

Computer records   ❏ Yes   ❏ No

Medicine summary for the prescription   ❏ Yes   ❏ No

The Child/Doctor Relationship Rules

❏ **Do** be happy and relaxed when going to the doctor.

❏ **Do** greet the doctor cheerfully.

❏ **Do** use the doctor's name.

❏ **Do** thank the doctor after the examination.

❏ **Don't** use going to the doctor as a threat against your child.

❏ **Don't** tell your child that something is going to hurt, or that it won't hurt if you really know that it will.

Going to the Doctor

	age	*check-up*
❏	1 week	exam
❏	2 weeks	exam and shots
❏	2 months	exam and shots
❏	4 months	exam and shots
❏	6 months	exam and shots
❏	9 months	exam and shots
❏	12 months	exam
❏	15 months	exam and shots
❏	18 months	exam
❏	2 years	exam
❏	3 years	exam
❏	5 years (or right before starting school)	exam and shots
❏	every 2-3 years afterward	general exams
❏	12 years	exams and shots
❏	15 years	exams and shots

Vision Problems
(when to go see your doctor)

❏ Your children squint or rub the eyes a lot (other than when tired).

❏ Your children's eyes move quickly either up or down or from side to side.

❏ Your children's eyes are watery, sensitive to light, or look different from the way they normally do.

❏ The pupil of the eyes have white, grayish-white, or yellow-colored material in it.

❏ The eyes stay red for several days.

❏ Your children's eyelids droop or the eyes look like they bulge.

❏ There is pus or crust in either eye that doesn't go away.

A Good Dental-Hygiene Program

❏ Clean your children's teeth daily. Preferably twice a day.

❏ Floss your children's teeth when the molars start touching.

❏ Give your kids, including your baby, water to drink.

❏ As soon as your children develop teeth, use a children's toothbrush and very gently brush their teeth.

❏ Use just a tiny amount of toothpaste (like baby pinky fingernail size) when brushing your children's teeth.

❏ Help your children brush their teeth until they are seven or eight years old.

❏ Don't forget to brush the tongue and the roof of the mouth.

Dental-Visit Guidelines

❏ **Do** allow your children to go back to the dental chair by themselves.

❏ **Do** always thank the dentist after the appointment is finished.

❏ **Do** check out books on going to the dentist. Find one that has pictures of things your children may see in the dental office.

❏ **Don't** use going to the dentist as a type of threat.

❏ **Don't** talk about any possible pain or anything hurting.

Appendix E
Keeping Your Children Well

· ·

*U*se this section as a reference to keep your children well. You should also read Chapter 23 for more information on keeping your children healthy.

Hot-Weather Guidelines

❑ Use sunscreen on your children anytime they're going to be in the sun (except for babies under six months old).

❑ Apply sunscreen on all body parts that are exposed to the sun (but avoid the eye area).

❑ Apply sunscreen liberally.

❑ Read the directions on your sunscreen.

❑ Don't go out into the sun between the hours of 10:00 a.m. and 3:00 p.m.

❑ Keep a hat on your children when they're in the sun.

❑ Keep a close eye on your kids when it's hot outside.

❑ Don't let your kids stay outside for more than an hour at a time without having them cool down.

❑ Provide your kids with a lot of liquids.

❑ Go through extra measures to keep babies cool because they don't sweat well.

Cold-Weather Guidelines

❑ Never send your kids outside in the cold without proper clothing.

❑ Keep children's fingers and toes dry when they play outdoors.

❑ Make sure boots and other winter shoes are not too tight.

❑ Limit the time your children spend outdoors.

Signs of Illness

These are all problem signs that indicate your child may be getting ill. Keep this list close at hand. If your children display any of these signs, get them to the doctor immediately. Don't ever take chances on your children's health.

❑ difficulty breathing

❑ screaming loud with knees drawn up

❑ pulling at ears

❑ swollen glands

❑ sleeping past feeding times or not eating as much as normal

❑ changes in sleeping schedules

❑ difficulty in waking up from sleep

❑ looking pale or gray

❑ dark circles under the eyes

❑ blue lips

❑ acting limp and without any energy

❑ bad breath (other than the fact that your child just ate three hard-boiled eggs)

❑ smelly private parts, even after a bath

Preventing the Spread of Germs

❑ Don't share towels.

❑ Don't share cups.

❑ Don't kiss your pets.

❑ Don't sit on a dirty toilet seat.

❑ Don't eat raw meat or eggs.

❑ Don't smoke.

❑ Don't touch your face.

❑ Do wash your hands.

❑ Do disinfect your house often.

Your Medicine Chest

❏ thermometer

❏ suction syringe

❏ eye dropper

❏ medicine dispenser

❏ children's or infants' Tylenol (acetaminophen)

❏ ice pack

❏ Band-Aids

❏ Pedialyte

❏ diaper-rash ointment

❏ petroleum jelly

❏ lip balm

❏ moisturizing soap and lotion

❏ anti-itch lotion

❏ tweezers

❏ scissors

❏ Syrup of Ipecac

❏ flashlight or penlight

❏ pad of paper and pen

❏ cool-mist humidifier or vaporizer (OK, try *under* your medicine chest)

Index

• F •

• G •

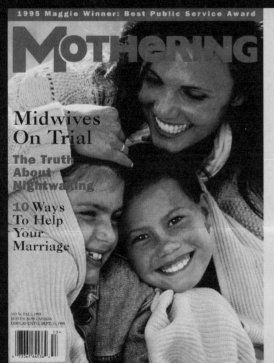

The Baby Jogger ®

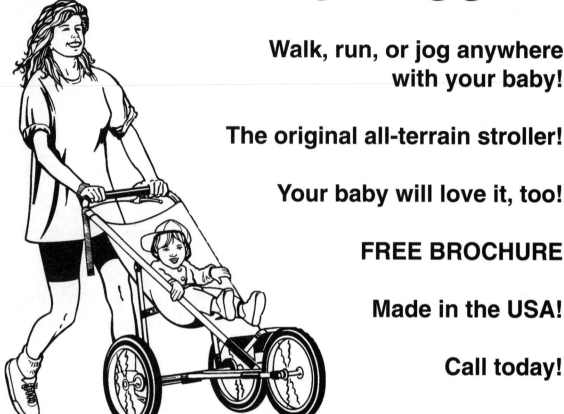

Walk, run, or jog anywhere with your baby!

The original all-terrain stroller!

Your baby will love it, too!

FREE BROCHURE

Made in the USA!

Call today!

Combine fitness, family and fun! At the park, along the trail or on the beach, you stay in shape and your baby rides in style. Now you can really enjoy life on the run!

1-800-241-1848

RACING STROLLERS INC. • PO Box 2189 • Yakima, WA 98907

- -

FREE GIFT

When you purchse any stroller manufactured by Racing Stollers Inc., we'll send you a free gift. Simply return this coupon with your completed warranty card to the above address. We'll send you a free water bottle with cage (retail value $15).

Title	Author	ISBN	Price

12/20/94

INTERNET / COMMUNICATIONS / NETWORKING

Title	Author	ISBN	Price
CompuServe For Dummies™	by Wallace Wang	1-56884-181-7	$19.95 USA/$26.95 Canada
Modems For Dummies™, 2nd Edition	by Tina Rathbone	1-56884-223-6	$19.99 USA/$26.99 Canada
Modems For Dummies™	by Tina Rathbone	1-56884-001-2	$19.95 USA/$26.95 Canada
MORE Internet For Dummies™	by John R. Levine & Margaret Levine Young	1-56884-164-7	$19.95 USA/$26.95 Canada
NetWare For Dummies™	by Ed Tittel & Deni Connor	1-56884-003-9	$19.95 USA/$26.95 Canada
Networking For Dummies™	by Doug Lowe	1-56884-079-9	$19.95 USA/$26.95 Canada
ProComm Plus 2 For Windows For Dummies™	by Wallace Wang	1-56884-219-8	$19.99 USA/$26.99 Canada
The Internet For Dummies™, 2nd Edition	by John R. Levine & Carol Baroudi	1-56884-222-8	$19.99 USA/$26.99 Canada
The Internet For Macs For Dummies™	by Charles Seiter	1-56884-184-1	$19.95 USA/$26.95 Canada

MACINTOSH

Title	Author	ISBN	Price
Macs For Dummies®	by David Pogue	1-56884-173-6	$19.95 USA/$26.95 Canada
Macintosh System 7.5 For Dummies™	by Bob LeVitus	1-56884-197-3	$19.95 USA/$26.95 Canada
MORE Macs For Dummies™	by David Pogue	1-56884-087-X	$19.95 USA/$26.95 Canada
PageMaker 5 For Macs For Dummies™	by Galen Gruman	1-56884-178-7	$19.95 USA/$26.95 Canada
QuarkXPress 3.3 For Dummies™	by Galen Gruman & Barbara Assadi	1-56884-217-1	$19.99 USA/$26.99 Canada
Upgrading and Fixing Macs For Dummies™	by Kearney Rietmann & Frank Higgins	1-56884-189-2	$19.95 USA/$26.95 Canada

MULTIMEDIA

Title	Author	ISBN	Price
Multimedia & CD-ROMs For Dummies™, Interactive Multimedia Value Pack	by Andy Rathbone	1-56884-225-2	$29.95 USA/$39.95 Canada
Multimedia & CD-ROMs For Dummies™	by Andy Rathbone	1-56884-089-6	$19.95 USA/$26.95 Canada

OPERATING SYSTEMS / DOS

Title	Author	ISBN	Price
MORE DOS For Dummies™	by Dan Gookin	1-56884-046-2	$19.95 USA/$26.95 Canada
S.O.S. For DOS™	by Katherine Murray	1-56884-043-8	$12.95 USA/$16.95 Canada
OS/2 For Dummies™	by Andy Rathbone	1-878058-76-2	$19.95 USA/$26.95 Canada

UNIX

Title	Author	ISBN	Price
UNIX For Dummies™	by John R. Levine & Margaret Levine Young	1-878058-58-4	$19.95 USA/$26.95 Canada

WINDOWS

Title	Author	ISBN	Price
S.O.S. For Windows™	by Katherine Murray	1-56884-045-4	$12.95 USA/$16.95 Canada
MORE Windows 3.1 For Dummies™, 3rd Edition	by Andy Rathbone	1-56884-240-6	$19.99 USA/$26.99 Canada

PCs / HARDWARE

Title	Author	ISBN	Price
Illustrated Computer Dictionary For Dummies™	by Dan Gookin, Wally Wang, & Chris Van Buren	1-56884-004-7	$12.95 USA/$16.95 Canada
Upgrading and Fixing PCs For Dummies™	by Andy Rathbone	1-56884-002-0	$19.95 USA/$26.95 Canada

PRESENTATION / AUTOCAD

Title	Author	ISBN	Price
AutoCAD For Dummies™	by Bud Smith	1-56884-191-4	$19.95 USA/$26.95 Canada
PowerPoint 4 For Windows For Dummies™	by Doug Lowe	1-56884-161-2	$16.95 USA/$22.95 Canada

PROGRAMMING

Title	Author	ISBN	Price
Borland C++ For Dummies™	by Michael Hyman	1-56884-162-0	$19.95 USA/$26.95 Canada
"Borland's New Language Product" For Dummies™	by Neil Rubenking	1-56884-200-7	$19.95 USA/$26.95 Canada
C For Dummies™	by Dan Gookin	1-878058-78-9	$19.95 USA/$26.95 Canada
C++ For Dummies™	by Stephen R. Davis	1-56884-163-9	$19.95 USA/$26.95 Canada
Mac Programming For Dummies™	by Dan Parks Sydow	1-56884-173-6	$19.95 USA/$26.95 Canada
QBasic Programming For Dummies™	by Douglas Hergert	1-56884-093-4	$19.95 USA/$26.95 Canada
Visual Basic "X" For Dummies™, 2nd Edition	by Wallace Wang	1-56884-230-9	$19.99 USA/$26.99 Canada
Visual Basic 3 For Dummies™	by Wallace Wang	1-56884-076-4	$19.95 USA/$26.95 Canada

SPREADSHEET

Title	Author	ISBN	Price
1-2-3 For Dummies™	by Greg Harvey	1-878058-60-6	$16.95 USA/$21.95 Canada
1-2-3 For Windows 5 For Dummies™, 2nd Edition	by John Walkenbach	1-56884-216-3	$16.95 USA/$21.95 Canada
1-2-3 For Windows For Dummies™	by John Walkenbach	1-56884-052-7	$16.95 USA/$21.95 Canada
Excel 5 For Macs For Dummies™	by Greg Harvey	1-56884-186-8	$19.95 USA/$26.95 Canada
Excel For Dummies™, 2nd Edition	by Greg Harvey	1-56884-050-0	$16.95 USA/$21.95 Canada
MORE Excel 5 For Windows For Dummies™	by Greg Harvey	1-56884-207-4	$19.95 USA/$26.95 Canada
Quattro Pro 6 For Windows For Dummies™	by John Walkenbach	1-56884-174-4	$19.95 USA/$26.95 Canada
Quattro Pro For DOS For Dummies™	by John Walkenbach	1-56884-023-3	$16.95 USA/$21.95 Canada

UTILITIES / VCRs & CAMCORDERS

Title	Author	ISBN	Price
Norton Utilities 8 For Dummies™	by Beth Slick	1-56884-166-3	$19.95 USA/$26.95 Canada
VCRs & Camcorders For Dummies™	by Andy Rathbone & Gordon McComb	1-56884-229-5	$14.99 USA/$20.99 Canada

WORD PROCESSING

Title	Author	ISBN	Price
Ami Pro For Dummies™	by Jim Meade	1-56884-049-7	$19.95 USA/$26.95 Canada
MORE Word For Windows 6 For Dummies™	by Doug Lowe	1-56884-165-5	$19.95 USA/$26.95 Canada
MORE WordPerfect 6 For Windows For Dummies™	by Margaret Levine Young & David C. Kay	1-56884-206-6	$19.95 USA/$26.95 Canada
MORE WordPerfect 6 For DOS For Dummies™	by Wallace Wang, edited by Dan Gookin	1-56884-047-0	$19.95 USA/$26.95 Canada
S.O.S. For WordPerfect™	by Katherine Murray	1-56884-053-5	$12.95 USA/$16.95 Canada
Word 6 For Macs For Dummies™	by Dan Gookin	1-56884-190-6	$19.95 USA/$26.95 Canada
Word For Windows 6 For Dummies™	by Dan Gookin	1-56884-075-6	$16.95 USA/$21.95 Canada
Word For Windows For Dummies™	by Dan Gookin	1-878058-86-X	$16.95 USA/$21.95 Canada
WordPerfect 6 For Dummies™	by Dan Gookin	1-878058-77-0	$16.95 USA/$21.95 Canada
WordPerfect For Dummies™	by Dan Gookin	1-878058-52-5	$16.95 USA/$21.95 Canada
WordPerfect For Windows For Dummies™	by Margaret Levine Young & David C. Kay	1-56884-032-2	$16.95 USA/$21.95 Canada

FOR MORE INFORMATION OR TO ORDER, PLEASE CALL ▶ 800. 762. 2974

For volume discounts & special orders please call Tony Real, Special Sales, at 415. 655. 3048

Fun, Fast, & Cheap!

CorelDRAW! 5 For Dummies™ Quick Reference
by Raymond E. Werner

ISBN: 1-56884-952-4
$9.99 USA/$12.99 Canada

Windows "X" For Dummies™ Quick Reference, 3rd Edition
by Greg Harvey

ISBN: 1-56884-964-8
$9.99 USA/$12.99 Canada

Word For Windows 6 For Dummies™ Quick Reference
by George Lynch

ISBN: 1-56884-095-0
$8.95 USA/$12.95 Canada

WordPerfect For DOS For Dummies™ Quick Reference
by Greg Harvey

ISBN: 1-56884-009-8
$8.95 USA/$11.95 Canada

Title	Author	ISBN	Price
DATABASE			
Access 2 For Dummies™ Quick Reference	by Stuart A. Stuple	1-56884-167-1	$8.95 USA/$11.95 Canada
dBASE 5 For DOS For Dummies™ Quick Reference	by Barry Sosinsky	1-56884-954-0	$9.99 USA/$12.99 Canada
dBASE 5 For Windows For Dummies™ Quick Reference	by Stuart J. Stuple	1-56884-953-2	$9.99 USA/$12.99 Canada
Paradox 5 For Windows For Dummies™ Quick Reference	by Scott Palmer	1-56884-960-5	$9.99 USA/$12.99 Canada
DESKTOP PUBLISHING / ILLUSTRATION/GRAPHICS			
Harvard Graphics 3 For Windows For Dummies™ Quick Reference	by Raymond E. Werner	1-56884-962-1	$9.99 USA/$12.99 Canada
FINANCE / PERSONAL FINANCE			
Quicken 4 For Windows For Dummies™ Quick Reference	by Stephen L. Nelson	1-56884-950-8	$9.95 USA/$12.95 Canada
GROUPWARE / INTEGRATED			
Microsoft Office 4 For Windows For Dummies™ Quick Reference	by Doug Lowe	1-56884-958-3	$9.99 USA/$12.99 Canada
Microsoft Works For Windows 3 For Dummies™ Quick Reference	by Michael Partington	1-56884-959-1	$9.99 USA/$12.99 Canada
INTERNET / COMMUNICATIONS / NETWORKING			
The Internet For Dummies™ Quick Reference	by John R. Levine	1-56884-168-X	$8.95 USA/$11.95 Canada
MACINTOSH			
Macintosh System 7.5 For Dummies™ Quick Reference	by Stuart J. Stuple	1-56884-956-7	$9.99 USA/$12.99 Canada
OPERATING SYSTEMS / DOS			
DOS For Dummies® Quick Reference	by Greg Harvey	1-56884-007-1	$8.95 USA/$11.95 Canada
UNIX			
UNIX For Dummies™ Quick Reference	by Margaret Levine Young & John R. Levine	1-56884-094-2	$8.95 USA/$11.95 Canada
WINDOWS			
Windows 3.1 For Dummies™ Quick Reference, 2nd Edition	by Greg Harvey	1-56884-951-6	$8.95 USA/$11.95 Canada
PRESENTATION / AUTOCAD			
AutoCAD For Dummies™ Quick Reference	by Ellen Finkelstein	1-56884-198-1	$9.95 USA/$12.95 Canada
SPREADSHEET			
1-2-3 For Dummies™ Quick Reference	by John Walkenbach	1-56884-027-6	$8.95 USA/$11.95 Canada
1-2-3 For Windows 5 For Dummies™ Quick Reference	by John Walkenbach	1-56884-957-5	$9.95 USA/$12.95 Canada
Excel For Windows For Dummies™ Quick Reference, 2nd Edition	by John Walkenbach	1-56884-096-9	$8.95 USA/$11.95 Canada
Quattro Pro 6 For Windows For Dummies™ Quick Reference	by Stuart A. Stuple	1-56884-172-8	$9.95 USA/$12.95 Canada
WORD PROCESSING			
Word For Windows 6 For Dummies™ Quick Reference	by George Lynch	1-56884-095-0	$8.95 USA/$11.95 Canada
WordPerfect For Windows For Dummies™ Quick Reference	by Greg Harvey	1-56884-039-X	$8.95 USA/$11.95 Canada

FOR MORE INFORMATION OR TO ORDER, PLEASE CALL ▶ 800. 762. 2974

For volume discounts & special orders please call
Tony Real, Special Sales, at 415. 655. 3048

12/20/94

Windows 3.1 SECRETS™
by Brian Livingston

ISBN: 1-878058-43-6
$39.95 USA/$52.95 Canada

Includes Software.

MORE Windows 3.1 SECRETS™
by Brian Livingston

ISBN: 1-56884-019-5
$39.95 USA/$52.95 Canada

Includes Software.

Windows GIZMOS™
by Brian Livingston & Margie Livingston

ISBN: 1-878058-66-5
$39.95 USA/$52.95 Canada

Includes Software.

Windows 3.1 Connectivity SECRETS™
by Runnoe Connally, David Rorabaugh, & Sheldon Hall

ISBN: 1-56884-030-6
$49.95 USA/$64.95 Canada

Includes Software.

Windows 3.1 Configuration SECRETS™
by Valda Hilley & James Blakely

ISBN: 1-56884-026-8
$49.95 USA/$64.95 Canada

Includes Software.

Internet SECRETS™
by John R. Levine & Carol Baroudi

ISBN: 1-56884-452-2
$39.99 USA/$54.99 Canada

Includes Software.
Available: January 1995

Internet GIZMOS™ For Windows
by Joel Diamond, Howard Sobel, & Valda Hilley

ISBN: 1-56884-451-4
$39.99 USA/$54.99 Canada

Includes Software.
Available: December 1994

Network Security SECRETS™
by David Stang & Sylvia Moon

ISBN: 1-56884-021-7
Int'l. ISBN: 1-56884-151-5
$49.95 USA/$64.95 Canada

Includes Software.

PC SECRETS™
by Caroline M. Halliday

ISBN: 1-878058-49-5
$39.95 USA/$52.95 Canada

Includes Software.

WordPerfect 6 SECRETS™
by Roger C. Parker & David A. Holzgang

ISBN: 1-56884-040-3
$39.95 USA/$52.95 Canada

Includes Software.

DOS 6 SECRETS™
by Robert D. Ainsbury

ISBN: 1-878058-70-3
$39.95 USA/$52.95 Canada

Includes Software.

Paradox 4 Power Programming SECRETS,™ 2nd Edition
by Gregory B. Salcedo & Martin W. Rudy

ISBN: 1-878058-54-1
$44.95 USA/$59.95 Canada

Includes Software.

Paradox For Windows "X" Power Programming SECRETS™
by Gregory B. Salcedo & Martin W. Rudy

ISBN: 1-56884-085-3
$44.95 USA/$59.95 Canada

Includes Software.

Hard Disk SECRETS™
by John M. Goodman, Ph.D.

ISBN: 1-878058-64-9
$39.95 USA/$52.95 Canada

Includes Software.

WordPerfect 6 For Windows Tips & Techniques Revealed
by David A. Holzgang & Roger C. Parker

ISBN: 1-56884-202-3
$39.95 USA/$52.95 Canada

Includes Software.

Excel 5 For Windows Power Programming Techniques
by John Walkenbach

ISBN: 1-56884-303-8
$39.95 USA/$52.95 Canada

Includes Software.
Available: November 1994

INFO WORLD

...SECRETS™

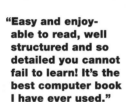

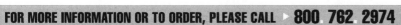

IDG BOOKS®

Order Center: **(800) 762-2974** *(8 a.m.–6 p.m., EST, weekdays)*

12/20/94

Quantity	ISBN	Title	Price	Total

Shipping & Handling Charges

	Description	First book	Each additional book	Total
Domestic	Normal	$4.50	$1.50	$
	Two Day Air	$8.50	$2.50	$
	Overnight	$18.00	$3.00	$
International	Surface	$8.00	$8.00	$
	Airmail	$16.00	$16.00	$
	DHL Air	$17.00	$17.00	$

*For large quantities call for shipping & handling charges.
**Prices are subject to change without notice.

Ship to:

Name _____

Company _____

Address _____

City/State/Zip _____

Daytime Phone _____

Payment: ☐ Check to IDG Books (US Funds Only)

☐ VISA   ☐ MasterCard   ☐ American Express

Card # _____ Expires _____

Signature _____

Subtotal _____

CA residents add
applicable sales tax _____

IN, MA, and MD
residents add
5% sales tax _____

IL residents add
6.25% sales tax _____

RI residents add
7% sales tax _____

TX residents add
8.25% sales tax _____

Shipping _____

Total _____

Please send this order form to:

IDG Books Worldwide
7260 Shadeland Station, Suite 100
Indianapolis, IN 46256

Allow up to 3 weeks for delivery.
Thank you!

IDG BOOKS WORLDWIDE REGISTRATION CARD

RETURN THIS
REGISTRATION CARD
FOR FREE CATALOG

Title of this book: Parenting For Dummies

My overall rating of this book: ❏ Very good [1]   ❏ Good [2]   ❏ Satisfactory [3]   ❏ Fair [4]   ❏ Poor [5]

How I first heard about this book:

❏ Found in bookstore; name: [6]

❏ Advertisement: [8]

❏ Word of mouth; heard about book from friend, co-worker, etc.: [10]

❏ Book review: [7]

❏ Catalog: [9]

❏ Other: [11]

What I liked most about this book:

What I would change, add, delete, etc., in future editions of this book:

Other comments:

Number of computer books I purchase in a year: ❏ 1 [12]   ❏ 2-5 [13]   ❏ 6-10 [14]   ❏ More than 10 [15]

I would characterize my computer skills as: ❏ Beginner [16] ❏ Intermediate [17] ❏ Advanced [18] ❏ Professional [19]

I use ❏ DOS [20] ❏ Windows [21] ❏ OS/2 [22] ❏ Unix [23] ❏ Macintosh [24] ❏ Other: [25]_____
(please specify)

I would be interested in new books on the following subjects:
(please check all that apply, and use the spaces provided to identify specific software)

❏ Word processing: [26]

❏ Data bases: [28]

❏ File Utilities: [30]

❏ Networking: [32]

❏ Other: [34]

❏ Spreadsheets: [27]

❏ Desktop publishing: [29]

❏ Money management: [31]

❏ Programming languages: [33]

I use a PC at (please check all that apply): ❏ home [35] ❏ work [36] ❏ school [37] ❏ other: [38] _____

The disks I prefer to use are ❏ 5.25 [39] ❏ 3.5 [40] ❏ other: [41]_____

I have a CD ROM: ❏ yes [42]   ❏ no [43]

I plan to buy or upgrade computer hardware this year: ❏ yes [44]   ❏ no [45]

I plan to buy or upgrade computer software this year: ❏ yes [46]   ❏ no [47]

Name: _____ Business title: [48] _____ Type of Business: [49] _____

Address (❏ home [50] ❏ work [51]/Company name: _____)

Street/Suite# _____

City [52]/State [53]/Zipcode [54]: _____ Country [55] _____

❏ **I liked this book!** You may quote me by name in future
IDG Books Worldwide promotional materials.

My daytime phone number is _____

IDG
BOOKS

THE WORLD OF
COMPUTER
KNOWLEDGE

❏ YES!

Please keep me informed about IDG's World of Computer Knowledge.
Send me the latest IDG Books catalog.

COMPUTER
BOOK SERIES
FROM IDG